THIS BOOK IS DEDICATED TO TIM'S TWO SONS
AND LARRY'S TWO DAUGHTERS

———————— ● ————————

ALSO BY LARRY GONICK

ALSO BY TIM KASSER

HYPER-CAPITALISM

The Modern Economy, Its Values, and How to Change Them

Larry Gonick & Tim Kasser

THE NEW PRESS

NEW YORK
LONDON

PERMISSIONS DEPARTMENT
THE NEW PRESS
120 WALL STREET, 31ST FLOOR
NEW YORK, NY 10005.

PUBLISHED IN THE UNITED STATES BY THE NEW PRESS, NEW YORK, 2018
DISTRIBUTED BY TWO RIVERS DISTRIBUTION

LIBRARY OF CONGRESS CATALOGING-IN-PUBLICATION DATA:

NAMES: GONICK, LARRY, AUTHOR. | KASSER, TIMOTHY, AUTHOR.
TITLE: HYPERCAPITALISM : THE MODERN ECONOMY, ITS VALUES, AND HOW TO CHANGE THEM / LARRY GONICK, TIMOTHY KASSER.
DESCRIPTION: NEW YORK : NEW PRESS, THE, 2018. | INCLUDES BIBLIOGRAPHICAL REFERENCES AND INDEX.
IDENTIFIERS: LCCN 2017030133 | ISBN 9781620972823 (PAPERBACK)
SUBJECTS: LCSH: CAPITALISM. | INDUSTRIES--MIDDLE WEST. | BISAC: BUSINESS & ECONOMICS / ECONOMIC HISTORY. | POLITICAL SCIENCE / PUBLIC POLICY / ECONOMIC POLICY.
CLASSIFICATION: LCC HB501 .G66 2018 | DDC 330.12/2—DC23 LC RECORD AVAILABLE AT HTTPS://LCCN.LOC.GOV/2017030133

THE NEW PRESS PUBLISHES BOOKS THAT PROMOTE AND ENRICH PUBLIC DISCUSSION AND UNDERSTANDING OF THE ISSUES VITAL TO OUR DEMOCRACY AND TO A MORE EQUITABLE WORLD. THESE BOOKS ARE MADE POSSIBLE BY THE ENTHUSIASM OF OUR READERS; THE SUPPORT OF A COMMITTED GROUP OF DONORS, LARGE AND SMALL; THE COLLABORATION OF OUR MANY PARTNERS IN THE INDEPENDENT MEDIA AND THE NOT-FOR-PROFIT SECTOR; BOOKSELLERS, WHO OFTEN HAND-SELL NEW PRESS BOOKS; LIBRARIANS; AND ABOVE ALL BY OUR AUTHORS.

WWW.THENEWPRESS.COM

BOOK DESIGN BY LARRY GONICK
COMPOSITION BY LARRY GONICK
THIS BOOK WAS SET IN AAVARMEDIUM, A CUSTOM TYPEFACE BUILT IN FONTOGRAPHER AND BASED ON LARRY GONICK'S HAND LETTERING.

PRINTED IN THE UNITED STATES OF AMERICA

2 4 6 8 10 9 7 5 3 1

PHOTO CREDITS: P.82, BUDWEISER PHOTO BY USER MBELL ON FLICKR; SEE HTTPS://WWW.FLICKR.COM/PHOTOS/MBELL1975/2619576066/IN/PHOTOSTREAM/. RUBBER WORKER ON P. 93 BY RYAN WOO, TAKEN FROM HTTPS://WWW.FLICKR.COM/PHOTOS/CIFOR/5701864787. WHANGANUI RIVER ON P. 185 BY JAMES SHOOK, TAKEN FROM HTTPS://COMMONS.WIKIMEDIA.ORG/WIKI/FILE:WHANGANUI_RIVER.JPG. RIGHTS TO THESE THREE PHOTOS WERE GRANTED UNDER THE CREATIVE COMMONS LICENSE. OTHER PHOTOS USED ARE EITHER IN THE PUBLIC DOMAIN, OF UNKNOWN PROVENANCE, OR WERE TAKEN BY THE FIRST AUTHOR.

P. 65. THE GRAPH IS REPRINTED WITH PERMISSION OF THE AMERICAN PSYCHOLOGICAL ASSOCIATION.

P. 170. DRAWING "EARLY SCHEMATIC DESIGN RENDERING OF JAMAICA PLAIN COHOUSING" BY LAURA FITCH, ARCHITECT. USED BY PERMISSION.

CONTENTS

Acknowledgments

LARRY GONICK:

THANKS TO TIM KASSER, FOR BRINGING ME THIS IDEA IN THE FIRST PLACE, AND FOR HIS UNFAILING PATIENCE IN ANSWERING ALL MY QUESTIONS AND OBJECTIONS. COLLABORATING ON A POLITICAL BOOK CAN SPARK VIGOROUS DISCUSSION, BECAUSE OPINIONS MAY VARY AND ARE RARELY MILD. TIM ALSO PROVIDED MANY ASTUTE EDITORIAL SUGGESTIONS.

THANKS TO MARC FAVREAU AND MAURY BOTTON AT THE NEW PRESS FOR EDITORIAL AND PRODUCTION GUIDANCE, RESPECTIVELY.

THANKS TO MY WIFE, LISA, FOR PUTTING UP WITH ME THROUGH THIS AND MANY OTHER MONSTER PROJECTS.

THANKS TO THE MESA REFUGE FOR TWO GLORIOUS WEEKS OF QUIET TIME IN THE GARDENS OF WEST MARIN COUNTY.

AND THANKS TO MY THURSDAY GUYS' LUNCH BUNCH FOR KEEPING UP MY MORALE IN TURBULENT POLITICAL TIMES.

TIM KASSER:

THANKS TO LARRY GONICK, FOR BRINGING TO LIFE A BOOK THAT HAD BEEN RATTLING IN MY HEAD FOR TEN YEARS, AND FOR MAKING THIS PROCESS BOTH CHALLENGING AND FUN.

THANKS TO THE MANY KNOX COLLEGE STUDENTS WHO TOOK *ALTERNATIVES TO CONSUMERISM* AND TO DIANA BECK, WHO HELPED ME DESIGN THE INITIAL VERSION OF THAT CLASS. THANKS ALSO TO MY COLLEAGUES AT KNOX WHO HAVE, FOR TWO DECADES, PROVIDED ME WITH THE EXCELLENT LIBRARY AND COMPUTER RESOURCES NEEDED TO COMPLETE THIS BOOK, AND WHO HAVE SUPPORTED MY OWN FORMS OF DOWNSHIFTING, ACTIVISM, AND ACADEMIC FREEDOM.

THANKS TO NEW DREAM (FORMERLY CENTER FOR A NEW AMERICAN DREAM), WHICH INVITED ME TO MAKE AN ANIMATED VIDEO ON MATERIALISM THAT PROVIDED THE INITIAL IDEA FOR THE FORM OF THIS BOOK.

THANKS TO SUSAN LINN FOR CONNECTING US WITH THE NEW PRESS, AND THANKS TO EVERYONE AT THE NEW PRESS FOR THEIR PATIENCE AND ENTHUSIASM.

THANKS TO THE MANY FRIENDS AND COLLEAGUES WHO HAVE HELPED ME THINK THROUGH THE IDEAS BEHIND THIS BOOK IN GENERAL AND WHO HAVE GIVEN ME FEEDBACK ABOUT SPECIFIC PARTS OF THIS BOOK IN PARTICULAR.

THANKS, AS ALWAYS, TO MY WIFE, VIRGINIA, FOR HER WONDERFUL ABILITY TO COMBINE A CRITICAL EAR WITH LOVE.

A Note on Gender, Ethnicity, and Cartoons

AUTHORS OF NON-CARTOON BOOKS CAN WRITE ABOUT CONSUMERS, INVESTORS, POLITICIANS, AND OTHER ROLES IN HYPERCAPITALIST ECONOMICS WHILE LEAVING READERS FREE TO IMAGINE THE ETHNICITY AND GENDER OF THE PEOPLE WHO INHABIT THOSE ROLES. A CARTOON BOOK, IN CONTRAST, MUST USE SPECIFIC CHARACTERS TO REPRESENT THOSE DIFFERENT ECONOMIC ACTORS, AND EVERY CHARACTER MUST BE A PARTICULAR PERSON. THIS CARTOON BOOK INCLUDES A DIVERSE CAST OF CHARACTERS WHO WERE ASSIGNED GENDER AND ETHNICITY SEMI-RANDOMLY (THE MAIN EXCEPTION BEING OUR INVESTOR, THE OWNER OF CAPITAL, WHO IS A WHITE MALE, AS ARE MOST HOLDERS OF CAPITAL). WE URGE THE READER NOT TO READ ANYTHING INTO THESE GENDER AND RACIAL ASSIGNMENTS. WE BY NO MEANS INTEND TO IMPLY THAT CONSUMERS ARE TYPICALLY WHITE FEMALES OR THAT POLITICIANS ARE TYPICALLY AFRICAN-AMERICAN MALES, FOR EXAMPLE. OUR FOCUS IS ON ECONOMIC BEHAVIORS AND ROLES, NOT GENDER AND ETHNICITY. WE RECOGNIZE THAT IN REAL LIFE THIS DISTINCTION IS LESS THAN CLEAR-CUT AND THAT GENDER AND ETHNICITY ARE RELEVANT TO ECONOMICS, BUT THOSE INTERACTIONS ARE BEYOND THE SCOPE OF THIS BOOK. WE WERE FORCED TO MAKE CHOICES, AND WE KNOW THAT OUR CHOICES WERE NECESSARILY IMPERFECT.

PREFACE

HI, I'M TIM KASSER, AND WHEN I'M NOT A CARTOON CHARACTER, I'M A PSYCHOLOGY PROFESSOR AT KNOX COLLEGE IN ILLINOIS!

FROM THE TIME I STARTED GRAD SCHOOL 30 YEARS AGO, I'VE BEEN STUDYING PEOPLE'S **VALUES** AND **GOALS**, AND IN PARTICULAR THEIR MATERIALISTIC VALUES AND GOALS FOR MONEY, POSSESSIONS, AND STATUS.

MY COLLEAGUES AND I WERE AMONG THE FIRST TO EXPLORE THE RELATIONSHIP BETWEEN **MATERIALISTIC VALUES** AND PEOPLE'S **WELL-BEING**.

OUR EARLY RESEARCH REVEALED THAT WHEN PEOPLE FOCUS THEIR LIVES ON CHASING MONEY AND STUFF, THEY TEND TO BE LESS HAPPY AND SATISFIED, AND MORE DEPRESSED AND ANXIOUS.

LATER STUDIES SHOWED THAT MATERIALISTIC VALUES ARE ALSO ASSOCIATED WITH DESTRUCTIVE ATTITUDES TOWARD OTHER PEOPLE AND THE ENVIRONMENT.

WHAT IS IT, I WONDERED, THAT LEADS PEOPLE TO PUT SUCH A HIGH PRIORITY ON MATERIAL GAIN? HOW DO THEY GET THIS WAY?

THIS QUESTION LED ME TO THINK ABOUT **ECONOMIC SYSTEMS** AND HOW THEY PUSH PEOPLE TOWARD SOME GOALS AND AWAY FROM OTHERS.

IT CERTAINLY SEEMS TO BE TRUE THAT MATER-IALISTIC TENDENCIES ARE A BASIC PART OF THE SPECIES *HOMO SAPIENS*, BUT THAT ISN'T THE WHOLE STORY.

SINCE THE LATE 1800S, AND ESPECIALLY SINCE THE 1950S, MUCH OF THE WORLD HAS BEEN LIVING UNDER A SYSTEM THAT CELEBRATES MATERIALISM, CONSUMPTION, AND STATUS.

IN THIS BOOK, WE CALL THAT SYSTEM **HYPERCAPITALISM.**

IT'S OVER THE TOP! OUT OF CONTROL! BLOATED! MISSHAPEN! FREAKISH!

THAT'S MY CO-AUTHOR, LARRY GONICK, THE CARTOONIST. HE HAS HIS OPINIONS, TOO... NOW WHERE WAS I?

OH, RIGHT! I WAS ABOUT TO SAY THAT HYPER-CAPITALISM DEPENDS FOR ITS VERY **SURVIVAL** ON MATERIALISTIC VALUES.

WITHOUT BUYING, IT'S DYING!

AS EXTENSIVE RESEARCH HAS SHOWN, THE MORE THAT PEOPLE AND SOCIETIES PRIORITIZE MATER-IALISTIC VALUES, THE LESS THEY CARE ABOUT PROMOTING WELL-BEING, FAIR TREATMENT OF OTHERS, AND ENVIRONMENTAL SUSTAINABILITY.

OUR ACCOUNT OF HYPERCAPITALISM IS DIVIDED INTO TWO PARTS, ONE DARKER AND ONE LIGHTER.

IN PART I, WE'LL DESCRIBE THE INTERPLAY OF HYPERCAPITALISM AND VALUES. WE'LL EXPLAIN THE THEORY AND PRACTICE OF CAPITALISM AND TRACE THE GROWTH OF ITS CURRENT "HYPER" INCARNATION.

WE'LL ALSO INTRODUCE YOU TO WHAT PSYCHOLOGISTS HAVE LEARNED ABOUT HUMAN VALUE SYSTEMS, AND WE'LL SHOW HOW THESE FINDINGS HELP TO ACCOUNT FOR HYPERCAPITALISM'S ASSAULT ON PERSONAL, SOCIAL, AND ECOLOGICAL WELL-BEING.

PART II OF THE BOOK IS ABOUT **ACTION!!**

WHEN I STARTED MY CAREER, I WAS MOSTLY INDIFFERENT TO POLITICS. BUT THE MORE I LEARNED, THE HARDER IT BECAME TO IGNORE THE SOCIAL AND POLITICAL IMPLICATIONS OF MY WORK. IN TIME, I BECAME AN **ACTIVIST** AS WELL AS A SCIENTIST.

PART II, THEN, WILL PROVIDE AN OVERVIEW OF THE MANY WAYS THAT PEOPLE ARE, RIGHT **NOW,** ACTIVELY WORKING TO RESIST HYPERCAPITALISM.

THESE PEOPLE ARE CREATING LIFESTYLES AND INSTITUTIONS ORIENTED AROUND HEALTHIER VALUES...

SO WHAT DO YOU SAY? LET'S GET STARTED!!

PART I

Chapter 1
A REVOLUTION OF VALUES

Wen in the course of human events, it becomes necessar... ...ate and equal station to which the Laws of Nature and of Nature... to the separation.— We hold these truths to be self-evident, that ...ng these are Life, Liberty and the pursuit of Happiness.—

BRILLIANT!

...ble to dissolve... ...them

WHEN THOMAS JEFFERSON WROTE "THE PURSUIT OF HAPPINESS" IN THE DECLARATION OF INDEPENDENCE, HE WAS MAKING A STARK DEPARTURE FROM AN EARLIER REVOLUTIONARY SLOGAN.

UNTIL THEN, THE CHANT OF BOSTON'S ANTI-TAX PROTESTORS HAD BEEN "LIBERTY AND **PROPERTY**," A PHRASE ECHOED IN THE 1774 *DECLARATION OF COLONIAL RIGHTS.*

LIBERTY AND PROPERTY!!

JEFFERSON, HOWEVER, DECIDED TO EDIT "PROPERTY" OUT.

IT SOUNDS SO... **CRASS**...

HE WANTED A DIFFERENT PRINCIPLE TO DESCRIBE PERSONAL ASPIRATIONS, SOMETHING MORE INTRINSIC TO HUMAN WELL-BEING.

AND BETTER NOT TO MENTION SOME OF **MY** PROPERTY, EH, SALLY?

WITH HIS CLASSICAL EDUCATION, THE VIRGINIAN HARKENED BACK TO AN ANCIENT GREEK IDEAL OF THE GOOD LIFE, IN GREEK *EUDAEMONIA.*

eu·daemonia

TRUE

SPIRITUALITY

THAT'S THE STUFF!

EUDAEMONIA MEANT LIVING A LIFE IN PURSUIT OF VIRTUE, MEANING, AND UNDERSTANDING.

AND THE PHILOSOPHERS AGREED: THIS VALUE RAN **OPPOSITE** TO THE PURSUIT OF PROPERTY!

"WHY DO YOU CARE SO MUCH ABOUT LAYING UP THE GREATEST AMOUNT OF MONEY AND HONOR AND REPUTATION, AND SO LITTLE ABOUT WISDOM AND TRUTH AND THE... IMPROVEMENT OF THE SOUL?"

"UNHAPPY ARE THOSE WHO HAVE MANAGED TO ACQUIRE MORE EXTERNAL GOODS THAN THEY CAN POSSIBLY USE AND ARE LACKING IN THE GOODS OF THE SOUL."

"IF YOU WANT TO MAKE A MAN HAPPY, ADD NOT TO HIS RICHES, BUT TAKE AWAY FROM HIS DESIRES."

SOCRATES

ARISTOTLE

EPICURUS

ONE HUNDRED NINETY-ONE YEARS AFTER JEFFERSON'S EDIT, AMERICANS STILL HADN'T GOTTEN THE MESSAGE... THE PROFIT MOTIVE STILL REIGNED SUPREME... AND ON APRIL 4, 1967, IN THE MIDST OF A U.S. WAR IN VIETNAM AND A TUMULTUOUS STRUGGLE FOR CIVIL RIGHTS AT HOME, THE REVEREND **MARTIN LUTHER KING JR.** HAD THIS TO SAY:

"WE AS A NATION MUST UNDERGO A RADICAL REVOLUTION OF VALUES. WE MUST RAPIDLY BEGIN THE SHIFT FROM A THING-ORIENTED SOCIETY TO A PERSON-ORIENTED SOCIETY. WHEN MACHINES AND COMPUTERS, PROFIT MOTIVES AND PROPERTY RIGHTS, ARE CONSIDERED MORE IMPORTANT THAN PEOPLE, THE GIANT TRIPLETS OF RACISM, EXTREME MATERIALISM, AND MILITARISM ARE INCAPABLE OF BEING CONQUERED."

KING, A BAPTIST MINISTER WHO ADMIRED GANDHI, NATURALLY HAD SOME BIBLICAL REFERENCES IN MIND, AND HE MAY HAVE BEEN THINKING OF THE BUDDHA, TOO...

"THOU SHALT NOT COVET..."

MILK
BAGELS
LETTUCE
ONIONS
TOMATOES
~~COVETOUS-~~
~~NESS~~

MOSES

"YOU CANNOT SERVE GOD AND MONEY."

IT IS EASIER FOR A CAMEL TO PASS THROUGH THE EYE OF A NEEDLE THAN FOR A RICH MAN TO ENTER THE KINGDOM OF HEAVEN."

JESUS

"DESIRE IS SUFFERING."

THE BUDDHA

DESPITE THESE PRECEDENTS, KING'S WORDS SEEMED SO CONTRARY TO CURRENT AMERICAN VALUES THAT FBI DIRECTOR **J. EDGAR HOOVER** CALLED THE MINISTER "A TRAITOR TO HIS COUNTRY AND HIS RACE."

LET'S GET A WIRETAP ON THIS JESUS, TOO, WHOEVER HE IS!

DR. KING'S REFERENCE TO VALUES WAS DIRECT. HE CHALLENGED AMERICANS TO SUBORDINATE THE PURSUIT OF MONEY TO SOMETHING MORE HUMANE. JEFFERSON EXPRESSED THE SAME VIEW IMPLICITLY. WHAT ARE THESE OTHER VALUES? WHAT DO PEOPLE AND SOCIETIES PURSUE WHEN THEY PURSUE HAPPINESS?

20% OFF, THAT'S WHAT I'M AFTER!

SALE

THE IDEA OF VALUES

TO PSYCHOLOGISTS, A VALUE IS A GUIDING PRINCIPLE, ANYTHING A PERSON HOLDS IN HIGH REGARD, BELIEVES IN, ASPIRES TO, OR CRAVES. VALUES ARE THE AIMS PEOPLE FIND WORTH-WHILE TO PURSUE.

OH— THOSE...

VALUES MAY BE PERSONAL, SUCH AS **INNER HARMONY, PHYSICAL PLEASURE, A SENSE OF BELONGING, CREATIVITY, INFLUENCE OVER OTHERS, SELF-DISCIPLINE,** OR **WEALTH;** OR SOCIAL, LIKE A DESIRE FOR **CONFORMITY, DIVERSITY, NATIONAL SECURITY, FREEDOM, EGALITARIANISM,** AND THE LIKE.

I VALUE FAMILY, SIMPLICITY, CREA-TIVITY, EGALITAR-IANISM, SOCIAL JUSTICE, AND COUNTRY LIVING. RIGHT, EARL?

N.B. THIS IS NOT A SYMBOLIC DONKEY. KASSER ACTUALLY HAS A DONKEY NAMED EARL.

I VALUE EXCITEMENT, NOVELTY, LOW PRICES, AND DEATH-DEFY-ING RIDES!

PLAINLY, VALUES MAY COMPETE WITH EACH OTHER. EACH PERSON PREFERS A MIX OF SOME VALUES OVER OTHERS, AND DIFFERENT VALUES CAN LEAD TO CONFLICT.

VALUES ARE STRONGLY BOUND UP WITH THEIR SOCIAL MILIEU. TRADITION, POLITICS, ECONOMICS, RELIGION, AND MEDIA ALL HAVE AN INFLUENCE.

THIS BOOK ARGUES THAT OUR CURRENT SYSTEM PROMOTES AND DEPENDS UPON VALUES INCOMPATIBLE WITH A SENSE OF PERSONAL WELL-BEING. THE NEVERENDING NEED TO SELL HAS OVERWHELMED WHAT DR. KING CALLED "PERSON-ORIENTED" VALUES. AND WE HAVE WAYS TO MEASURE THIS!

NOW THAT WE'VE CLARIFIED WHAT VALUES ARE, LET'S ASK IF THEY HAVE SHOWN ANY MEASURABLE CHANGES RECENTLY.

PERSONAL GOALS:

SINCE THE LATE 1960S, FIRST-YEAR AMERICAN COLLEGE STUDENTS NATIONWIDE HAVE BEEN SURVEYED ABOUT THE IMPORTANCE THEY PLACE ON VARIOUS ASPECTS OF LIFE.

ASKED TO RATE THE IMPORTANCE OF BEING VERY **WELL-OFF FINANCIALLY,** THE PERCENTAGE WHO RESPONDED "VERY IMPORTANT" OR "ESSENTIAL" HAS RISEN STEADILY FROM UNDER **40%** TO OVER **80%**.

ON THE OTHER HAND, THOSE WHO REGARDED "DEVELOPING A MEANINGFUL PHILOSOPHY OF LIFE" AS VERY IMPORTANT OR ESSENTIAL HAS FALLEN STEEPLY.

HOW WE DESCRIBE OURSELVES

THIS GRAPH SHOWS A GOOGLE nGRAM OF FIVE MILLION ENGLISH-LANGUAGE BOOKS PUBLISHED BETWEEN THE YEARS 1800 AND 2000. ONE CURVE SHOWS THE FREQUENCY WITH WHICH THE WORD "CITIZEN" APPEARED, WHILE THE OTHER CURVE PLOTS THE FREQUENCY OF THE WORD "CONSUMER."

CITIZEN

FREQUENCY

CONSUMER

1800　1840　1880　1920　1960　2000

YEAR OF PUBLICATION

AS YOU SEE, REFERENCES TO CONSUMERS WERE VERY RARE BEFORE 1900, WHEN THEY STARTED TO CLIMB.

> BEFORE THAT, EVERYONE WAS A FARMER, ANYWAY!

MEANWHILE, MENTIONS OF "CITIZEN" PEAKED AROUND 1920 AND HAVE FALLEN EVER SINCE, WITH AN ESPECIALLY STEEP DROP AFTER 1970.

> CITIZEN!

> YOU TALKIN' TO ME?

THE CURVES CROSSED BEFORE 1980, AND NOW PEOPLE ARE CALLED "CONSUMERS" NEARLY **TWICE** AS OFTEN AS "CITIZENS." CLEARLY, WE NOW THINK OF EACH OTHER MORE AS BUYERS OF STUFF THAN AS PARTICIPANTS IN A SHARED SOCIETY.

> HOW DID WE GET SO CUT OFF FROM EACH OTHER?

WEALTH & INCOME INEQUALITY

PROMOTING ECONOMIC INEQUALITY IS ANOTHER SIGN OF SOCIAL VALUES. GOVERNMENT POLICIES AND PRIVATE BEHAVIOR COMBINE TO HELP THE ALREADY-RICH GROW EVEN RICHER, WHILE EVERYONE ELSE STAGNATES OR FALLS BEHIND.

IT'S AN OFFICIAL BLESSING FOR MONEY-LUST, AT THE EXPENSE OF VALUES LIKE SOCIAL JUSTICE AND EQUALITY. A SENSE OF COMMUNITY IS ERODED AS THE TOP DOGS LOCK THEMSELVES INTO GATED KENNELS TO AVOID MIXING WITH MUTTS LIKE THE REST OF US.

HOW BAD HAS IT GOTTEN? CONSIDER THE FRACTION OF ALL WEALTH—STOCKS, BONDS, REAL ESTATE, CASH, ETC.—OWNED BY THE RICHEST **0.1%** OF THE AMERICAN POPULATION. ACCORDING TO A STUDY BY THE LONDON SCHOOL OF ECONOMICS, THIS FRACTION **TRIPLED** BETWEEN 1975 AND 2012, TO 22% OF THE TOTAL.

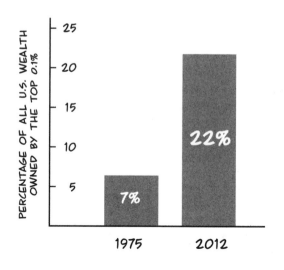

14

TO PUT IT ANOTHER WAY, MORE THAN ONE DOLLAR IN EVERY FIVE IS NOW OWNED BY A GROUP OF AROUND 300,000 AMERICANS (0.1% OF 300 MILLION).

WE ALL HAVE OUR BURDENS.

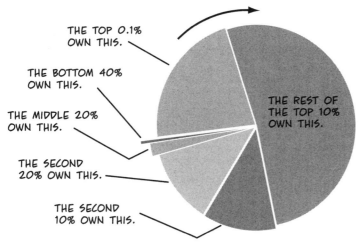

THE TOP 0.1% OWN THIS.

THE BOTTOM 40% OWN THIS.

THE MIDDLE 20% OWN THIS.

THE SECOND 20% OWN THIS.

THE SECOND 10% OWN THIS.

THE REST OF THE TOP 10% OWN THIS.

ALMOST ALL THE REST BELONGS TO A SLIGHTLY LARGER ELITE. ESTIMATES FOR 2007 SHOWED THAT THE RICHEST 10% HAD **73%** OF THE WEALTH; THE NEXT 10% OWN **12%,** MAKING A TOTAL OF **85%;** OF WHAT REMAINS, THE BOTTOM 40% OWN A SHOCKINGLY TINY **0.2%.**

OTHER MEASUREMENTS SHOW A SIMILAR TREND. THE INCOME OF CEOS (CHIEF EXECUTIVE OFFICERS) OF THE TOP 350 COMPANIES, FOR EXAMPLE, ROSE MORE THAN **NINEFOLD** FROM 1978 TO 2013, WHILE WORKER PAY STAGNATED. IN 2013, THE AVERAGE CEO MADE ABOUT **300 TIMES** AN AVERAGE WORKER'S PAY, UP FROM A RATIO OF **30** TO **1** IN 1978.

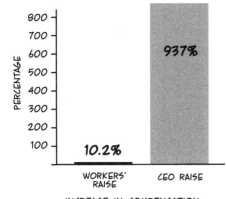

INCREASE IN COMPENSATION
1978–2013 (INFLATION-ADJUSTED)

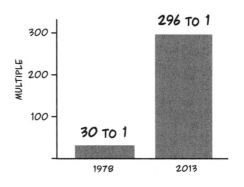

LARGE-COMPANY CEO PAY
RELATIVE TO WORKER PAY

15

WHY HAVE AMERICANS TOLERATED (AND SOMETIMES EVEN CHEERED) THIS RISE OF MATERIALISTIC, COMPETITIVE VALUES? THAT QUESTION HAS MANY ANSWERS, BUT SURELY ONE OF THEM IS THIS: IT'S BEEN HEAVILY **SOLD**. WE'RE TALKING ABOUT

MORE THAN JUST A WAY TO SELL STUFF, COMMERCIALS ALSO ADVERTISE A VISION OF THE GOOD LIFE AS ONE FILLED WITH GLISTENING NEW TOYS. ADS PROMOTE THE IDEA THAT BUYING PRODUCTS WILL MAKE US HAPPY.

THEY ALSO KEEP US FROM THINKING TOO MUCH. ADVERTISING IS DESIGNED TO AROUSE INSTANT RESPONSES, TO MANIPULATE, TO ASSOCIATE OBJECTS WITH VIEWERS' PRIMAL EMOTIONS. RARE IS THE AD THAT HONESTLY DESCRIBES THE PRODUCT IT PUSHES.

MEN! DRINK BEER AND ATTRACT VOLUPTUOUS FEMALES IN HALTER TOPS!*

HMMMFF... MAYBE THE NEXT ROUND WILL DO IT...

*PARAPHRASE OF ACTUAL COMMERCIAL

IT'S POSSIBLE, WE SUPPOSE, THAT ADVERTISERS THINK THEY ARE DOING SOMETHING GOOD, CONTRIBUTING TO THE HEALTH OF SOCIETY, AND PROMOTING PRODUCTIVE, HEALTHY VALUES. JUDGING BY THEIR OWN WORDS, HOWEVER, PROBABLY NOT.

"IF YOU OWN THIS CHILD AT AN EARLY AGE, YOU CAN OWN THIS KID FOR YEARS TO COME."

—MIKE SEARLES, FORMER PRESIDENT OF KIDS "R" US

"YOU CAN MANIPULATE CONSUMERS INTO WANTING AND THEREFORE BUYING YOUR PRODUCTS... IS IT ETHICAL? I DON'T KNOW. IT'S A GAME. OUR ROLE... IS TO MOVE PRODUCTS."

—LUCY HUGHES, MARKETING CONSULTANT

MS HUGHES, BY THE WAY, IS CREDITED WITH INVENTING THE "NAG FACTOR," WHICH MEASURES HOW MUCH KIDS CAN BE PERSUADED TO PESTER THEIR PARENTS.

MY WORK HERE IS DONE...

THE TOTAL VOLUME OF ADVERTISING DEFIES BE-LIEF. IN 2016, AMERICAN BUSINESS WILL SPEND AN ESTIMATED

$550

ON ADVERTISING FOR EVERY INDIVIDUAL MAN, WOMAN, AND CHILD IN THE U.S.—MORE THAN DOUBLE THE TOTAL OF 50 YEARS AGO, AND STILL RISING STEEPLY. SEE HOW THEY VALUE US?

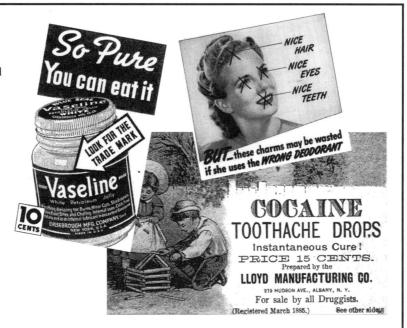

ALL THESE TRENDS SUGGEST THAT THE COUNTRY—AND WITH IT THE WHOLE WORLD—HAS ENTERED INTO SOME CRAZY, EXTREME, OVERPOWERING STAGE OF THE CAPITALIST SYSTEM, NOW IT'S CAPITALISM ON STEROIDS... CAPITALISM EVERYWHERE ALL THE TIME... IT'S THE JUGGERNAUT WE CALL

HYPER-CAPITALISM.

WHAT DEFINES HYPERCAPITALISM? SOME OF ITS FEATURES, LIKE UBIQUITOUS ADVERTISING AND EXTREME INEQUALITY, APPEARED IN THE PREVIOUS PAGES.

BUT THOSE ARE **SYMPTOMS** OF HYPERCAPITALISM, NOT ITS UNDERLYING PRINCIPLES. THEY ARE **RESULTS** OF THE SYSTEM, NOT ITS CAUSES.

IN THIS BOOK, WE AIM TO EXPOSE THE STRUCTURES THAT SUPPORT HYPERCAPITALISM, THE FUEL THAT RUNS ITS ENGINE, THE GOALS THAT ANIMATE ITS RELENTLESS ADVANCE.

TO DO SO, WE FIRST NEED TO EXAMINE ITS BASIC FOUNDATIONS, THE CHASSIS ON WHICH THE JUGGERNAUT IS BUILT.

FIRST, IN OTHER WORDS, WE NEED TO UNDERSTAND PLAIN, OLD, ORDINARY **CAPITALISM**; ONLY THEN CAN WE SEE HOW IT GOT TO BE SO HYPER!

Chapter 2
THE BASICS OF CAPITALISM

CAPITALISM IS A WAY TO ORGANIZE THE MAKING, TRADING, AND OWNERSHIP OF **STUFF**. IN OTHER WORDS, IT'S AN **ECONOMIC** SYSTEM.

IT ISN'T THE BE-ALL AND END-ALL OF EVERYTHING, DESPITE HOW THINGS MAY LOOK AT COSTCO SOMETIMES.

THERE'S MORE??

BEFORE SAYING WHAT CAPITALISM IS, WE SHOULD FIRST SAY WHAT IT **ISN'T**, NAMELY GOD-GIVEN AND ETERNAL. COUNTLESS SOCIAL AND ECONOMIC SYSTEMS HAVE HELD SWAY AS THE CENTURIES RUMBLED PAST.

ANOTHER 500 YEARS, ANOTHER SYSTEM!

FOR 99% OF HUMAN EXISTENCE, NEARLY EVERYONE LIVED BY FORAGING, WITH NO FIXED HOME, NO GOVERNMENT, AND FEW POSSESSIONS. PEOPLE TRAVELED LIGHT.

WHAT SAY WE DUMP THE DEAD WEIGHT...?

ONCE FARMING BEGAN, SYSTEM-ORGANIZERS LET THEIR IMAGINATIONS RUN WILD, INTO **FEUDAL-ISM** (PEASANTS ATTACHED TO A PIECE OF LAND RULED BY A LORD); **SLAVERY** (WORKERS OWNED PERSONALLY BY THE BOSS); AND THE NAMELESS WAY OF NATIVE NORTH AMERICANS, WHO HAD NO NOTION OF PRIVATE LAND OWNERSHIP WHATSOEVER.

WE BELONG TO **IT**, ACTUALLY!

BIZARRE!

22

CAPITALISM, IN FACT, IS A NOVELTY. IT CAME OF AGE IN INDUSTRIAL BRITAIN, EUROPE, AND THE UNITED STATES IN THE 1800S, WHICH EXPLAINS THE ICONIC CAPITALIST'S *FIN-DE-SIECLE* SIDEWHISKERS, TOP HAT, AND TAILCOAT.

BIZARRE!

AS REALISTS, YOUR AUTHORS PREFER TO DEPICT MODERN CAPITALISTS AS THEY ACTUALLY ARE, DRESSED IN SWEATERS, SLACKS, TASSEL LOAFERS, AND MAYBE A TEE SHIRT OR HOODIE. THESE DAYS IT'S HARD TO TELL A TITAN OF FINANCE FROM ANYONE ELSE WITHOUT INSPECTING HIS LABELS.

"CRAFTED BY ROYAL CUSTOM TAILORS, DUBAI"

AND WE SAY "HIS" ADVISEDLY. MEN STILL CONTROL THE VAST BULK OF BUSINESS, WITH SOME EXCEPTIONS.

CUTE!

I OWN 10,000 OF THESE, JACK!

LEMONAD

23

A CAPITALIST LOOKS AT CAPITALISM

WHAT THEN IS CAPITALISM? TO EXPLAIN IT, WE'VE INVITED A GUEST NARRATOR, **CAPPY FREEMARK,** WHO HAS VERY FINE LABELS INDEED!

I CAN'T WAIT TO SEE THE LOOK ON THEIR FACES WHEN WE CRUSH THOSE LOSERS, HEH HEH—OOPS!

AHEM! (COUGH) OH, HI! LET'S START WITH A LITTLE **STORY**...

ONCE UPON A TIME, IN A LITTLE COTTAGE NESTLED IN THE VILLAGE OF COTTAGEVILLE, LIVED A LITTLE OLD WOMAN NAMED **BETTY BAKER** WHO LIKED TO MAKE **BREAD.**

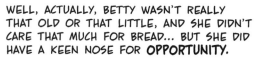

WELL, ACTUALLY, BETTY WASN'T REALLY THAT OLD OR THAT LITTLE, AND SHE DIDN'T CARE THAT MUCH FOR BREAD... BUT SHE DID HAVE A KEEN NOSE FOR **OPPORTUNITY.**

SMELLS LIKE MONEY...

SHE NOTICED THAT EVERY HOME IN THE NEIGHBORHOOD DID ITS OWN BAKING. THE AROMA WAS DIVINE, BUT ALL THE MEASURING, MIXING, KNEADING, PUNCHING, RISING, SHAPING, BAKING, AND COOLING TOOK HOURS OUT OF EVERYBODY'S DAY.

A WORSE TIME-SUCK THAN THE INTERNET...

BETTY MUSED THAT SHE COULD HELP PEOPLE SAVE TIME AND EFFORT BY BAKING EVERYONE'S BREAD **HERSELF.**

I'LL FILL A SOCIAL NEED!

AND I CAN TURN THAT BREAD INTO, UM, DOUGH...

OW! A LOW PUN!

24

TO START A BAKERY, BETTY NEEDED TO BUY EQUIPMENT AND SUPPLIES, WHICH COST **MONEY**. LUCKILY, BETTY HAD SOMETHING SAVED FROM AN EARLIER VENTURE BUYING AND SELLING CONDEMNED COTTAGES.

BUT NEVER MIND ABOUT **THAT**...

THE MINUTE SHE DECIDED TO INVEST IT, THIS MONEY UNDERWENT AN UNCANNY CONCEPTUAL TRANSFORMATION.

WHA—?

DEET
DOOT
BEEP
BOOP

IT STOPPED BEING MERE MONEY AND SUDDENLY TURNED INTO **CAPITAL**.

GASP! WHO ARE **YOU**?

THE **ENTREPRENEURIAL SPIRIT!!**

GO ON! MAKE A WISH! MAKE THREE WISHES! MAKE A HUNDRED!

I CAN'T PROMISE TO **GRANT** ANY OF 'EM, BUT IT'S GOOD TO SET **GOALS**...

HOW ABOUT A HAND HERE?

NOT MY JOB, SORRY!

BETTY SPENDS SOME OF HER CAPITAL ON EQUIPMENT: AN OVEN, MIXERS, BOWLS, PANS, AND WHATEVER ELSE SHE NEEDS. THIS STUFF FORMS HER **FIXED** OR **SUNK** CAPITAL, MONEY THAT STAYS IN THE BUSINESS. PRESUMABLY, SHE CAN RECOUP THESE EXPENSES BY SELLING THE GOODS.

ALWAYS BE CONFIDENT!

HE'S EVERY-WHERE...

SHE ALSO HAS TO PAY **OPERATING EXPENSES,** THE COST OF FUEL FOR THE OVEN, FLOUR, YEAST, SALT, CLEANING SUPPLIES, AND ANYTHING ELSE **USED UP** IN MAKING BREAD OR MAINTAINING THE BAKERY.

YES!

BETTY'S BUNS

AT LAST, BETTY PUTS UP A SIGN, FIRES THE OVENS, BAKES A BATCH OF LOAVES, AND THROWS OPEN THE DOORS TO A HUNGRY PUBLIC. NOW MONEY STARTS COMING IN.

THIS DIAGRAM SHOWS THE INITIAL CAPITAL BEING DIVIDED BETWEEN THE FIXED CAPITAL, WHICH REMAINS IN THE BUSINESS, AND THE OPERATING COSTS, WHICH FLOW OUT.

FIXED CAPITAL

OPERATING EXPENSES

THE LITTLE SHOP OF ARROWS!

ORIGINAL CAPITAL

FOR THE BUSINESS TO BE VIABLE, INCOME MUST EXCEED OPERATING COSTS. BETTY ALSO NEEDS SOMETHING TO PAY FOR HER OWN LIVING EXPENSES—FOOD, SHELTER, CLOTHES, A MASERATI—AND THEN THERE'S A LITTLE SOMETHING MORE, THE **EXTRA** MONEY THAT MAKES CAPITALISM GO:

PROFIT.

OPERATING EXPENSES

PROFIT

CONSUMERS' MONEY IN

LIVING EXPENSES (SALARY)

27

WHAT'S THE POINT OF PROFIT? IF BETTY CAN COVER THE BAKERY'S EXPENSES AND EARN A SALARY, WHY DOES SHE NEED ANY MORE?

YEAH... WITHOUT PROFIT, SHE COULD CUT PRICES!!

SH! DON'T BOTHER THE NICE MAN!

TRUE... BUT THE POINT IS THAT PROFIT IS **SOCIALLY USEFUL!!**

HUH?

IN THE FIRST PLACE, PROFIT IS AN **INCENTIVE** TO **INVEST**. REMEMBER, BETTY PUT HERSELF AT RISK OF **LOSING** HER MONEY IF THE BAKERY FAILED. PROFIT IS HER **REWARD** FOR TAKING THAT RISK!

IN THE SECOND PLACE, PROFIT CAN BECOME **CAPITAL** FOR INVESTMENT IN NEW BUSINESS. PROFIT GENERATES ECONOMIC GROWTH!

HMM... IF IT'S SO SOCIALLY IMPORTANT, WHY DOESN'T SOCIETY OWN IT?

I'LL PRETEND I DIDN'T HEAR THAT!

SUPPOSE BETTY'S BUNS ARE SO POPULAR THAT THE BREAD RUNS OUT BEFORE EVERYONE IS SERVED.

SORRY!

WITH HER PROFITS, BETTY CAN **EXPAND**: BUY A NEW OVEN, MORE SUPPLIES, ETC. THIS WILL SATISFY MORE PEOPLE **AND** MAKE MORE PROFIT. EVERYONE WINS!

PROFIT MAKES DREAMS COME TRUE!

LATELY I'VE BEEN DREAMING OF WORLD DOMINATION... IS THAT HEALTHY?

ALL OUT

AND SO...

NOW THAT THE BUSINESS IS TOO MUCH FOR ONE PERSON TO HANDLE, BETTY POSTS A HELP-WANTED SIGN. SHE'S GOING TO HIRE A **WORKER**.

HELP WANTED

AFTER INTERVIEWING HALF THE PEOPLE IN COTTAGEVILLE, BETTY OFFERS THE ASSISTANT JOB TO **ERNIE WAGES**.

I'M A **JOB CREATOR**...

HOW MUCH DOES BETTY PAY HER NEW HIRE? HER SELF-INTEREST TELLS HER: **AS LITTLE AS POSSIBLE.**

I FEEL SO GOOD ABOUT MYSELF!

ON THE ONE HAND, ERNIE HAS TO HAVE ENOUGH TO KEEP HIMSELF IN BREAD, BEANS, RAGS, AND A HOVEL. OTHERWISE, HE WOULD WASTE AWAY AND BE BAD FOR BUSINESS.

A LIVING SKELETON BEHIND THE COUNTER MIGHT CREEP OUT THE CUSTOMERS.

ON THE OTHER HAND, IF BETTY PAYS ANY MORE, HER PROFIT GOES DOWN, ALSO BAD FOR BUSINESS... AND SO, THERE BEING NO OTHER JOBS IN COTTAGEVILLE, ERNIE SIGNS ON FOR SUBSISTENCE WAGES.

BE GRATEFUL I'M GIVING YOU WORK!

FUNNY, I THOUGHT **I** WAS GIVING **YOU** WORK...

WITH THE BUN BARN UP AND RUNNING, A NEW ISSUE ARISES:

COMPETITION,

THE HEART AND SOUL OF CAPITALISM.

FOR SOME REASON, THEY CALL IT A "RAT RACE."

FOR EXAMPLE, BREAD BUYERS MAY COMPETE WITH EACH OTHER. WHEN BREAD IS IN SHORT SUPPLY, THEY BID UP THE PRICE.

$10!
$20!
$50!!

ERNIE WAGES COMPETED FOR HIS JOB. WHEN JOBS ARE SCARCE, WORKERS BID DOWN THE WAGE THEY ARE WILLING TO TAKE.

I'LL TAKE $8 AN HOUR...
I'LL TAKE $7.75!
I'LL TAKE... SIGH... $7...

THEN, ONE MOMENTOUS DAY, BETTY IS HORRIFIED TO DISCOVER A NEW BUSINESS, **BOB'S BAGELBOX,** OPENING ACROSS THE STREET. SUDDENLY, SHE ALSO FACES COMPETITION!

WHY DIDN'T YOU SAY THIS WAS AN OPEN RELATIONSHIP??

I THOUGHT YOU KNEW...

BOB'S

SUDDENLY THERE'S MORE BREAD, SO **CONNIE SUMER**, BETTY'S BEST CUSTOMER, STOPS BIDDING AND CROSSES THE STREET.

B-BUT—BRAND LOYALTY?

NOT MY ROLE HERE, BETS'!

NOW BUSINESSES BID FOR CUSTOMERS. BOB SETS HIS PRICES BELOW BETTY'S, SO SHE HAS TO CUT HERS TO MATCH. PROFIT FALLS.

10% OFF everything

WELL, NOW...

BOB HITS BACK BY INTRODUCING NEW FLAVORS. AGAIN CONNIE CHEERS AND BETTY MOANS.

THIS AND THE THERAPY BILLS ARE KILLING ME...

OO! STRAWBERRY BACON!

AS THESE BUSINESSES GROW, SO DO OPPOR-TUNITIES FOR MORE BUSINESS. SOON COTTAGE-VILLE SEES NEW FLOUR MILLS, TRUCKING FIRMS, BURLAP-BAG MAKERS, BUILDING CONTRACTORS, BANKS...

EVENTUALLY, THE NUMBER OF JOB OPENINGS OUT-STRIPS THE SUPPLY OF WORKERS, AND COMPANIES COMPETE FOR LABOR BY BIDDING UP WAGES.

I'LL PAY YOU **$10** AN HOUR!

I'LL PAY $11!

$12!

$13!

$16!

$14!

IN SUM:

COMPETITION EXPANDS CONSUMER CHOICE, LOWERS PRICES, CUTS PROFITS, AND, IN A GROWING ECONOMY, RAISES WAGES.

WHY CAN'T EVERYONE **ELSE** COMPETE BESIDES ME?

TRULY, COMPETITION IS MARVELOUS...

... AS LONG AS IT DOESN'T GET OUT OF HAND, LIKE THE DAY BOB DECIDED TO INCREASE HIS MARKET SHARE BY SETTING BETTY'S BUN BARN ON **FIRE**.

WAY TO THINK OUTSIDE THE BOX, BOBBO!

BOB'S PYROMANIA HIGHLIGHTS THE NEED FOR RULES AND REFEREES IN THE CAPITALIST GAME, IN OTHER WORDS, **LAWS** AND **GOVERNMENT**. THE POLICE ARREST BOB AND TAKE HIM AWAY.

GOVERNMENT IS THE PROBLEM, NOT THE SOLUTION!!

GOVERNMENT'S ROLE IN CAPITALISM IS MORE COMPLEX AND DIFFUSE THAN THE SIMPLE SELF-INTEREST OF OWNERS, WORKERS, AND CONSUMERS. **PAUL ITTICKS,** MAYOR OF COTTAGEVILLE, HAS ALL SORTS OF GOALS AND DREAMS.

HI HOWAYA

MAKE PEOPLE HAPPY

BALANCE BUDGET

ENFORCE LAW AND ORDER

BOSS PEOPLE AROUND...

STIMULATE BUSINESS

SAVE THE WORLD

BE JUST AND MERCIFUL

CRUSH MY OPPONENTS

BUILD SOMETHING HUGE AND VISIBLE WITH MY NAME ON IT.

"PURE" CAPITALISM, HOWEVER, WANTS GOVERNMENT TO AVOID EXPENSIVE PROGRAMS, OR ANY ACTIVITIES THAT MAY STIFLE THE ENTREPRENEURIAL SPIRIT.

STAND ASIDE, ITTICKS!

WAIT—AREN'T YOU THE ARSONIST'S ACCOMPLICE?

NOT THAT CAPITALISM IS AGAINST SOCIAL WELFARE... BUT ITS MAIN CONCERN IS THAT GOVERNMENT SHOULD CONCENTRATE ON ENCOURAGING **MORE CAPITALISM.**

BECAUSE WHAT COULD GO WRONG?

WHAT ARE THESE CAPITALISM-FRIENDLY FUNCTIONS OF GOVERNMENT? ONE WE'VE ALREADY SEEN: PUTTING AWAY CRIMINALS.

YOU DIDN'T JUST ROB A HOUSE, PAL; YOU ROBBED AN INSURANCE COMPANY.

DON'T YOU SEE? I'M STIMULATING THE ECONOMY BY INCREASING CONSUMPTION!

GOVERNMENT ALSO ACTS AS THE FINAL JUDGE OF PRIVATE DISPUTES. THAT IS, GOVERNMENT **ENFORCES CONTRACTS.**

FOR INSTANCE, BETTY PROMISES TO PAY HER FLOUR SUPPLIER 30 DAYS AFTER DELIVERY.

THE CHECK WILL BE IN THE MAIL ON TUESDAY.

IF SHE DOESN'T KEEP HER PROMISE AND PAY, THE FLOUR COMPANY CAN TAKE HER TO COURT—A GOVERNMENT INSTITUTION.

YOUR HONOR, MY CLIENT WAS CLEARLY REFERRING TO TUESDAY, FEBRUARY 15, 3025!

HOOEY!

GESUNDHEIT.

IF THE JUDGMENT GOES AGAINST BETTY, GOVERNMENT CAN COMPEL HER TO PAY. IT CAN EVEN DRAW MONEY DIRECTLY FROM HER BANK ACCOUNT IF NECESSARY.

ALL IN THE INTERESTS OF FAIR PLAY!

THE GOVERNMENT ALSO
HELPS BUSINESS WITH

INFRASTRUCTURE

PROJECTS LIKE ROADS,
BRIDGES, DAMS, ELECTRIC
GRIDS, AND SEWERS. THESE
JOBS ARE OFTEN TOO BIG OR
UNPROFITABLE FOR PRIVATE
BUSINESS, SO GOVERNMENT
BUILDS AND MAINTAINS THEM.

WELCOME TO THE
PAUL ITTICKS HOLE
IN THE GROUND.

INFRASTRUCTURE DOES MORE THAN IMPROVE PUBLIC LIFE. IT ALSO AIDS THE CAPITALIST GOALS
OF MORE **COMPETITION** AND **OPPORTUNITY**. ROADS AND CANALS ENABLE DISTANT BUSINESSES
TO COMPETE WITH EACH OTHER, ALLOW WORKERS AND CONSUMERS TO MOVE MORE EASILY, AND
CUT THE COST OF MOVING GOODS AND SUPPLIES.

RATS!

AND LET'S NOT FORGET THE

MILITARY!!

BESIDES PROTECTING THE NATION
FROM INVASION, GOVERNMENT'S
ARMED FORCES ALSO SECURE
ACCESS TO RAW MATERIALS,
TRADE ROUTES, AND MARKETS
FOR THE NATION'S BUSINESSES.

FOLLOW YOUR
NOSE 'TIL YOU
SMELL OIL...

DOING ALL THIS COSTS MONEY, SO GOVERNMENT MUST RAISE REVENUE. THIS IT DOES BY **BORROWING**—SELLING GOVERNMENT BONDS TO WHOEVER WILL BUY THEM—AND BY **TAXING,** COMPELLING CITIZENS AND COMPANIES TO GIVE IT CASH.

GOSH, FOR ME?

NOBODY LIKES HAVING MONEY TAKEN AWAY, SO EVERYONE COMPLAINS ABOUT TAXES DESPITE ALL THE BENEFITS.

I JUST DON'T SEE WHERE IT GOES...

BECAUSE THE AMOUNT OF TAX REVENUE DEPENDS ON PROFITS, PURCHASES, AND INCOME, GOVERNMENT HAS A STRONG INTEREST IN ECONOMIC ACTIVITY. THE MORE BUYING AND SELLING, THE BETTER!

"WE CANNOT LET THE TERRORISTS ACHIEVE THE GOAL OF FRIGHTENING OUR NATION TO THE POINT... WHERE PEOPLE DON'T SHOP."

—PRES. GEORGE W. BUSH

AT LAST! AN HONEST POLITICIAN!

THESE, THEN, ARE THE FOUR BASIC ROLES IN CAPITALISM'S CAST OF CHARACTERS: **BUSINESS OWNER-OPERATOR, CONSUMER, WORKER,** AND **GOVERNMENT.**

OWNERS, CONSUMERS, AND WORKERS ARE SUPPOSED TO ACT PURELY IN THEIR OWN **INDIVIDUAL SELF-INTEREST.** IT'S THEIR JOB TO BE SELFISH AND COMPETITIVE.

I WANT THE GREATEST POSSIBLE PROFIT!

I WANT THE BEST POSSIBLE DEAL ON EVERY-THING!

I WANT TO MAKE THE BEST LIVING I CAN!

OWNER

CONSUMER

WORKER

GOVERNMENT IS DIFFERENT. ITS MAIN GOAL IS A ROBUST CAPITALIST ECONOMY, RUNNING ACCORDING TO THE RULES. GOVERNMENT SHOULD FOSTER COMPETITION AND OPPORTUNITY, MEANING THAT CITIZENS MAY ALL SEEK GAIN WITHIN THE LAW.

I WANT THE BEST POSSIBLE RAT RACE!

37

THIS CAPITALIST IDEAL WAS FIRST DESCRIBED BY SCOTSMAN

ADAM SMITH

(1723–1790), THE GRANDDADDY OF FREE-MARKET THEORY.

HIS INFLUENCE IS AS GREAT AS HIS CHIN!

HIS CELEBRATED 1776 MASTERPIECE **THE WEALTH OF NATIONS** ARGUES FORCEFULLY FOR TWO PRINCIPLES, CONSIDERED HIGHLY DARING AT THE TIME.

1. AN ECONOMY, IN FACT, A SOCIETY, DOES BEST WHEN PEOPLE ARE FREE TO ACT IN THEIR OWN **SELF-INTEREST.** CAPITAL'S PURSUIT OF PROFIT LEADS TO INVESTMENT IN THE MOST PRODUCTIVE AND USEFUL ACTIVITIES. IN SMITH'S FAMOUS PHRASE, THE INDIVIDUAL IS "LED BY AN INVISIBLE HAND TO PROMOTE AN END WHICH WAS NO PART OF HIS INTENTION... BUT PURSUING HIS OWN END, HE FREQUENTLY PROMOTES THAT OF SOCIETY MORE EFFECTUALLY."

STRANGE... I AM HAVING AN URGE TO INVEST IN TACO TRUCKS...

2. **COMPETITION IS GOOD.** BUSINESS COMPETITION REDUCES PRICES, RAISES QUALITY, ENHANCES CHOICE, AND—WHEN COMBINED WITH POINT 1—FOSTERS GROWTH, WHICH, IN TURN, RAISES WAGES. EVERYBODY WINS, EXCEPT FOR THOSE WHO FAIL BY MAKING STUPID INVESTMENTS IN SOCIALLY USELESS PURSUITS.

CAPITALISM HAS AN INVISIBLE FOOT, TOO!

ADAM SMITH'S IDEAS SHOCKED MANY PEOPLE. AFTER ALL, HE WAS ADVOCATING **UNIVERSAL SELFISHNESS.** TO ACHIEVE PROGRESS, HE SAID, EVERYONE MUST STRIVE TO GET **MORE**: MORE PROFIT, MORE PAY, MORE STUFF FOR THEIR MONEY. THIS WAS UNHEARD OF, AGAINST COMMON SENSE, AND SURELY UNCHRISTIAN. HOW CAN GREED BE GOOD?

MANY PEOPLE STILL FIND IT A CHALLENGING THOUGHT. DOES HUMANITY'S WELL-BEING REALLY DEPEND ON MAXIMIZING ECONOMIC ACTIVITY?

YET, SHOCKING OR NO, ADAM SMITH'S IDEAS HAVE TAKEN HOLD. ECONOMICS DEPARTMENTS AND GOVERNMENTS, ESPECIALLY IN THE ENGLISH-SPEAKING WORLD, HAVE MADE *THE WEALTH OF NATIONS* THEIR BIBLE.

STILL, NO SYSTEM IS PERFECT, AND CAPITALISM DOES HAVE POTENTIAL FOR **CONFLICT.** BUSINESS OWNERS' INTERESTS IN SOME WAYS RUN AGAINST THE INTERESTS OF WORKERS AND CONSUMERS. BETTY WANTS TO MAXIMIZE PROFIT AND TO CHARGE THE HIGHEST PRICES THE MARKET WILL BEAR, WHILE ERNIE WANTS HIGH WAGES AND CONNIE WANTS LOW PRICES.

	OWNER WANTS	WORKER WANTS
WAGES	LOWER	HIGHER
PROFITS	HIGHER	LOWER

	OWNER WANTS	CONSUMER WANTS
PRICES	HIGHER	LOWER
PROFITS	HIGHER	LOWER

YOU WERE PERFECTLY WELL AWARE OF THIS, WEREN'T YOU, A.S.?

"THE INTEREST OF... DEALERS... IS ALWAYS IN SOME RESPECTS DIFFERENT FROM, AND EVEN OPPOSITE TO, THAT OF THE PUBLIC."

SMITH WOULD HAVE THESE CONFLICTS RESOLVED BY A WISE AND PRINCIPLED GOVERNMENT, DEDICATED TO **MORE** FREEDOM AND COMPETITION. ONLY ECONOMIC **GROWTH,** HE ARGUED, COULD BRING PROSPERITY FOR ALL.

IN THE YEARS SINCE HIS CLASSIC WAS PUBLISHED, CAPITALISM HAS SUCCEEDED SPECTACULARLY, LIFTING BILLIONS OF PEOPLE, FROM SEOUL TO BANGALORE, OUT OF POVERTY.

I'M SORRY I MISSED IT...

NO WONDER SO MANY LEADERS AND THINKERS HAVE CHEERED FOR THIS GREAT WAY OF DOING BUSINESS!

"A PEOPLE... WHO ARE POSSESSED OF THE SPIRIT OF COMMERCE, WHO SEE, AND WHO WILL PURSUE THEIR ADVANTAGES, MAY ACHIEVE ALMOST ANYTHING."

—GEORGE WASHINGTON

"THE ONLY WAY THAT HAS EVER BEEN DISCOVERED TO HAVE A LOT OF PEOPLE COOPERATE TOGETHER VOLUNTARILY IS THROUGH THE FREE MARKET."

—MILTON FRIEDMAN, ECONOMIST

"THE CAPACITY TO ENVISION A SET OF FUTURE EVENTS AND THEN ACT TO FULFILL THEM IS A CENTRAL SOURCE OF CAPITALISM'S STRENGTH."

—WILLIAM GREIDER, WRITER

"CAPITALISM HAS CREATED THE HIGHEST STANDARD OF LIVING EVER KNOWN ON EARTH."

—AYN RAND, WRITER

"I'VE ALWAYS BEEN A STRONG BELIEVER IN THE POWER OF THE FREE MARKET."

—BARACK OBAMA

"THE AMERICAN FREE ENTERPRISE SYSTEM HAS BEEN THE GREATEST ENGINE FOR PROSPERITY THE WORLD HAS EVER SEEN."

—TED CRUZ, SENATOR

THANKS FOR THE SNAPPY PRESENTATION, CAPPY... BUT AREN'T THERE SOME **OTHER** QUOTES YOU MIGHT HAVE MENTIONED?

HM?

YOU KNOW... WHAT ADAM SMITH WROTE IN *THE WEALTH OF NATIONS* ABOUT THE **PITFALLS** OF FREE ENTERPRISE!

OH... THAT...

ON HOW OWNERS BEHAVE:

"PEOPLE OF THE SAME TRADE SELDOM MEET TOGETHER, EVEN FOR MERRIMENT AND DIVERSION, BUT THE CONVERSATION ENDS IN A CONSPIRACY AGAINST THE PUBLIC, OR IN SOME CONTRIVANCE TO RAISE PRICES."

ON POLITICAL INFLUENCE:

"WHENEVER THE LEGISLATURE ATTEMPTS TO REGULATE THE DIFFERENCES BETWEEN MASTERS AND THEIR WORKMEN, ITS COUNSELLORS ARE ALWAYS THE MASTERS."

ON WHAT THAT INFLUENCE TENDS TO BE:

"A PROPOSAL OF ANY NEW LAW OR REGULATION OF COMMERCE WHICH COMES FROM [OWNERS] OUGHT ALWAYS TO BE LISTENED TO WITH GREAT PRECAUTION, AND OUGHT NEVER TO BE ADOPTED TILL AFTER HAVING BEEN LONG AND CAREFULLY EXAMINED NOT ONLY WITH THE MOST SCRUPULOUS, BUT WITH THE MOST SUSPICIOUS ATTENTION. IT COMES FROM AN ORDER OF MEN WHOSE INTEREST IS NEVER EXACTLY THE SAME WITH THAT OF THE PUBLIC, WHO HAVE GENERALLY AN INTEREST TO DECEIVE AND EVEN TO OPPRESS THE PUBLIC, AND WHO ACCORDINGLY HAVE, UPON MANY OCCASIONS, BOTH DECEIVED AND OPPRESSED IT."

THESE CAUTIONS SUGGEST THAT **REAL-WORLD** CAPITALISM MAY NOT BE THE PURE COMPETITION IMAGINED BY ADAM SMITH...

IN THE NEXT CHAPTER, WE LOOK AT HOW FAR CAPITALISM CAN BE FROM CAPPY'S LITTLE FOUR-CHARACTER FABLE... AND IN THE PROCESS, WE DISCOVER THE ANSWER TO THIS QUESTION: HOW DOES CAPPY FREEMARK MAKE **HIS** MONEY?

HEY! THAT'S **MY** BUSINESS!

Chapter 3
CORPORATIONS AND THEIR OWNERS

AS CAPPY SHOULD HAPPILY ADMIT, HIS ACCOUNT OF CAPITALISM WAS A SORT OF **TOY,** A MODEL SYSTEM.

WELL, YEAH, OKAY...

TO SEE HOW THE SYSTEM REALLY WORKS, AND HOW IT GOT HYPER, WE NEED TO INTRODUCE TWO NEW AND POWERFUL PLAYERS IN THE ECONOMIC DRAMA: **CORPORATIONS** AND **INDEPENDENT INVESTORS.**

SO BEAUTIFUL ...

INCORPORATION IS A WAY OF **LIMITING LIABILITY**, I.E., THE AMOUNT OF MONEY AT RISK OF BEING LOST. THIS IS SOMETHING THAT WORRIES BETTY BAKER!

BETTY ONCE HAD A COMPETITOR, **MANYA LOAF**, WHO, LIKE BETTY, OWNED A BAKERY...

... UNTIL ONE DAY, LOAF'S EMPLOYEE, ROB "OATMEAL" RAZIN, FELL INTO THE KNEADING MACHINE.

RAZIN'S REMAINS FOUND THEIR WAY INTO SEVERAL HUNDRED PUMPERNICKEL LOAVES.

THAT'S NOT A CARAWAY SEED, IT'S A BUTTON...

THE RAZIN FAMILY **SUED** MANYA LOAF AND WON THE ENORMOUS JUDGMENT THEY DESERVED.

NOT ONLY DID LOAF LOSE HER BAKERY AND EVERYTHING IN IT, BUT ALSO HER HOUSE, CAR, AND SAVINGS—EVERYTHING BUT A BARREL, WHICH SHE WEARS IN HER NEW HOME UNDER A BRIDGE.

SNARL!

MANYA'S PROBLEM WAS THAT HER **LIABILITY** WAS **UNLIMITED.** SHE WAS VULNERABLE TO LOSING EVERYTHING SHE OWNED. NEEDLESS TO SAY, BETTY DOESN'T WANT THIS HAPPENING TO **HER!**

I'M WEARING A RUT IN MY WALL-TO-WALL!

HAPPILY FOR BETTY, THE LAW PROVIDES A CHEAP, SIMPLE SOLUTION. ALL BETTY NEEDS TO DO IS FILL OUT SOME **INCORPORATION FORMS** AND REGISTER THEM WITH THE STATE FOR A SMALL FEE.

STILL DONE ON PAPER IN MOST PLACES.

SUDDENLY, THE BUSINESS IS A **CORPORATION,** SEPARATE FROM BETTY'S PERSONAL ASSETS!

AND LIFE GOES ON AS BEFORE, EXCEPT FOR THE EXTRA TAX FORMS, LAWYERS, AND ACCOUNTANTS!

INCORPORATION CHANGES THE LEGAL STANDING OF A BUSINESS. **ALL LIABILITY BELONGS TO THE CORPORATION,** NOT TO ITS INDIVIDUAL OWNER(S). CLAIMANTS LIKE THE RAZIN ESTATE CAN USUALLY WIN JUDGMENTS ONLY AGAINST THE **CORPORATION, NOT AGAINST ITS OWNER(S) PERSONALLY.**

I'D BETTER INCORPORATE TO PROTECT THE BARREL.

IN OTHER WORDS, BETTY'S PERSONAL HOUSE, CAR, AND BANK ACCOUNTS ARE IMMUNE TO CLAIMS AGAINST BETTCO'S ASSETS.

IT'S LIKE AN ECONOMIC FLU SHOT!

NOW IT'S BETTCO'S CREDITORS WHO PACE THE FLOOR!

45

CORPORATE PROTECTION **STIMULATES INVESTMENT.** PEOPLE ARE READIER TO RISK MONEY WHEN LIABILITY IS LIMITED. AT WORST, THEY MAY LOSE WHAT THEY PUT IN, BUT NO MORE, SO THERE'S LESS TO FEAR. THIS EXTRA INCENTIVE TO INVEST IS EXACTLY WHY THE GOVERNMENT LICENSES CORPORATIONS IN THE FIRST PLACE. MORE INVESTMENT SPURS ECONOMIC GROWTH.

RISK IS GOOD, BUT THERE'S NO SENSE GOING NUTS WITH IT!

NOT EVERY INVESTOR WANTS TO START A NEW BUSINESS, HOWEVER. IT'S EASIER TO BUY A PIECE—A **SHARE**—OF AN EXISTING ONE. CAPPY HERE WOULD LIKE TO BUY INTO BETTCO.

I WANT A PIECE OF YOUR BUNS!

STEP BACK!

I MEAN BETTCO'S BUNS—**BETTCO'S!**

WELL, THAT'S DIFFERENT...

AND HE'S NOT THE ONLY ONE! THE COMPANY'S PROFITS ATTRACT OTHER INVESTORS, TOO..

BETT-CO! BETT-CO!! BETT-CO!

46

BETTY PONDERS HER OPTIONS. RIGHT NOW SHE OWNS 100% OF A MEDIUM-SIZED BUSINESS, BUT SHE HAS LITTLE CASH ON HAND. THE INVESTORS AT THE DOOR OFFER **CAPITAL** IN EXCHANGE FOR **PART OWNERSHIP**. IF SHE SELLS, SHE LOSES SOME CONTROL, BUT...

100% OF A **LITTLE** VERSUS PART OF A **TON**...

HMMM...

WHERE'S MY ACCOUNTANT??

BETTY'S ADVISERS CALCULATE THE COMPANY'S VALUE AT **$40 MILLION**. THEY PROPOSE THAT BETTY KEEP 1/4 FOR HERSELF AND SELL THE REMAINING 3/4 FOR **$30 MILLION**.

GET OUT!

AND BETTY'S DECISION IS...

ARE YOU KIDDING?

THREE-QUARTERS OF THE COMPANY'S TOTAL "STOCK" IS DIVIDED INTO 3 MILLION EQUAL **SHARES**, WORTH $10 APIECE. THE SHARES ARE "TENDERED" TO THE PUBLIC IN AN **INITIAL PUBLIC OFFERING (IPO)**, AND BETTCO'S GOES WELL. EVERY SHARE OF STOCK IS SOLD.

BUY A THOUSAND SHARES, GET A FREE MUFFIN!

WITH $30 MILLION TO PLAY WITH, BETTY BEGINS BUILDING THE GLOBAL EMPIRE OF HER DREAMS. NEW BETTCO BUNNERIES RISE LIKE POPOVERS, SPREADING THEIR IRRESISTIBLE AROMA FAR BEYOND COTTAGEVILLE.

AND **I** GET A VERY INTIMIDATING DESK!

(BY THE WAY, YOU MAY WONDER WHY BETTY SOLD MORE THAN HALF THE COMPANY RATHER THAN KEEPING AT LEAST 51% OF THE STOCK. THE REASON IS THAT SHE CAN STILL DOMINATE BETTCO WITH HER MINORITY SHARE. THE OTHER 3 MILLION SHARES ARE DISPERSED AMONG MANY INVESTORS, WHO HAPPILY DEFER TO BETTY'S JUDGMENT AND EXPERIENCE.)

BETTY IS THRILLED, BUT WHAT DO THE INVESTORS GET FOR THEIR MONEY? TWO THINGS, POTENTIALLY:

** A PORTION OF BETTCO'S PROFIT, PAID OUT IN REGULAR CASH **DIVIDENDS**.

** A PIECE OF A GROWING BUSINESS. AS BETTCO'S VALUE RISES, SO DOES THE VALUE OF EVERY SHARE.

GROW! GROW! GROW! GROW!

IF BETTCO GROWS, HOW DOES A SHAREHOLDER REALIZE MONEY FROM THE INCREASED VALUE OF HIS OR HER INVESTMENT? ONE WAY IS TO **SELL SHARES** TO SOMEONE ELSE AT A **STOCK EXCHANGE,** WHERE SELLERS MEET BUYERS.

HERE CAPPY, THE SELLER, MAY FACE A RUDE AWAKENING. POTENTIAL BUYERS TYPICALLY OFFER LESS THAN WHAT CAPPY IS ASKING FOR HIS SHARES. IN TRUTH, A SHARE OF STOCK IS **REALLY** WORTH ONLY WHAT PEOPLE ARE WILLING TO PAY FOR IT.

WHAT PEOPLE WILL PAY DEPENDS NOT ONLY ON BETTCO'S SIZE AND PERFORMANCE, BUT ALSO ON OVERALL ACTIVITY IN THE STOCK MARKET; EXPECTATIONS ABOUT BETTCO'S FUTURE PROSPECTS; THE FASHIONABILITY OF THE FOOD SECTOR COMPARED TO BIOTECH OR OTHER INDUSTRIES; AND A HOST OF OTHER FACTORS.

STOCK TRADING HAS ITS OWN SPECIAL LIFE AND LANGUAGE, HAVING NOTHING TO DO WITH THE PRODUCTS OR SERVICES OFFERED BY THE UNDERLYING COMPANY.

EVEN THOUGH CAPPY FREEMARK AND BETTY BAKER BOTH OWN PART OF THE COMPANY, THEIR INTERESTS MAY NOW BE AT ODDS. BETTY, THE OWNER-OPERATOR, FOCUSES ON PRODUCT, WHILE INVESTORS KEEP THEIR EYE ON THE **SHARE PRICE.**

IS SOMETHING WRONG WITH THE MUFFIN, CAPPY?

GRRR... WHO EVEN CARES?

DING

SET TO SOUND ALERT WHEN SHARE PRICE FALLS

AT TIMES, BETTY MAY THINK IT WISE TO DO SOMETHING UNPROFITABLE. MAYBE SHE BUYS SOME NEW EQUIPMENT OR GIVES EXTRA SICK LEAVE TO HER EMPLOYEE ERNIE WAGES. THESE MOVES LOOK TO BETTY LIKE GOOD BUSINESS IN THE LONG RUN.

LET ME KNOW WHEN YOU'RE FEELING BETTER, ERN'!

DING
DING
DING
DING
DING

CAPPY, ON THE OTHER HAND, THINKS **SHORT-TERM.** INVESTORS KNOW THAT EVEN A TEMPORARY DROP IN PROFIT CAN BRING DOWN SHARE PRICES. CAPPY WANTS BETTCO TO GET THE **MOST PRODUCTION** AT THE **LOWEST COST** AT ALL TIMES!

SQUEEZE 'EM, DAMMIT!

AGAIN, CAPPY ISN'T THE ONLY ONE. MANY OTHER DISGRUNTLED SHAREHOLDERS FEEL THE SAME WAY. THEY MOUNT A CHALLENGE TO BETTY'S LEADERSHIP BY ELECTING A NEW **BOARD OF DIRECTORS,** THE COMMITTEE THAT OVERSEES CORPORATE MANAGEMENT.

ON THE DEMOCRATIC PRINCIPLE OF ONE SHARE, ONE VOTE!

BETTY NOW FACES A HOSTILE BOARD, MORE IN LINE WITH CAPPY'S VIEWS. THEY TELL HER TO LAY OFF SOME WORKERS AND SPEED UP THE REST, WASTE NO MONEY (EXCEPT ON BOARD-MEMBER COMPENSATION), USE CHEAPER FLOUR, MAKE SMALLER LOAVES, ETC., ETC., ETC.

MORE PROFIT NOW!

MORE PROFIT NOW!

BETTY REPLIES THAT SHE CAN'T FUNCTION IF SHE ALWAYS HAS TO LOOK OVER HER SHOULDER AT QUARTERLY PROFIT WHILE ALSO TRYING TO MANAGE FLOUR, WATER, AND YEAST. THE BOARD "RELUCTANTLY ACCEPTS HER RESIGNATION," I.E., FIRES HER FROM THE BUSINESS SHE HERSELF STARTED (AS HAPPENED TO APPLE FOUNDER STEVE JOBS IN 1997*).

WELL, AT LEAST I'M IN GOOD COMPANY!

*THOUGH NOT FOR THE SAME REASON

51

AS BETTY, ERNIE, PAUL, AND CONNIE STAND BY STUNNED, BETTCO'S NEW MANAGEMENT REORGANIZES THE COMPANY.

WAGES AND OTHER COSTS ARE CUT, WORKERS ARE SPED UP OR LAID OFF...

OW!

OW!

OW!

THE BUSINESS ACQUIRES A SHIPPING COMPANY, AN EQUIPMENT MANUFACTURER, A SOFTWARE VENDOR, A FINANCIAL-SERVICES ARM, AND ANY NUMBER OF OTHER NEW UNITS.

CALL ME ALGI!

BETTCO REBRANDS ITSELF AS THE **AMALGAMATED GIGANTIC** CORPORATION, THE NEXT CHARACTER IN OUR CAPITALIST TRAGICOMEDY.

AMALGAMATED GIGANTIC TOWER

HOW CAN A CORPORATION BE A CARTOON CHARACTER, WHEN LEGALLY IT'S ONLY A GOVERNMENT-LICENSED ENTITY ORGANIZED FOR A SPECIFIC PURPOSE?

ONE REASON IS A U.S. SUPREME COURT CASE FROM 1886, *SANTA CLARA COUNTY V. SOUTHERN PACIFIC RAILROAD.* THE DECISION, WHICH HAD TO DO WITH TAXES ON RAILROAD RIGHTS OF WAY, INCLUDED A REMARK WITH FAR-REACHING LEGAL CONSEQUENCES:

"THE FOURTEENTH AMENDMENT TO THE CONSTITUTION, WHICH FORBIDS A STATE TO DENY TO ANY PERSON WITHIN ITS JURISDICTION THE EQUAL PROTECTION OF THE LAWS, APPLIES TO THESE CORPORATIONS."

IN EFFECT, IT LIKENED CORPORATIONS TO "PERSONS," AND FROM THAT DAY TO THIS, THE LAW HAS REGARDED THE CORPORATION AS A SPECIAL SORT OF **FLESH-AND-BLOOD HUMAN BEING!**

53

So... what sort of "persons" are corporations? Very rich ones, sometimes, surpassing entire nations in economic output. This list shows the top 50 countries and companies, by total revenue, in 2015. (Companies are marked with gray bars.)

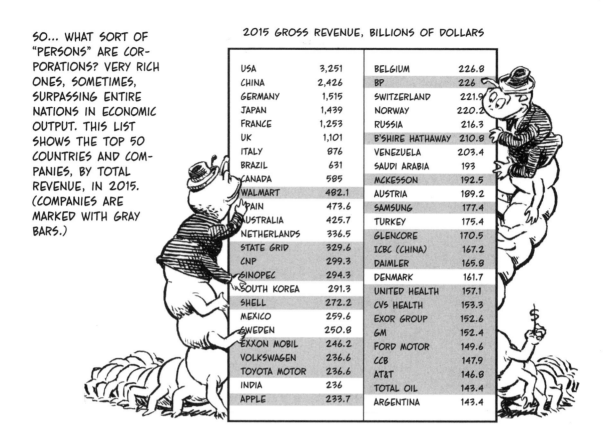

2015 GROSS REVENUE, BILLIONS OF DOLLARS

USA	3,251	BELGIUM	226.8
CHINA	2,426	BP	226
GERMANY	1,515	SWITZERLAND	221.9
JAPAN	1,439	NORWAY	220.2
FRANCE	1,253	RUSSIA	216.3
UK	1,101	B'SHIRE HATHAWAY	210.8
ITALY	876	VENEZUELA	203.4
BRAZIL	631	SAUDI ARABIA	193
CANADA	585	MCKESSON	192.5
WALMART	482.1	AUSTRIA	189.2
SPAIN	473.6	SAMSUNG	177.4
AUSTRALIA	425.7	TURKEY	175.4
NETHERLANDS	336.5	GLENCORE	170.5
STATE GRID	329.6	ICBC (CHINA)	167.2
CNP	299.3	DAIMLER	165.8
SINOPEC	294.3	DENMARK	161.7
SOUTH KOREA	291.3	UNITED HEALTH	157.1
SHELL	272.2	CVS HEALTH	153.3
MEXICO	259.6	EXOR GROUP	152.6
SWEDEN	250.8	GM	152.4
EXXON MOBIL	246.2	FORD MOTOR	149.6
VOLKSWAGEN	236.6	CCB	147.9
TOYOTA MOTOR	236.6	AT&T	146.8
INDIA	236	TOTAL OIL	143.4
APPLE	233.7	ARGENTINA	143.4

These giants operate across national borders worldwide. They build factories where wages are low... take profits where taxes are light... stash assets where no one can see... and generally make it hard for national governments to understand the full scope of corporate operations, much less hold them legally accountable.

I can't tell my headquarters from my hindquarters...

AND, LEST GOVERNMENT BALK, CORPORATIONS DEPLOY PUBLIC RELATIONS SPECIALISTS, ADVERTISING AGENCIES, LOBBYISTS, CAMPAIGN CONTRIBUTIONS, AND, YES, BRIBES TO DEMONSTRATE TO OUR ELECTED REPRESENTATIVES THE RIGHTNESS OF ALGI'S OPINIONS.

YOUR ONE O'CLOCK IS HERE, MR. ITTICKS!

CORPORATIONS ALSO WORM THEIR WAY INTO OUR MINDS. LARGE MEDIA COMPANIES—ALL CORPORATE THEMSELVES—DEPEND ON CORPORATE ADVERTISING FOR THEIR SURVIVAL. CORPORATIONS, UNLIKE ORDINARY PERSONS, SEND US A CONSTANT STREAM OF MESSAGES ABOUT PRODUCTS, PREFER-ENCES, AND POLICY.

ANYONE WHO INTERRUPTS THE FLOW OF OIL IS A TERRORIST. GLOBAL WARMING IS A HOAX. IT ISN'T CAUSED BY HUMANS. IT'S GOOD FOR YOU. BAKERIES ARE WARM, AREN'T THEY?

AND THEY CALL IT **NEWS**

IN SHORT, IT IS VERY HARD FOR GOVERNMENT (OR ANYONE ELSE) TO RESIST THE INFLUENCE OF CORPORATIONS.

PAULIE, DARLING, **PLEASE** LET'S INVADE SOMEPLACE...

SIGH... WHERE ARE **MY** AD AGENCIES AND LOBBYISTS?

CORPORATIONS DO RESEMBLE PER-
SONS IN ONE RESPECT: CORPOR-
ATIONS HAVE **VALUES**—OR RATHER,
A VALUE. A PUBLICLY TRADED
CORPORATION BELIEVES IN THE
PURSUIT OF A SINGLE THING...

SHARE
PRICE!

THIS PURSUIT OF
SHARE PRICE, WHICH
DEPENDS ON PROFIT,
WHICH DEPENDS ON
SALES AND EXPENSES,
HAS ITS IMPLICATIONS.
IN THE NEXT CHAPTER,
WE DISCUSS WHAT
HAPPENS WHEN COR-
PORATE VALUES MEET
COMPETING VALUES.

AK! NO!
NO!

BUT I THOUGHT
COMPETITION
WAS GOOD...

Chapter 4
CAPITALISM AND VALUES

TIM GOES WEST TO VISIT LARRY!

NOW WE HAVE TO CHANGE OUR POINT OF VIEW A LITTLE BIT...

FROM A STORY ABOUT ECONOMIC RELATIONSHIPS, WE NEED TO MOVE INTO THE ARENA OF HUMAN VALUES...

IT MIGHT BE CHALLENGING...

BECAUSE WE'LL HAVE TO USE VISUALS TO TALK ABOUT PEOPLE'S STATES OF MIND...

THINK YOU CAN HANDLE THAT, LARRY?

WHAT?

IT'S PRETTY CLEAR, ISN'T IT, THAT CAPITALISM INVOLVES MORE THAN JUST MONEY AND PROPERTY? THE SYSTEM ALSO DEPENDS ON A SET OF **BELIEFS**!

YEAH... OKAY...

CAPITALISM'S "THOUGHT-SPACE," ITS **IDEOLOGY**, ENCOURAGES THE IDEA THAT IT'S **GOOD** TO PURSUE MONEY, PROFIT, POSSESSIONS, COMPETITION, AND STATUS.

HMM... ISN'T COMPETITION FOR STATUS PART OF BEING AN ANIMAL?

SURE, BUT IT STILL HAS TO BE BALANCED BY MORE **COOPERATIVE** PURSUITS, IF A SPECIES IS TO SURVIVE!

YEAH! SOMETIMES YOU DO HAVE TO SLAM ON THE BRAKES—

LOOK OUT!

THAT WAS CLOSE... ANYWAY, THESE BELIEFS ABOUT WHAT'S WORTH PURSUING IN LIFE ARE WHAT PSYCHOLOGISTS CALL **VALUES**. THESE ACT AS **GUIDING PRINCIPLES** FOR PEOPLE'S ATTITUDES AND BEHAVIORS.

$#%*&!!!

THE POINT IS, CAPITALISM PROMOTES SOME VALUES AT THE EXPENSE OF OTHERS!

HOW DO YOU KNOW **THAT?**

KNOW WHAT?

THAT ONE VALUE IS AT THE **EXPENSE** OF ANOTHER? WHY COULDN'T THE GREEDIEST GUY IN THE WORLD ALSO BE A COOPERATIVE, HELPFUL HUMAN BEING?

FOR THAT MATTER, HOW DO YOU KNOW WHAT SOMEONE'S VALUES **ARE?** YOU CAN'T EXACTLY LOOK INTO PEOPLE'S HEADS, CAN YOU?

NOT EXACTLY...

BUT PSYCHOLOGISTS HAVE DEVELOPED A BRILLIANT TECHNIQUE FOR ASSESSING PEOPLE, A TECHNIQUE REFINED BY DECADES OF PAINSTAKING ANALYSIS AND EXPERIENCE!

OH. WHAT'S THAT?

WE ASK THEM.

WHY DIDN'T I THINK OF THAT?

ONE WAY TO GET INFORMATION ABOUT PEOPLE IS BY HAVING THEM FILL OUT A **SURVEY.** PSYCHOLOGISTS DO THIS ALL THE TIME.

HERE'S A SLIGHTLY MODIFIED EXCERPT FROM A WIDELY USED VALUES SURVEY:

VALUES SURVEY

In the space below, write the number (−1,0,1,2,3,4,5,6,7) that indicates the importance of that value for you personally.

−1 means the value is opposed to the principles that guide you
0 means the value is not at all important
3 means the value is important
6 means the value is very important
7 means the value is of supreme importance

___ EQUALITY (equal opportunity for all)

___ OBEDIENCE (dutiful, meeting obligations)

___ SOCIAL POWER (control over others, dominance)

___ PLEASURE (gratification of desires)

___ FREEDOM (freedom of action and thought)

___ HUMILITY (modesty, being self-effacing)

___ SUCCESS (achieving goals)

___ SOCIAL ORDER (stability of society)

___ AN EXCITING LIFE (stimulating experiences)

___ LOYALTY (being faithful to my friends and/or group)

THAT PARTICULAR SURVEY WAS THE WORK OF

SHALOM SCHWARTZ,

WHO PIONEERED MODERN VALUES RESEARCH IN THE 1980S AND '90S.

SCHWARTZ'S IDEAS AND METHODS HAVE HAD WIDE INFLUENCE. HIS SURVEYS HAVE BEEN FILLED OUT IN MORE THAN 70 COUNTRIES BY TENS OF THOUSANDS OF SUBJECTS (MOSTLY STUDENTS AND HIGH-SCHOOL TEACHERS, WHO ARE EASY TO CORRAL).

IN THIS WORK, SCHWARTZ CAME TO IDENTIFY CERTAIN VALUES AS FUNDAMENTAL TO HUMAN EXPERIENCE. THE ITEMS ON THE SURVEY ARE MEANT TO EXEMPLIFY ONE OR MORE OF THESE...

10 BASIC VALUES.

SELF-DIRECTION, INDEPENDENCE OF THOUGHT AND ACTION

TRADITION, RESPECT FOR CULTURAL PRACTICES

SECURITY, SAFETY, HARMONY, STABILITY

ACHIEVEMENT, SUCCESSFUL ACCOMPLISHMENT

STIMULATION, NOVELTY, EXCITEMENT

BENEVOLENCE, HELPING AND SUPPORTING THE PEOPLE AROUND ONE

CONFORMITY, FITTING IN, RESTRAINING THE SELF TO BE LIKE OTHERS

UNIVERSALISM, HELPING AND SUPPORTING ALL PEOPLE AND NATURE

SAVE THE WHALES, RHINOS, BATS, BEES, BIRDS, FISH....

HEDONISM, SENSUAL PLEASURE

POWER, STATUS, PRESTIGE, DOMINANCE OVER PEOPLE OR NATURE

NOW THE QUESTION IS: **WHICH VALUES "GO TOGETHER"** AND WHICH ARE IN **CONFLICT?** FOR INSTANCE, IS SOMEONE WHO CRAVES STIMULATION LIKELY TO CARE ABOUT SECURITY?

STATISTICALLY, THIS IS A QUESTION OF **CORRELATION**—AND SCHWARTZ'S DATA ANALYSIS POPS OUT THIS BEAUTIFUL CIRCLE OF CORRELATED RESULTS.

NOT ME!

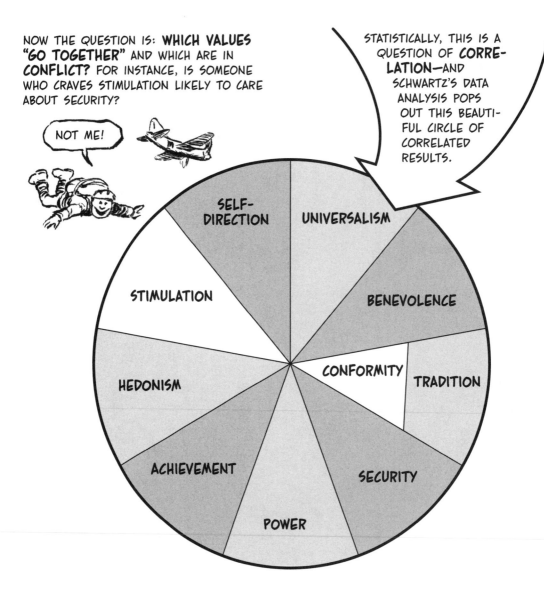

SELF-DIRECTION

UNIVERSALISM

STIMULATION

BENEVOLENCE

HEDONISM

CONFORMITY

TRADITION

ACHIEVEMENT

SECURITY

POWER

IN THE "SCHWARTZ CIRCUMPLEX," EACH VALUE HAS ITS HIGHEST POSITIVE CORRELATIONS WITH ITS IMMEDIATE NEIGHBORS. A PERSON WHO VALUES POWER IS ALSO VERY LIKELY TO GIVE HIGH MARKS TO SECURITY AND ACHIEVEMENT.

CONFORMITY CORRELATES WITH **TRADITION.** PEOPLE MAY CONFORM FOR THE SAKE OF PRESERVING CONTINUITY.

CONFORMITY ALSO GOES WITH **SECURITY.** PEOPLE GO ALONG TO PRESERVE HARMONY.

ACHIEVEMENT IS NEAR **HEDONISM.** PEOPLE'S ACCOMPLISHMENTS MAY BE PLEASING.

LOOKIN' GOOD!

ON THE OTHER HAND, VALUES ON **OPPOSITE** SIDES OF THE CIRCLE ARE EXPERIENCED AS BEING IN **CONFLICT.** THEY ARE **NEGATIVELY CORRE-LATED** IN THE SURVEY RESULTS. SOMEONE WHO GIVES HIGH MARKS TO GAINING POWER IS UNLIKELY TO CARE MUCH ABOUT SAVING THE WORLD (UNIVERSALISM).

IT'S NOT ABOUT YOU, IT'S ABOUT **ME**...

THIS TENDENCY OF PEOPLE TO EXPERIENCE ONE VALUE AS BEING IN CONFLICT WITH ANOTHER IS CALLED THE **SEESAW EFFECT.** THE GREATER THE DESIRE FOR ACHIEVEMENT AND POWER, THE LOWER THE REGARD FOR BENEVOLENCE, UNIVERSALISM, AND SELF-DIRECTION (AUTONOMY).

SOMETIMES YOU HAVE TO BE CRUEL JUST TO BE CRUEL.

SCHWARTZ'S FINDINGS BEGIN TO SHOW THE ROLE OF VALUES IN A SOCIETY OBSESSED WITH MONEY, STATUS, AND STUFF. WE CAN FIND THE SEESAW EFFECT IN MANY OTHER AREAS OF PSYCHOLOGICAL RESEARCH.

MINE, FOR EXAMPLE!

63

A FEW YEARS LATER, MY COLLEAGUES AND I DEVELOPED A VALUES SURVEY LINKING PEOPLE'S VALUES TO THEIR **PERSONAL GOALS.**

EACH SURVEY ITEM ASKED FOR A RATING OF A SPECIFIC GOAL'S IMPORTANCE TO THE SURVEY TAKER.

"I WILL BE FINANCIALLY SUCCESSFUL"... "I WILL HAVE MANY GOOD FRIENDS"... ETC.

WE ASSOCIATED SPECIFIC GOALS TO THIS SET OF VALUES, WHICH OBVIOUSLY BEARS A FAMILY RESEMBLANCE TO SCHWARTZ'S.

- SPIRITUALITY
- COMMUNITY FEELING AND ENGAGEMENT
- AFFILIATION (HAVING MEANINGFUL PERSONAL RELATIONSHIPS)
- SELF-ACCEPTANCE/PERSONAL GROWTH (FEELING COMPETENT AND FREE)
- PHYSICAL HEALTH

- SAFETY/SECURITY
- HEDONISM (HAVING PLEASURABLE EXPERIENCES)
- FINANCIAL SUCCESS
- IMAGE (LOOKING GOOD TO OTHERS, MAKING A GOOD IMPRESSION)
- POPULARITY (BEING ADMIRED BY MANY PEOPLE)
- CONFORMITY (FITTING IN TO SOCIETY)

FOR EXAMPLE, THESE GOALS EXPRESS THE VALUE OF **SELF-ACCEPTANCE/PERSONAL GROWTH:**

"I WILL DEAL WITH PROBLEMS EFFECTIVELY."

"I WILL CHOOSE WHAT I DO, RATHER THAN BEING PUSHED ALONG BY LIFE."

THE VALUE **COMMUNITY FEELING** IS EXPRESSED IN GOALS LIKE THESE:

"I WILL DO THINGS THAT IMPROVE OTHERS' LIVES."

"I WILL ASSIST PEOPLE WHO NEED IT WITHOUT EXPECTING ANYTHING IN RETURN."

BASED ON MORE THAN 1,800
RESPONSES IN 15 COUNTRIES,
OUR STATISTICAL ANALYSIS
PRODUCED THIS GRAPH.

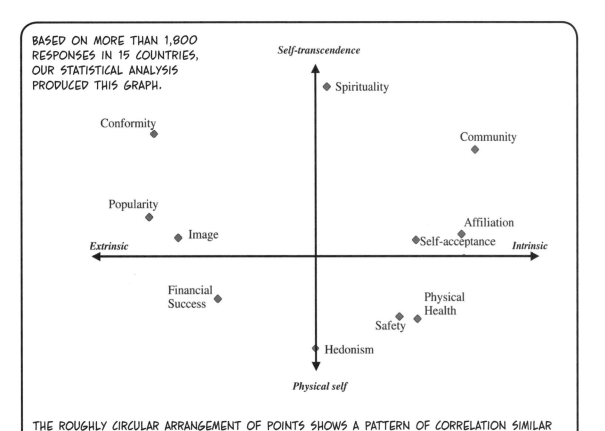

Self-transcendence

◆ Spirituality

Conformity ◆

Community ◆

Popularity ◆

Affiliation

◆ Image

◆ Self-acceptance

Extrinsic ←————————————→ *Intrinsic*

Financial ◆
Success

Physical
Health ◆

Safety ◆

◆ Hedonism

Physical self

THE ROUGHLY CIRCULAR ARRANGEMENT OF POINTS SHOWS A PATTERN OF CORRELATION SIMILAR
TO SCHWARTZ'S. NEARBY VALUES ARE POSITIVELY CORRELATED, WHILE OPPOSITE VALUES ARE
REPORTED AS CONFLICTING OR INCOMPATIBLE.

THE ARRAY OF GOALS ALSO FELL NATURALLY ALONG TWO
DIMENSIONS: **EXTRINSIC** TO **INTRINSIC** (HORIZONTAL AXIS),
AND **TRANSCENDENT** TO **PHYSICAL** (VERTICAL AXIS).

EXTRINSIC GOALS
ARE ASSOCIATED
WITH REWARDS
FROM THINGS OR
PEOPLE.

PURSUING
INTRINSIC
VALUES BRINGS
INNER SATIS-
FACTION.

THROUGHOUT THE
REST OF THIS BOOK,
WE'LL OFTEN REFER
TO INTRINSIC AND
EXTRINSIC VALUES.

THE IMPORTANT POINT FOR NOW IS THAT, LIKE THE SCHWARTZ CIRCUMPLEX, OUR RESULTS ALSO SHOWED A BASIC CONFLICT BETWEEN INTRINSIC AND EXTRINSIC VALUES.

ANOTHER BALANCING ACT!

EXTRINSIC

Intrinsic

THE SEESAW EFFECT EMERGES NOT ONLY FROM SURVEY RESULTS, BUT ALSO FROM

EXPERIMENTAL EVIDENCE.

PROBABLY THE MOST FAMOUS EXPERIMENTS ON VALUE TRADE-OFFS WERE DONE BY PSYCHOLOGIST **KATHLEEN VOHS** AND HER COLLEAGUES.

VOHS WANTED TO KNOW WHETHER PEOPLE WITH **MONEY** ON THEIR MINDS BEHAVED DIFFERENTLY FROM PEOPLE WHO WERE THINKING ABOUT SOMETHING ELSE.

THE EXPERIMENT: FIRST, EACH PARTICIPANT WAS ASKED TO PUT A FEW SCRAMBLED WORDS IN ORDER. HALF THE PEOPLE WERE GIVEN PHRASES ABOUT MONEY; THE OTHER HALF GOT NEUTRAL PHRASES.

"SALARY THE HIGH IS"

"OFF UMBRELLAS RAIN KEEP"

PSYCHOLOGISTS WOULD SAY THAT SOME PARTICIPANTS WERE **PRIMED** TO HAVE THOUGHTS OF MONEY, WHILE OTHERS WERE NOT.

WHO WROTE THIS STUFF ANYWAY, YODA?

NEXT, EACH PARTICIPANT WENT TO A PRIVATE ROOM WITH A FORM TO FILL OUT.

AT THIS POINT CAME AN INTERRUPTION. ONE OF THE RESEARCHERS BROUGHT IN A NEW PERSON TO SHARE THE ROOM.

UNFORTUNATELY, WE RAN OUT OF SPACE...

ONCE SETTLED, THE NEWCOMER BEGAN ASKING THE OTHER PARTICIPANT TO CLARIFY SOMETHING ABOUT THE FORM.

SORRY... I DON'T QUITE GET THIS...

THE SEEMINGLY CONFUSED PERSON WAS ACTUALLY PART OF THE EXPERIMENT. THE OBJECT WAS TO COMPARE HOW **HELPFUL** THE MONEY-PRIMED PARTICIPANTS WERE, RELATIVE TO THE NEUTRALLY PRIMED CONTROL GROUP.

CAN YOU SPELL "MILD DECEPTION"?

THE RESULTS WERE DRAMATIC: NEUTRALLY PRIMED PARTICIPANTS SPENT AN AVERAGE OF

150 SECONDS HELPING THE "CONFUSED" PERSON.

ARE WE SUPPOSED TO WRITE OUR MIDDLE INITIAL? WHERE'S THE BATHROOM?

WHILE THE MONEY-PRIMED SUBJECTS AVERAGED LESS THAN HALF AS LONG, JUST

67 SECONDS.

$$

BUT—

IT'S HARD TO RESIST THE IMPLICATION: EVEN RANDOM, SEEMINGLY IRRELEVANT THOUGHTS ABOUT MONEY SUPPRESS PEOPLE'S HELPFUL IMPULSES, AS PREDICTED BY THE VALUE-CIRCUMPLEX MODELS.

NOT ONLY THAT, BUT VOHS FOUND THAT MONEY-PRIMED SUBJECTS PUT GREATER **PHYSICAL DISTANCE** BETWEEN THEMSELVES AND OTHERS, AND WERE MORE LIKELY TO WORK ON PROBLEMS **ALONE,** GIVEN THE CHOICE.

WHAT'S WITH THEM?

ANOTHER VOHS EXPERIMENT: SUBJECTS PRIMED EITHER WITH THOUGHTS OF MONEY OR NEUTRAL IDEAS WERE EACH GIVEN $2 IN QUARTERS AND THEN ASKED TO DONATE A PORTION TO CHARITY. THE AVERAGE DONATION WAS QUITE DIFFERENT, DEPENDING ON PRIMING!

$

77¢

$1.34

IN A TRIAL DESIGNED BY **EUGENE CARUSO**, SUBJECTS RESPONDED TO A COMPUTER QUESTIONNAIRE ABOUT CAPITALISM. ON SOME PEOPLE'S SCREENS, THE BACKGROUND WAS A BLURRED IMAGE OF A ONE-HUNDRED-DOLLAR BILL.

"IN YOUR OPINION, DOES CAPITALISM SERVE MOST PEOPLE'S NEEDS?"

SUBJECTS SEEING THE BLURRED BILL HAD MORE POSITIVE RESPONSES ABOUT CAPITALISM THAN OTHERS DID! (THIS IS CALLED THE "BLEED-OVER EFFECT.")

STRONGLY AGREE

SOMEWHAT DISAGREE

MY COLLEAGUE **MONIKA BAUER** HAS SHOWN THAT SIMPLY REFERRING TO SOME SUBJECTS AS "CONSUMERS" AND OTHERS AS "CITIZENS" AFFECTS THEIR RESPONSES TO VALUE-LADEN WORDS.

THERE'S NO GETTING AROUND IT: VALUES ARE IN CONFLICT, AND OUR ENVIRONMENT AFFECTS OUR VALUES IN WAYS WE DON'T EVEN NOTICE.

20% OFF!

SALE

NO.

DON'T LET ME SPEND ANY MORE! PLEASE! HELP ME! HELP... MEEEE...

WE CAN ALSO SEE THIS DISPLACEMENT OF VALUES IN THE PUBLIC LIFE OF OUR COUNTRY. ONE NOTORIOUS EXAMPLE IS THE OIL INDUSTRY'S HANDLING OF **CLIMATE SCIENCE.**

IN THE LATE 1970S, THE **AMERICAN PETROLEUM INSTITUTE** OR API (THE INDUSTRY TRADE ORGANIZATION) FORMED A PANEL OF SENIOR SCIENTISTS FROM EXXON, MOBIL, SHELL, TEXACO, AND OTHER MAJOR OIL COMPANIES TO LOOK AT THE EFFECT OF EXHAUST GASES ON CLIMATE.

SCIENCE HELPS US **EXPLORE, DRILL,** AND **REFINE!** WE **LUHHHVVVE** SCIENCE!

BY 1980, THE GROUP HAD BECOME CONVINCED THAT THE NONSTOP RELEASE OF CARBON DIOXIDE GAS FROM BURNING FOSSIL FUELS WOULD SOON COOK THE EARTH.

UM... WHAT?

THEY BEGAN MAKING PLANS FOR CUTTING EMISSIONS, CHANGING REFINERY TECHNOLOGY, AND MOVING TO ALTERNATIVE FUELS, IN THE INTERESTS OF PRESERVING A HABITABLE PLANET!

SOUNDS EXPENSIVE....

70

MANAGEMENT'S RESPONSE:

WE HATE SCIENCE.

THE OIL GIANTS DISBANDED THE SCIENTIFIC COMMITTEE AND CREATED A NEW GROUP, THE **GLOBAL CLIMATE COALITION**, MORE FOCUSED ON CORPORATE GOALS.

ALL IN FAVOR OF HIGHER PROFITS...

IN THE WORDS OF AN INTERNAL API ACTION PLAN, "UNLESS 'CLIMATE SCIENCE' BECOMES A NON-ISSUE... THERE MAY BE NO... VICTORY FOR OUR EFFORTS."

LOVE THE QUOTATION MARKS AROUND "CLIMATE SCIENCE"!

SINCE THE 1990S, THE GCC HAS BEEN BUSY:

* SUPPRESSING SCIENTISTS' FINDINGS

* CREATING BOGUS "SCIENTIFIC" ORGANIZATIONS THAT SPREAD DOUBT AND MISINFORMATION

* SMEARING INDIVIDUAL CLIMATE SCIENTISTS

* "INVESTING" HEAVILY IN POLITICIANS TO DERAIL EMISSION REGULATIONS

AND IT WORKED! THE U.S. PULLED OUT OF A GLOBAL CLIMATE AGREEMENT IN 2017... A MAJOR AMERICAN POLITICAL PARTY NOW CONSIDERS CLIMATE SCIENCE A HOAX... OBSTRUCTION TO PROGRESS IS RAMPANT... AND WHY? BECAUSE MANAGEMENT'S NEED FOR PROFIT TRUMPS THE VALUES OF BENEVOLENCE, UNIVERSALISM, COMMUNITY FEELING, AND PLAIN OLD HONESTY.

DON'T YOU PEOPLE HAVE **CHILDREN?**

I DON'T KNOW ABOUT YOU, BUT **MY** KIDS HAVE AIR CONDITIONING!

71

SPEAKING OF CHILDREN, PSYCHOLOGISTS AGREE THAT YOUNG CHILDREN DO NOT HAVE THE COGNITIVE CAPABILITIES NEEDED TO EVALUATE **ADVERTISING.** KIDS TAKE ADS AT FACE VALUE.

WANNIT.

AFTER HEARING SCIENTIFIC TESTIMONY TO THIS EFFECT, THE FEDERAL TRADE COMMISSION (FTC) IN THE 1970S PROPOSED A BAN ON ADVERTISING AIMED AT CHILDREN UNDER 8 YEARS OLD.

AT LEAST UNTIL THEY CAN TELL LIES FROM TRUTH...

TOY COMPANIES, CEREAL MAKERS, AND CANDY PRODUCERS, WHICH NEED TO MOVE PRODUCT, JOINED FORCES WITH TV BROADCASTERS, WHICH RELY ON AD REVENUE.

THE NATION'S RIGHT TO WHITE SUGAR IS IN PERIL!

THEY MOUNTED A MULTI-MILLION DOLLAR LOBBYING EFFORT STRESSING AMERICAN VALUES.

"IN AN AMERICAN, DEMOCRATIC, CAPITALIST SOCIETY, WE MUST ALL LEARN... TO CARE FOR OURSELVES."*

*TESTIMONY OF KELLOGG'S LAWYER FRED FURTH

ALSO, FREE FRUIT-LOOPS FOR OUR FRIENDS HERE!

AND SO PRESIDENT JIMMY CARTER SIGNED INTO LAW THE **FTC IMPROVEMENTS ACT OF 1980,** WHICH BARRED THE FTC FROM REGULATING ADVERTISING TO CHILDREN ON THE BASIS OF ITS BEING UNFAIR. THE WELL-BEING OF CHILDREN FELL VICTIM TO... WELL, YOU KNOW WHAT...

KELLOGG'S KNOWS HOW TO TAKE CARE OF ITSELF! WHY DON'T **YOU?**

BY NOW IT SHOULD BE CLEAR THAT THE PURSUIT OF MATER-IALISTIC, EXTRINSIC VALUES SUPPRESSES INTRINSIC VALUES SUCH AS COMMUNITY AND UNIVERSALISM.

IS THERE AN ALTERNATIVE? IS IT REALISTIC TO CALL FOR A SOCIETY MORE FOCUSED ON INTRINSIC VALUES? I THINK THE ANSWER TO THAT QUESTION IS **YES.**

AS A HISTORICAL EXAMPLE, LOOK AT THE **GREAT LAW OF THE IROQUOIS,** WHICH ONCE GOVERNED A FEDERA-TION OF NATIVE NATIONS IN EASTERN NORTH AMERICA.

IT SAID THIS:

"IN ALL YOUR DELIBERATIONS, IN ALL YOUR EFFORTS AT LAW-MAKING, IN ALL YOUR OFFICIAL ACTS, SELF-INTEREST SHALL BE CAST INTO OBLIVION. LOOK AND LISTEN FOR THE WELFARE OF THE WHOLE PEOPLE, AND HAVE ALWAYS IN VIEW NOT ONLY THE PRESENT, BUT ALSO THE COMING GENERATIONS... THE UNBORN OF THE FUTURE NATIONS."

THE IROQUOIS MANAGED TO BASE THEIR SOCIETY ON PRINCIPLES OF PRESERVA-TION AND SUSTAINABILITY, WHILE EXPLICITLY REJECTING EXTRINSIC VALUES LIKE PERSONAL POWER AND MATERIAL GAIN.

DON'T YOU HAVE A LAW LIKE THAT?

IT'D NEVER GET PAST THE SUGAR LOBBY...

INSTEAD OF ENSHRINING INTRINSIC VALUES, MODERN AMERICA HAS GONE IN THE OPPOSITE DIRECTION.

THE UNITED STATES NOW EXALTS CAPITALISM'S SELF-SERVING, COMPETITIVE VALUES ABOVE EVERYTHING ELSE.

IT'S GOOD TO BE HOME...

OUR HYPERCOMPETITIVE, HYPERCONSUMERIST, AND GENERALLY HYPER SOCIETY HAS SPREAD THESE VALUES INTO NEARLY EVERY ASPECT OF LIFE. THAT'S WHY WE CALL THE CURRENT SYSTEM **HYPERCAPITALISM.**

IN THE NEXT CHAPTER, WE DESCRIBE THIS SYSTEM'S BASIC FEATURES. LATER WE SHOW HOW MATERIALISTIC VALUES RUN AMOK HAVE CROWDED OUT THE INTRINSIC VALUES THAT SUPPORT WELL-BEING, FAIR PLAY, EQUALITY, HONESTY, AND ECOLOGICAL SUSTAINABILITY.

SO POP A COUPLE OF ANTI-NAUSEA TABLETS, BECAUSE WE'RE ABOUT TO DISSECT THE MONSTER KNOWN AS **HYPERCAPITALISM!**

SCALPEL!

Chapter 5
THE FIVE COMMANDMENTS
OF HYPERCAPITALISM

Every way of life needs its code of conduct. Buddhism has its eightfold path... the American constitution has its articles and amendments... biblical law has its ten commandments... and hypercapitalism adds a few new rules all its own...

YO, MOSES, CAN YOU HANDLE FIVE MORE?

AS MOSES LEADS HIS HIS PEOPLE IN SEARCH OF THE ORGANIC AISLE, LET'S SEE HOW CAPPY'S FIVE COMMANDMENTS ARE PLAYING OUT TODAY, STARTING WITH #1.

MOMMY, CAN WE EAT AT BURGER PROPHET?

Thou shalt CONSUME.

WHAT **IS** CONSUMPTION? PEOPLE ARE SO USED TO THE WORD THAT WE THINK IT MEANS "BUYING," BUT THAT ISN'T RIGHT AT ALL...

NO, TO "CONSUME" MEANS TO DEVOUR OR BURN UP, AS IN "THE HOUSE WAS CONSUMED BY FLAME."

A SPECTAC-ULAR BUYING OPPORTUNITY!

CAPITALISM, WITH ITS NEED FOR ENDLESS SALES, IS WELL AWARE OF THE DIFFERENCE BETWEEN BUYING AND CONSUMING. IN THE WORDS OF THE 1932 BUSINESS BOOK *CONSUMER ENGINEERING*,

"GOODS FALL INTO TWO CLASSES: THOSE THAT WE USE, SUCH AS MOTOR CARS OR SAFETY RAZORS, AND THOSE THAT WE USE **UP**, SUCH AS TOOTHPASTE OR SODA BISCUITS. CONSUMER ENGINEERING MUST SEE TO IT THAT WE USE **UP** THE KIND OF GOODS WE NOW MERELY USE."

TRUE PIONEERS OF WASTE!

78

BUSINESS HAS EMBRACED THIS PYROMANIACAL ADVICE BY PEDDLING DISPOSABLE PENS, RAZORS, CIGARETTE LIGHTERS, DIAPERS, BAGS, BOTTLES, CUPS... WHILE MORE DURABLE ITEMS GET REGULAR STYLE MAKEOVERS TO TEMPT CONSUMERS INTO PURCHASING NEW ONES.

1959 CHEVY

CONSUMPTION, BEING THE OPPOSITE OF PRESERVATION, CARRIES A HUGE COST IN WASTE DISPOSAL AND POLLUTION, BUT NEVER MIND! BY NOW, CONSUMER ENGINEERING HAS WORKED SO WELL THAT THE STUFF WE BUY IS KNOWN AS **CONSUMER "GOODS."**

THEN WHAT'S ALL THAT STUFF?

CONSUMER BADS.

AND THE CREATURES FORMERLY KNOWN AS HUMAN BEINGS HAVE BECOME **CONSUMERS.**

GOSH, WHAT CAN I TORCH TODAY?

TO "ENGINEEER" PEOPLE INTO
CONSUMERS, BUSINESS USES MASSIVE

"TO MAKE PEOPLE BUY MORE GOODS, IT IS NECESSARY TO DIS- PLACE WHAT THEY ALREADY HAVE."

EARNEST ELMO CALKINS, "DEAN OF ADVERTISING MEN" IN THE EARLY 1900S AND GRANDDADDY OF THE SOFT SELL.

SINCE THE EARLY TWENTIETH CENTURY, ADVERTISERS HAVE PERFECTED WAYS TO APPEAL TO PEOPLE'S IRRATIONAL IMPULSES.

NOW WE'RE AWASH IN MESSAGES THAT SELL EMOTIONS, IMAGES, AND ATTITUDES, MESSAGES THAT ARE NOT TO BE TAKEN LITERALLY.

NOW THAT'S MORE LIKE IT!

ADVERTISERS ADAPT TO EVERY NEW MEDIA TECHNOLOGY. IN THE 1950S, **TELEVISION** BROUGHT VISUAL ADVERTISING INTO VIRTUALLY EVERY HOME IN AMERICA. TODAY, 99% OF U.S. HOUSEHOLDS HAVE AT LEAST ONE TV.

PLOP PLOP FIZZ FIZZ!

THESE BROADCAST ADS HAVE THEIR LIMITATIONS: ADVERTISERS HAVE NO DIRECT WAY OF KNOWING EXACTLY WHO IS WATCHING OR HOW VIEWERS REACT TO THE AD.

DOGGONE THING IS A SCREEN, WHEN WHAT I NEED IS A WINDOW!

GREAT TASTE!

LESS FILLING!

BUT TECHNOLOGY MARCHES ON, AND NOW ADVERTISERS CAN TRACK YOUR CLICKS TO LEARN WHAT YOU LIKE. THE SCREEN WATCHES YOU!

THAT'S TOTALLY FAIR...

ONLINE ADS CAN BE "NARROWCAST," OR DIRECTLY AIMED (SUPPOSEDLY) AT SPECIFIC VIEWERS WITH SPECIFIC INTERESTS.

I WANT TO HELP!

OKAYYY... THEN YOU MIGHT STOP TRYING TO SELL ME WHAT I BOUGHT YESTERDAY.

SOMEDAY SOON (IF NOT ALREADY), ADVERTISERS WILL TRACK YOUR PHONE'S LOCATION AND SEND COUPONS FOR DISCOUNTS IN NEARBY STORES.

824

ATTENTION! TARGET IS SHOWING RESISTANCE... COMMENCE FIRING IN 10...9...8...

FACED WITH THIS ONSLAUGHT, MANY PEO-PLE SIMPLY TUNE OUT ADS BY INSTAL-LING AD-BLOCKING SOFTWARE, FAST-FORWARDING PAST COMMERCIALS, OR HITTING MUTE AND LEAVING THE ROOM.

HEH HEH HEH!

SOLUTION? **INESCAPABLE ADS.** COMPANIES PAY TO PUT ADS ON HIGHWAY TOLL BOOTHS, ESCA-LATOR HANDRAILS, TOILET STALLS... RONALD M°DONALD EVEN SHOWED UP ON SCHOOL REPORT CARDS IN FLORIDA.

NO LO QUIERO...

WE'VE ALL SEEN CORPORATE NAMES ON PUBLIC VENUES. HERE'S FENWAY PARK'S **BUDWEISER RIGHT FIELD** (IRONICALLY, THE ONLY PLACE IN THE STADIUM WHERE YOU CAN'T SEE THE SIGN).

OR TRY SAYING "MATTEL CHILDREN'S HOSPITAL" (IN LOS ANGELES) WITHOUT BEING A SHILL FOR A TOY COMPANY.

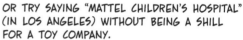

EXIT THROUGH THE GIFT SHOP, KIDS!

GOLDENPALACE.COM BOUGHT NAMING RIGHTS TO A **MONKEY** WITH A $650,000 GIFT TO A BOLIVIAN NATURE RESERVE.

"THOUSANDS OF YEARS FROM NOW, THE GOLDENPALACE.COM MONKEY WILL LIVE TO CARRY OUR NAME THROUGH THE AGES."

—RICHARD ROWE, GOLDENPALACE.COM CEO

THIS IS GETTING COMPLETELY OUT OF HAND! I WANT **MY** GOVERNMENT TO **DO** SOMETH—

THE T-MOBIL CITY COUNCIL WILL COME TO ORDER!

WHOK

NEW HERE?

ANOTHER WAY AROUND PEOPLE'S RESISTANCE IS

STEALTH MARKETING,

WHICH MAKES ITS PITCH ON THE SLY.

SOMEONE IN A BAR IS TALKING UP **BLITZ BEER.** WHO'S TO KNOW HE'S A PAID ACTOR?

BLITZ IS AWESOME!

I WORK FOR BLATZ.

MOVIE ACTORS SMOKE ON SCREEN BECAUSE TOBACCO COMPANIES PAY THE PRODUCERS.

PUTTING CIGARETTES IN CINEMA IS CALLED **PRODUCT PLACEMENT.** ANOTHER EXAMPLE: THE **FUBU** CLOTHING BRAND WAS FIRST PITCHED TO YOUNG AFRICAN-AMERICAN MEN BY HAVING HIPHOP STARS WEAR IT IN CONCERT AND ON TV.

FUBAR!

AND THEN THERE'S THE **GIRLS INTELLIGENCE AGENCY.** THE **GIA** HIRES YOUNG WOULD-BE SLEUTHS TO DO MARKET RESEARCH.

I'VE ALWAYS WANTED TO SERVE MY COUNTRY BY REPORTING PEOPLE TO A HIGHER AUTHORITY!

THE "AGENT" INVITES HER UNSUSPECTING PALS TO A SLEEPOVER AND HANDS OUT GIFT BOXES.

INSIDE ARE COUPONS, FREE SAMPLES OF THIS AND THAT, TRIAL SUBSCRIPTIONS, ETC.

HUH!

GUESTS ARE ASKED TO FILL OUT A FORM SAYING WHAT THEY LIKED MOST AND LEAST.

A PARTY WITH HOMEWORK...?

THE INTELLIGENCE GOES INTO GIA'S MARKETING DATABASES.

I HAVEN'T HAD THIS MUCH FUN SINCE DERMABRASION...

NOW, HOWEVER, CAPITALISM HAS A PROBLEM. IT'S BEEN WILDLY SUCCESSFUL AT PUMPING UP PEOPLE'S **DESIRE** TO BUY—UH, CONSUME...

PANT
PANT
PANT
JACKET

BUT HOW TO **AFFORD** IT? AS WE'LL SEE, HYPERCAPITALISM IS NO FAN OF HIGH WAGES... SO SOMEHOW, CONSUMERS ARE EXPECTED TO BUY MORE STUFF WITH NO MORE CASH.

THE PROBLEM IS SOLVED IN TWO WORDS:

VISA!

MASTERCARD!

O.K.... AMERICAN EXPRESS AND DISCOVER CARD, TOO, SO IT'S REALLY MORE THAN TWO WORDS, BUT THE POINT IS THE SAME: HYPERCAPITALIST CONSUMERISM DEPENDS ON

EASY CREDIT.

HOW CREDIT CARDS WORK (FOR THE BANKS THAT ISSUE THEM):

WHEN CONNIE SUMER BUYS AN ITEM WITH PLASTIC, SHE IS ACTUALLY BORROWING MONEY FROM A BANK. SHE NEVER SEES THIS MONEY, AS THE BANK PAYS IT DIRECTLY TO THE SELLER, BUT CONNIE HAS INCURRED A DEBT.

BUSINESS PROFITS IN TWO WAYS:

THE MERCHANT MAKES AN IMMEDIATE SALE

THE BANK CHARGES CONNIE **INTEREST** ON THE LOAN.

AT A MODEST LI'L RATE OF 20%!

MOST CREDIT CARDS ARE **"REVOLVING,"** MEANING THAT CONNIE MUST SEND THE BANK ONLY A SMALL AMOUNT EACH MONTH, RATHER THAN PAY OFF THE FULL DEBT AT ONCE.

ONLY $36! SO-O-O-O-O EASY!

MOST OF THAT MINIMUM PAYMENT IS INTEREST, SO THE UNPAID BALANCE DROPS ONLY A LITTLE, AND CONNIE CONTINUES TO OWE.

I **KNEW** THERE WAS A REASON I ALWAYS HATED ARITHMETIC...

RESULT?

EVERY JACKET SHOULD HAVE A CALCULATOR FUNCTION...

MAKING ONLY THE MINIMUM PAYMENT, CONNIE TAKES **YEARS** TO PAY OFF THE DEBT. IN THAT TIME, THE INTEREST TYPICALLY ADDS UP TO SOMETHING **NEARLY EQUAL TO THE ORIGINAL PUR-CHASE PRICE.** FOR THE CONVENIENCE OF GETTING A JACKET **NOW,** CONNIE ULTI-MATELY PAYS **DOUBLE.**

USE OF REVOLVING CREDIT IN THE U.S. BEGAN GROWING IN THE 1970S. HERE'S HOW AMERICA'S TOTAL HOUSEHOLD DEBT AS A PERCENTAGE OF INCOME HAS CHANGED SINCE THEN.

AND LET'S NOT FORGET

STUDENT LOANS.

STUDENTS BORROW THEIR TUITION, THEN PAY ZERO WHILE THEY STAY IN SCHOOL.

ZERO! THEY'RE SO NICE TO ME!

STUDENT LOANS MAY NOT LOOK LIKE PART OF CONSUMERISM— THEY PROMOTE EDUCATION, AFTER ALL—BUT THEY DO STIMULATE SPENDING ON **SERVICES**—THE WORK OF TEACHERS, ADMINISTRATORS, OFFICE STAFF, JANITORS, ETC.

AND WHY NOT PROFIT FROM PROMOTING A NOBLE GOAL?

SMELLING MONEY, BUSINESSPEOPLE OPENED **FOR-PROFIT COLLEGES** BUILT ON STUDENT LOANS. THE COLLEGES ACT LIKE MERCHANTS IN A CREDIT-CARD TRANSACTION, WITH THE STUDENT IN THE ROLE OF INDEBTED CONSUMER.

IT'S **GENIUS!** THE EDUCATION UNIT TAKES FROM THE BANK UNIT!

I'M LEARNING SOMETHING ALREADY...

IF YOU THINK THE ANALOGY IS FAR-FETCHED, TRY EAVESDROPPING ON A DEAN. CHANCES ARE YOU'LL HEAR STUDENTS REFERRED TO AS "CONSUMERS."

IN OUR HYPERCAPITALIST ERA, ADMINISTRATORS OFTEN SAY THAT A SCHOOL'S "BUSINESS" IS TO "SELL" WHAT PLEASES THE "CUSTOMER."

WE'RE HERE TO MOVE PRODUCT, SO YOU'RE BEING REPLACED BY A VENDING MACHINE.

AMERICAN STUDENTS AND FORMER STUDENTS CARRY A TOTAL DEBT OF AROUND

$1.1 TRILLION,

AND 7 MILLION PEOPLE ARE BEHIND ON THEIR PAYMENTS. (BY COMPARISON, CREDIT CARD DEBT IS "ONLY" $700 BILLION.)

TAKE VISA?

CONSUMERISM HAS NON-FINANCIAL COSTS AS WELL.

WAIT. SOMETHING IS NON-FINANCIAL?

SEEING ADVERTISING EVERYWHERE, OUR MINDS FILL UP WITH THOUGHTS OF STUFF... WE GET USED TO BEING MANIPULATED... POLITICS BECOMES A GAME OF IMAGES... AND WE BUY INTO ALL SORTS OF CRAZINESS, LIKE THE IDEA THAT DRINKING BEER MAKES MEN SEXY.

BY NOW I'M **TOTALLY** IRRESISTIBLE...

THE BIBLE SAYS THAT DEBT IS THE END OF FREEDOM: "THE BORROWER IS THE SLAVE TO THE LENDER" (PROVERBS 22:7).

HOW CAN SO MUCH NICE STUFF BE SUCH A **LOAD**?

IN SHORT:

Thou shalt OPERATE GLOBALLY.

AND NOW, FOR OUR NEXT COMMANDMENT...

TOOT TOOT!

GLOBALIZATION IS NOT EXACTLY NEW. HISTORIANS PINPOINT ITS BIRTH TO THE 1570s, WHEN SPANISH SHIPS IN THE PHILIPPINES FIRST TRADED AMERICAN SILVER FOR CHINESE SILK AND PORCELAIN.

WHAT **IS** NEW IS THE VOLUME OF TRADE, THE INDEPENDENCE OF THE TRADING COMPANIES, THE SPEED OF TRAVEL AND COMMUNICATION, THE TERMS OF TRADE TREATIES, AND MORE...

IN TIMES PAST, RULERS NURTURED THEIR OWN NATIONS' COMPANIES WHILE DAMAGING FOREIGN RIVALS, LIKE A SEMI-RATIONAL CHICKEN SMASHING HER NEIGHBORS' EGGS.

A SEAGOING NATION, FOR INSTANCE, WOULD GIVE WORK TO ITS OWN SHIPBUILDERS. SHIPBUILDERS MADE NAVIES, AND NAVIES COULD GRAB NATURAL RESOURCES AND CAPTIVE CUSTOMERS FOR THE NATION'S TRADERS.

INDIA SHALL BE OURS!!

IT'S NOT ALWAYS GOOD TO BE WANTED...

KINGS ALSO LICENSED PRIVATE BUSINESSMEN TO COMMIT **PIRACY** AGAINST FOREIGN SHIPS. THE PIRATES THEN SPLIT THE TAKE WITH THE ROYAL TREASURY.

FOR CROWN, COUNTRY, AND CUT!

MERDE.

BUT PROBABLY GOVERNMENTS' MOST COMMON "PROTECTIONIST" TACTIC, GOOD IN WAR AND PEACE ALIKE, WAS THE

tariff.

AH, TARIFF, FRIEND TO WORKER AND OWNER ALIKE...

DEAR OLD TARIFF...

WHAT IS THAT, A SMALL DOG??

A TARIFF IS SIMPLY A TAX ON IMPORTS. TAXING IMPORTS RAISES THEIR PRICE; RAISING THEIR PRICE MAKES THEM MORE EXPENSIVE THAN HOMEGROWN ALTERNATIVES; AND SO THE TARIFF "TILTS THE MARKET" TOWARD HOME-PRODUCED MERCHANDISE. HERE IS A PURELY MADE-UP EXAMPLE:

COST IN FOREIGN COUNTRY $10,000

IMPORTER PAYS 100% TARIFF, AN EXTRA COST OF $10,000.

THE IMPORT'S PRICE MUST BE AT LEAST $20,000.

DOMESTIC ITEM COSTS LESS.

$17,500

A CRIME AGAINST BUYERS!

(BECAUSE TARIFFS STIFLE COMPETITION, THEY WERE POISON TO ADAM SMITH, INCIDENTALLY.)

PROTECTIONISM HAD A LONG RUN, MORE THAN 350 YEARS, UNTIL, NEAR THE END OF WORLD WAR II, CAME THE YEAR...

IN THAT YEAR, THE U.S., BRITAIN, FRANCE, AND A FEW DOZEN OTHER COUNTRIES TOOK A PLEDGE. THEY AGREED TO EASE PROTECTIONISM (GRADUALLY) AND MOVE TOWARD A NEW INTERNATIONAL POSTWAR ERA OF (MORE OR LESS) **FREE TRADE.**

AARGH! DOES NOTHING LAST?

MOUNT WASHINGTON HOTEL, BRETTON WOODS, NEW HAMPSHIRE, SITE OF THE ECONOMIC CONFERENCE

THE U.S., PRIME MOVER OF THE CHANGE, ARGUED THAT PROTECTIONISM ONLY BRINGS WAR.

JUST LOOK AT THE WORLD OUTSIDE NEW HAMPSHIRE!

FREE TRADE, SAID THE AMERICANS, PROMOTED PEACE. COUNTRIES BOUND BY COMMERCE WOULD SETTLE THEIR DIFFERENCES IN A FRIENDLIER, MORE BUSINESSLIKE WAY.

GROUP HUG!

THE U.S. CITED THE ECONOMIC **THEORY OF COMPARATIVE ADVANTAGE.** THIS SAYS THAT FREE TRADE PUSHES EVERY NATION TO PURSUE ITS MOST PROFITABLE OPTIONS, SO THAT EVERY NATION GROWS RICHER THAN IT WOULD HAVE DONE OTHERWISE.

DAVID RICARDO (1772–1823), ORIGINATOR OF THE THEORY OF COMPARATIVE ADVANTAGE

IT'S MATHEMATICAL! YOU WANT THIS... REALLY!

THE BRETTON WOODS AGREEMENTS ALSO CREATED AN INFANT **INTERNATIONAL MONETARY FUND** (IMF) TO HELP POOR COUNTRIES THROUGH TEMPORARY HARD TIMES. AS WE'LL SEE IN A BIT, THIS BABY GREW UP TO BE A KIND OF ENFORCER OF THE FREE-TRADE REGIME.

COME AND GET IT...

NOT EVERYONE JOINED THE BRETTON WOODS FUN. THE COMMUNIST U.S.S.R. COMPLAINED THAT FREE TRADE WAS NOTHING BUT A SCHEME TO ENRICH AMERICAN BUSINESS.

WATCH YOUR POCKETS!

STILL, MORE THAN 40 COUNTRIES SIGNED... SLOWLY, TARIFFS FELL... CLOSED MARKETS OPENED... COLONIES WON THEIR FREEDOM... JAPAN AND GERMANY BOUNCED BACK... COMMUNISM COLLAPSED IN RUSSIA... AND U.S. PRESIDENT GEORGE BUSH THE FIRST PROCLAIMED A "NEW WORLD ORDER."

AS IN, "YOUR ORDER IS READY"...

AND SO AMERICAN COMPANIES CLOSED U.S. FACTORIES AND "OFF-SHORED" PRODUCTION TO ASIA AND LATIN AMERICA... JAPANESE CARS WENT WORLDWIDE... ARABS BOUGHT WESTERN BANKS... CHINA INVESTED IN AFRICA... CAPITAL, GOODS, AND SERVICES SWAM FREELY... BUSINESS ORGANIZATIONS BECAME TRULY **MULTI-NATIONAL,** AND OPERATIONS BECAME FULLY GLOBALIZED.

WHAT COULD POSSIBLY GO WRONG?

LET'S SAY THIS UP FRONT: GLOBALIZATION ABSOLUTELY COMES WITH SOME **PLUSES.**

SWELL OF YOU!

IT BRINGS MONEY AND INDUSTRY TO POOR COUNTRIES... THEIR FACTORIES MAKE LOW-PRICED PRODUCTS, SO MORE PEOPLE WORLDWIDE CAN AFFORD CLOTHING AND OTHER NECESSITIES.

ALL-MART

ON THE OTHER HAND, GLOBALIZATION IS ALSO FREIGHTED WITH SOME HEAVY NEGATIVES...

FOR YOU, MAYBE! NOT FOR ME!

SOME OF THESE WILL COME UP IN LATER SECTIONS ON LABOR AND REGULATION. FOR NOW, WE'LL JUST MENTION TWO ISSUES THAT AFFECT EVERYONE...

NAMELY...

FOOD AND THE ENVIRONMENT.

YOU'RE STARTING WITH THE SMALL, UNIMPORTANT STUFF, EH?

ALL PEOPLE NEED BASIC FOODSTUFFS, BUT WHEN IT COMES TO FARMING, THE GLOBAL ECONOMY HAS OTHER IDEAS. BUSINESS DEMANDS RUBBER, COTTON, SILK, PALM AND OTHER SEED OILS, SISAL, JUTE, COCOA, COFFEE, AND TROPICAL MANGOES FOR NORTHERN TABLES.

WHY ARE YOU WASTING MY TIME GROWING YOUR OWN FOOD?

MANY WARM, UNINDUSTRIALIZED COUNTRIES FIND COMPARATIVE ADVANTAGE BY SELLING THESE **RAW AGRICULTURAL PRODUCTS** TO THE WORLD MARKET.

THE COMPANIES THAT MARKET THIS STUFF—OFTEN LARGE CORPORATIONS LIKE CONAGRA, NESTLÉ OR DOLE—TAKE OVER FARMLAND ONCE DEVOTED TO FOOD.

GIVE IT UP! THE WORLD HAS NEEDS TOO!

FOR EXAMPLE, UNDER **NAFTA**, THE FREE TRADE PACT BETWEEN MEXICO, THE U.S., AND CANADA, MEXICO SENDS TONS OF TABLE FRUIT NORTH, WHILE MEXICAN TORTILLA PRICES SOAR ON ACCOUNT OF THE SHORTAGE OF CORN.

WHERE'S **MY** COMPARATIVE ADVANTAGE?

A COUNTRY RELYING ON AGRICULTURAL EXPORTS IS DOUBLY VULNERABLE: IT SUFFERS BOTH FROM DROPS IN THE WORLD PRICE OF ITS CASH CROPS AND FROM INCREASES IN THE PRICE OF IMPORTED FOOD.

YOUR COUNTRY LACKS ROLLER COASTERS, SO WE'RE GIVING YOU ANOTHER KIND OF THRILL...

IF A COUNTRY TRIES TO PROTECT ITS OWN FOOD PRODUCERS, THE "INTERNATIONAL COMMUNITY" HAS WAYS OF MAKING ITS FEELINGS KNOWN.

TSK TSK!

FOR EXAMPLE, **HAITIAN RICE GROWERS** WOULD HAVE GONE BANKRUPT SELLING AT THE LOW WORLD PRICE, SO THE HAITIAN GOVERNMENT PROTECTED THEM WITH A 30% TARIFF ON IMPORTED RICE. THIS BLOCKED FREE TRADE!

TARIFF BARRIER

IN THE 1990s, HAITI ASKED FOR AN EMERGENCY LOAN FROM THE IMF. THE **CLINTON ADMINISTRATION** TOLD HAITI THAT **ENDING THE RICE TARIFF** MIGHT SPEED THE LOAN APPLICATION.

C'MON, MANNN... FREE TRADE IS COOOL...

HAITI CAVED AND DROPPED THE TARIFF TO NEARLY ZERO, AND THE ISLAND WAS SWAMPED WITH CHEAP IMPORTED RICE—MUCH OF IT GROWN IN CLINTON'S HOME STATE OF ARKANSAS, BY THE WAY.

WHAT A COINCIDENCE!

PREDICTABLY, HAITIAN RICE FARMERS LOST THEIR LAND AND FLOCKED TO THE CITY AS PAUPERS. A POOR NATION HAD LOST A PRECIOUS, HOME-GROWN FOOD STAPLE, PROBABLY FOREVER.

SIMILAR THINGS HAPPENED TO RICE FARMERS IN WEST AFRICA...

CRAZIEST OF ALL, **AMERICAN** RICE GROWERS GET GOVERNMENT SUBSIDIES!! (SO DO THOSE OF SEVERAL OTHER RICH NATIONS.) BUT HAITI IS IN NO POSITION TO DICTATE FREE-TRADE POLICY TO ITS MIGHTY NEIGHBOR TO THE NORTH.

THEY HAVE A COMPARATIVE ADVANTAGE IN MILITARY COUPS!

LARGE-SCALE PRODUCTION OF CASH CROPS ALSO SIMPLIFIES ECOSYSTEMS.

FOR EFFICIENCY'S SAKE, AGRIBUSINESS TYPICALLY SOWS VAST PLANTATIONS WITH A SINGLE CROP, I.E., A **MONOCULTURE**.

MONOCULTURE PLANTATIONS PLOW UNDER MORE DIVERSIFIED FARMS WITH MULTIPLE CROPS, TREES, AND ANIMALS...

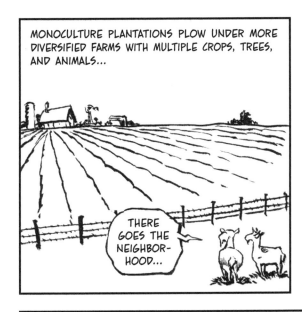

THERE GOES THE NEIGHBORHOOD...

OR THEY INVADE FORESTS AND OTHER COMPLEX NATURAL ENVIRONMENTS.

BRRAZZZZZZZ

THERE GO TEN THOUSAND NEIGHBORHOODS...

PLANTATIONS USE CHEMICAL PESTICIDES, HERBICIDES, AND FERTILIZER. THE CROPS, ALL ALIKE, ARE EXTRA-SUSCEPTIBLE TO DEVASTATING PESTS AND BLIGHT AND USUALLY LACK THE NUTRIENTS OF "HEIRLOOM" VARIETIES.

I HATE GMO CROPS! AN HOUR LATER YOU'RE HUNGRY AGAIN, IF YOU'RE STILL ALIVE!

RESULT: A DRASTIC, WORLDWIDE SIMPLIFICATION OF THE WEB OF LIFE. CASH-CROP MONOCULTURE IS A MAJOR DRIVER OF THE CURRENT, ONGOING MASS EXTINCTION OF IRREPLACEABLE SPECIES.

WHERE'S **MY** COMPARATIVE ADVANTAGE?

WELL, IN THAT CASE, SHALL WE...?

PUKPUK OKAY...

GLOBAL TRADE, AS WE SAID, HAS EXISTED FOR CENTURIES, AND SO HAVE ITS EFFECTS ON LAND USE AND ECOLOGY. THEY'RE NOT NEW...

20 ACRES FOR SALE

WHAT IS NEW IS THE INSTANT ELECTRONIC TRANSFER OF **MONEY** FROM ONE PLACE TO ANOTHER.

LIKE FROM A PHONE! WOW!

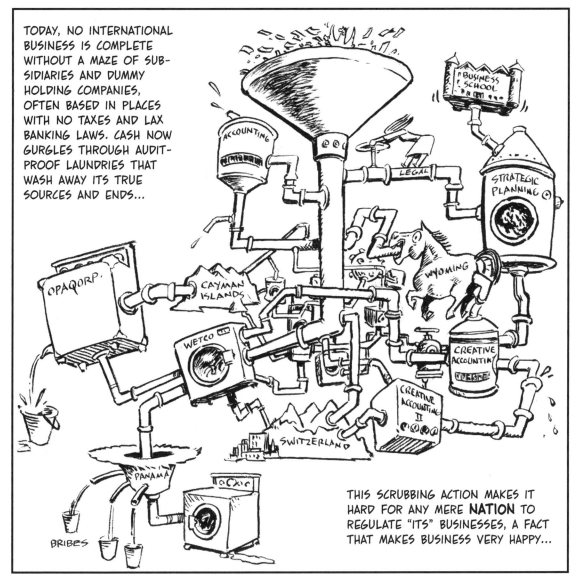

TODAY, NO INTERNATIONAL BUSINESS IS COMPLETE WITHOUT A MAZE OF SUBSIDIARIES AND DUMMY HOLDING COMPANIES, OFTEN BASED IN PLACES WITH NO TAXES AND LAX BANKING LAWS. CASH NOW GURGLES THROUGH AUDIT-PROOF LAUNDRIES THAT WASH AWAY ITS TRUE SOURCES AND ENDS...

THIS SCRUBBING ACTION MAKES IT HARD FOR ANY MERE **NATION** TO REGULATE "ITS" BUSINESSES, A FACT THAT MAKES BUSINESS VERY HAPPY...

Thou shalt not REGULATE.

EVER SINCE BUSINESS AND GOVERNMENT HAVE EXISTED, GOVERNMENT HAS REGULATED BUSINESS, AND BUSINESS HAS COMPLAINED.

GOVERNMENT SEES REGULATION AS A WAY TO PROTECT SOCIETY AND THE ENVIRONMENT, WHILE BUSINESS SEES IT AS A SORT OF RED-TAPE DISPENSER CREATING ALL KINDS OF TROUBLE AND EXPENSE. IN OTHER WORDS, REGULATION REDUCES PROFIT.

ANYONE WHO HAS EVER WRESTLED WITH A TAX FORM OR A CITY BUILDING DEPARTMENT CAN TELL YOU HOW SENSELESSLY, ANNOYINGLY COMPLICATED GOVERNMENT REGULATIONS CAN SEEM SOMETIMES.

BUT IT'S A LONG WAY FROM THERE TO A BLANKET REJECTION OF REGULATION, A LA PRESIDENT **RONALD REAGAN:**

"GOVERNMENT IS NOT THE SOLUTION TO OUR PROBLEM; GOVERNMENT **IS** THE PROBLEM."

I'M IN LUVVV!

WAIT—AREN'T **YOU** IN GOVERNMENT?

HYPERCAPITALISM MAKES DEREGULATION AN ARTICLE OF FAITH, AND THE RESULTS ARE NOT ALWAYS PRETTY. REAGAN, FOR EXAMPLE, DROPPED RULES THAT HELD BACK **SAVINGS AND LOAN** ASSOCIATIONS. THESE SOBER, LOCAL BANKS USED TO BE LIMITED TO ISSUING LOW-RISK HOME MORTGAGES.

BORRRING...

SUDDENLY, S&LS COULD MAKE RISKIER LOANS TO BUSINESSES THEY KNEW NOTHING ABOUT. A LENDING FRENZY FOLLOWED...

FREE AT LAST!!

HUGE NUMBERS OF LOANS FAILED, AND WITH THEM THE ENTIRE S&L BUSINESS. THE GOVERNMENT SPENT **$124 BILLION** TO RESCUE DEPOSITORS.

THAT WAS FUN, WASN'T IT?

DESPITE THIS FIASCO, THE CLINTON ADMINISTRATION FURTHER DEREGULATED THE BANKING INDUSTRY IN THE 1990S— WITH AN EVEN WORSE RESULT, THE BANKING MELTDOWN AND GOVERNMENT BAILOUT OF 2008.

WHAT'S LIFE WITHOUT A MELTDOWN AND BAILOUT EVERY NOW AND THEN?

GLOBALIZATION OFFERS NEW OPPORTUNITIES TO DODGE REGULATIONS. FOR EXAMPLE, BACK IN THE '90S, AMERICAN CORPORATIONS NOTICED THAT MEXICAN LAW BANNED THE SALE OF CERTAIN COMMUNALLY OWNED LANDS.

BUT THE U.S., MEXICO, AND CANADA WERE DISCUSSING THE ADVANTAGES OF FREE TRADE. CERTAIN LOBBYISTS WHISPERED IN CERTAIN EARS...

AMERICAN MINING AND AGRIBUSINESS COMPANIES NOW OWN LARGE TRACTS IN MEXICO, THANKS TO THIS STRATEGIC ACT OF DEREGULATION. (AND THE CORPORATIONS GET THE BONUS OF MEXICO'S WEAKER ENVIRONMENTAL LAWS.)

IN 1993, THE U.S., CANADA, AND MEXICO SIGNED THE FAMOUS NORTH AMERICAN FREE TRADE AGREEMENT, OR **NAFTA.** THE COUNTRIES' BUSINESSES COULD NOW TRADE ACROSS BORDERS WITHOUT GOVERNMENT OBSTACLES.

AND SO FLEETS OF MEXICAN CARGO TRUCKS, SPEWING MORE DIESEL FUMES THAN ALLOWED BY U.S. LAW, HEADED NORTH.

TIGHTENING MEXICAN EMISSION STANDARDS WOULD AMOUNT TO A NEW TAX ON TRUCKERS, SAYS MEXICO. THIS WOULD VIOLATE **NAFTA!** SO FAR, THE U.S. HAS AGREED, AND THE DIESEL FUMES SPEW ON.

I CAN'T SEE **YOU,** BUT I CAN SEE YOUR POINT.

THESE EXAMPLES SHOW HOW BUSINESS CAN USE FREE-TRADE IDEAS TO PIT ONE COUNTRY'S REGULATIONS AGAINST ANOTHER'S.

TRADE OR BREATHE FREELY? A NO-BRAINER!

BUSINESS ALSO CHAFED UNDER REGULATIONS CONTROLLING **MEDIA** ACCESS AND OWNERSHIP. IN OUR MEDIA-DRENCHED AGE, HYPERCAPITALISM WANTS TO SEND US ITS MESSAGE!

IT'S ALL FOR YOUR OWN GOOD...

YOUR OWN GOOD...

YOUR OWN...

AT ONE TIME, AMERICANS THOUGHT OF THE AIRWAVES AS A VIRTUAL **PUBLIC SPACE,** TO BE PROTECTED FROM THE UNDUE INFLUENCE OF PRIVATE MONEY. THE LAW LIMITED HOW MANY RADIO AND TV STATIONS A SINGLE COMPANY COULD OWN.

HOW ARE WE SUPPOSED TO **EXPRESS OURSELVES??**

ONE HAND TIED BEHIND BACK

THEN, IN THE 1980S, THE REAGAN ADMINISTRATION CHOSE TO LOOK THE OTHER WAY AS BIG MEDIA COMPANIES BEGAN EATING SMALLER ONES.

ME AGAIN!

THE OLD RULES

DEREGULATION CONTINUED UNDER THE DEMOCRATS WITH THE TELECOMMUNICATIONS ACT OF 1996. THE LAST RESTRAINTS CAME OFF, AND NOW ONLY **SIX** COMPANIES CONTROL 90% OF THE EYEBALLS.

FIVE TOO MANY, BUT I CAN LIVE WITH THAT, FOR NOW...

GE (NBC, UNIVERSAL, A&E, BRAVO, CNBC, COMCAST SPORTS, TELEMUNDO)

NEWSCORP (FOX, MULTIPLE NEWSPAPERS, SKY NEWS)

VIACOM (PARAMOUNT, REPUBLIC, NICKOLODEON, BET, COMEDY CENTRAL)

TIMEWARNER (HBO, TURNER, CNN, WARNER BROTHERS)

DISNEY (ABC, LUCAS, MARVEL, ESPN)

CBS (CBS, SHOWTIME, MULTIPLE BOOK PUBLISHERS)

WHAT DIFFERENCE DOES IT MAKE? ONLY THIS: CORPORATE MEDIA HAVE A CORPORATE POINT OF VIEW. BESIDES THAT, THEIR REVENUE COMES FROM CORPORATE AD SALES... SO WE'VE NEVER HEARD MUCH DIVERSITY OF OPINION IN THE "OFFICIAL" MEDIA.

WE SHOULD BOMB PETROLISTAN.

NO, WE SHOULD BLOCKADE AND SUBVERT PETRO-LISTAN.

THANK YOU BOTH FOR THIS WIDE-RANGING DISCUSSION.

MEDIA GIANTS WON'T EVEN RUN **PAID ADS** IF THEY DON'T LIKE THE MESSAGE. WHEN ACTIVIST **KALLE LASN,** FOUNDER OF *ADBUSTERS* MAGAZINE, TRIED TO BUY TIME FOR AN ANTI-CONSUMERISM SPOT, ALMOST NO ONE WOULD TAKE HIS MONEY. BROADCASTERS FEARED THAT IT MIGHT RUFFLE THE FEATHERS OF OTHER ADVERTISERS.

THEY'RE LIKE FRAGILE, DELICATE BIRDS...

THERE ALSO USED TO BE A THING CALLED THE **FAIRNESS DOCTRINE:** IF A STATION AIRED ONE POLITICAL PARTY'S OPINION, THEN THE OTHER PARTY'S VOICE HAD TO RECEIVE EQUAL TIME. THAT'S ALL GONE NOW, AND A NETWORK CAN BE AS ONE-SIDED AS IT LIKES.

WE SHOULD BOMB PETROLISTAN.

NO, WE SHOULD BOMB PETROLISTAN **YESTERDAY.**

NOT SOON ENOUGH!!

IN 2010, A MEDIA-RELATED LAWSUIT ATTACKED THE REGULATION OF

CAMPAIGN FINANCING.

THE CASE INVOLVED A 90-MINUTE VIDEO AGAINST CANDIDATE HILLARY CLINTON, SLATED TO AIR DURING THE 2008 PRIMARY SEASON.

SHE EATS TUNA. WOULD YOU CARE TO RESPOND?

THE FEDERAL ELECTION COMMISSION BLOCKED THE BROADCAST AS IMPROPER ELECTIONEERING.

BUREAUCRATS HAVE **NO** APPRECIATION OF THE FINE ART OF DEFAMATION...

THEY CITED THE 2002 CAMPAIGN REFORM ACT (CRA), WHICH LIMITED EXPENSES ON ELECTIONEERING BY OUTSIDE GROUPS.

IF THAT'S CONSTITUTIONAL, IT SURE ISN'T HYPER—CAPITALISTICAL...

THE CRA IS BASED ON A SIMPLE FACT: **MONEY INFLUENCES LAWMAKING.** THESE GRAPHS, BASED ON A PRINCETON-NORTHWESTERN STUDY, SHOW THE EFFECT. THE LEFT-HAND PICTURE SHOWS THE PROBABILITY OF VARIOUS PROPOSALS BEING PASSED INTO LAW, GIVEN DIFFERENT LEVELS OF PUBLIC SUPPORT. ON THE RIGHT WE SEE THE SAME OUTCOMES GRAPHED AGAINST THE OPINION OF THE **RICH.**

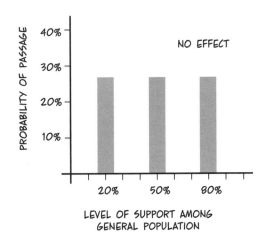

LEVEL OF SUPPORT AMONG GENERAL POPULATION

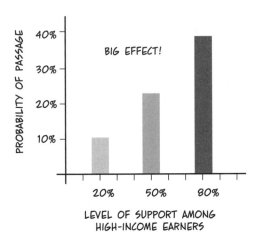

LEVEL OF SUPPORT AMONG HIGH-INCOME EARNERS

CITIZENS UNITED, THE CORPORATE-BACKED PRODUCERS OF THE MOVIE, SUED THE FEC. THE CASE WAS HEARD BY THE U.S. SUPREME COURT.

IN 2010, THE COURT RULED 5-4 IN FAVOR OF CITIZENS UNITED. THE MAJORITY OPINION SAID THAT CORPORATE **EXPENSES** ON SPEECH MUST NOT BE LIMITED!

IT'S DISCRIMINATION AGAINST THE RICH, YOUR HONORS!

"... PROHIBITION ON CORPORATE INDEPENDENT EXPENDITURES IS AN OUTRIGHT BAN ON SPEECH."

JUSTICE ANTHONY KENNEDY

THE MINORITY'S DISSENT NOTED THAT THERE WAS NO "BAN," ONLY A 30-DAY AD BLACKOUT, AND BESIDES,

"UNLIKE NATURAL PERSONS, CORPORATIONS HAVE 'LIMITED LIABILITY' FOR THEIR OWNERS AND MANAGERS, 'PERPETUAL LIFE,' SEPARATION OF OWNERSHIP AND CONTROL, 'AND FAVORABLE TREATMENT OF THE ACCUMULATION AND DISTRIBUTION OF ASSETS.' ... CORPORATIONS HAVE NO CONSCIENCES, NO BELIEFS, NO FEELINGS, NO THOUGHTS, NO DESIRES... THEY ARE NOT THEMSELVES MEMBERS OF 'WE THE PEOPLE.'"

JUSTICE JOHN PAUL STEVENS

MAJORITY RULES, AND NOW CORPORATIONS CAN POOL **UNLIMITED** FUNDS FOR CAMPAIGNS, AS LONG AS THE FUNDERS OPERATE "INDEPENDENTLY" OF ANY CANDIDATE.

PRETEND WE'VE NEVER MET!

BUT NO WORRIES! THE SUPREME COURT'S MAJORITY ASSURES US THAT

"INDEPENDENT EXPENDITURES, INCLUDING THOSE MADE BY CORPORATIONS, DO NOT GIVE RISE TO CORRUPTION OR THE APPEARANCE OF CORRUPTION."

NOW THERE'S A RELIEF!

I SEE WHY THEY CALL IT THE HIGH COURT... THEY MUST HAVE BEEN HIGH WHEN THEY WROTE THAT...

BUSINESS COMPLAINS ABOUT REGULATIONS, BUT BY AND LARGE BUSINESS HAS FRIENDLY RELATIONS WITH GOVERNMENT. GOVERNMENT ACTIVELY PROMOTES AND PROTECTS BUSINESS. GOVERNMENT LISTENS!

A LITTLE TO THE RIGHT...

RELATIONS BETWEEN BUSINESS AND WORKERS ARE LESS COZY.

EVERY DOLLAR PAID IN WAGES OR BENEFITS IS A DOLLAR OFF THE BOTTOM LINE. EVERY REQUEST FOR A RAISE LOOKS TO THE OWNER LIKE A LITTLE ACT OF TREASON.

FROM WITHIN MY VERY WALLS!

TO A WORKER, LABOR CAN BE MANY THINGS: A CALLING, A LIVELIHOOD, AN IDENTITY, A SOCIAL NETWORK, AND/ OR A WAY TO PAY THE BILLS. TO BUSINESS, ON THE OTHER HAND, LABOR IS ONLY ONE THING...

A COST.

PAYROLL

SO, IN HYPERCAPITALISM'S PROFIT-MAXIMIZING UNIVERSE, THE FOURTH COMMANDMENT IS

Thou shalt spend less on LABOR.

LESS THAN WHAT?

PICK A NUMBER, ANY NUMBER...

IN "PURE" CAPITALISM, WAGES ARE DETERMINED IN THE "LABOR MARKET." IN THIS MYTHICAL MARKETPLACE, BUYERS (EMPLOYERS) SHOP FOR A PRODUCT (LABOR) SOLD BY WORKERS. WORKERS COMPETE AGAINST EACH OTHER AND SO DRIVE DOWN WAGES, JUST AS BUSINESS COMPETITION HOLDS DOWN PRICES. (SEE P. 31.)

(SEE P. 31.)

SO QUAINT... SO MEDIEVAL!

ACTUALLY, MEDIEVAL WAGES WERE OFTEN REGULATED...

JOBBE FAIRE

STEALS AND DEALS

PRICES SLASHED

20% OFF!!

DON'T MISS OUR SHROVETIDE SALES EVENT!

IN MODERN TIMES, WORKERS HAVE BANDED TOGETHER TO FORM **LABOR UNIONS.** UNION WORKERS AGREE **NOT TO COMPETE** WITH EACH OTHER, BUT TO STAND OR FALL TOGETHER. A UNION NEGOTIATES WAGES FOR ALL ITS MEMBERS COLLECTIVELY, AND, IF IT CAN'T REACH AGREEMENT WITH MANAGEMENT, THE WORKERS WALK OFF THE JOB AND PICKET THE SITE.

THE WORST PART IS THAT IT'S PERFECTLY LEGAL...

107

IN THE UNITED STATES, UNION MEMBERSHIP PEAKED IN THE 1950S, AT AROUND

35% OF ALL WAGE- AND SALARY-EARNERS.

UNION JOBS WERE CONCENTRATED IN THE INDUSTRIAL NORTHEAST, MIDWEST, AND WEST COAST, WHILE ALL AMERICA DROVE UNION-MADE FINTAILED FANTASIES FROM DETROIT.

THEN, IN THE 1960S, A LITTLE GERMAN BUG-SHAPED THING APPEARED ON THE ROADS.

IT WAS SOON FOLLOWED BY JAPANESE CARS, SMALL, BOXY, RELIABLE, FUEL-EFFICIENT, AND CHEAP.

DETROIT LOST SALES... AND NOT ONLY DETROIT. CHEAPER, BETTER JAPANESE **CONSUMER ELECTRONICS** DROVE THEIR AMERICAN COMPETITORS OUT OF BUSINESS COMPLETELY. (ZENITH? ADMIRAL? RCA? REMEMBER THEM?) MILLIONS OF AMERICAN WORKERS FOUND THEMSELVES FURLOUGHED, WORKING SHORT SHIFTS, OR LAID OFF.

IN OTHER NEWS, TEXTILE FACTORIES ARE CLOSING IN NEW ENGLAND!

SIGH... AT LEAST I HAVE PLENTY OF FREE TIME TO APPRECIATE THIS VIBRANT SONY TRINITRON COLOR...

EVEN WHEN UNIONS AGREED TO TAKE PAY CUTS, COMPANIES LOOKED FOR OTHER WAYS TO REDUCE COSTS. UNIONS, THEY DECIDED, WERE THE PROBLEM.

NEVER DID LIKE 'EM...

CORPORATIONS ABANDONED THEIR OLD FACTORIES—AND THEIR WORKERS. NEW FACTORIES AROSE WHERE WAGES WERE LOW: NON-UNION PARTS OF THE U.S., LIKE THE SOUTH, AND, INCREASINGLY, ABROAD. GLOBALIZATION!

THESE FACTORIES EMPLOYED LOWER-PAID WORKERS—AND FEWER OF THEM. OWNERS INSTALLED NEW **AUTOMATION** TECHNOLOGY, BECAUSE ROBOTS TAKE NO WAGES!!!

GREAT... ANOTHER ONE... WHAT DOES **THIS** THING DO?

OH...

WITHIN A COUPLE OF DECADES, ONLY **11%** OF U.S. WORKERS BELONGED TO A UNION. AMERICANS WERE NOW IN COMPETITION NOT ONLY WITH EACH OTHER, BUT ALSO WITH WORKERS ALL OVER THE WORLD. WAGES STAGNATED, MANUFACTURING SHRANK, AND THE OLD INDUSTRIAL HEARTLAND BECAME THE

RUST BELT.

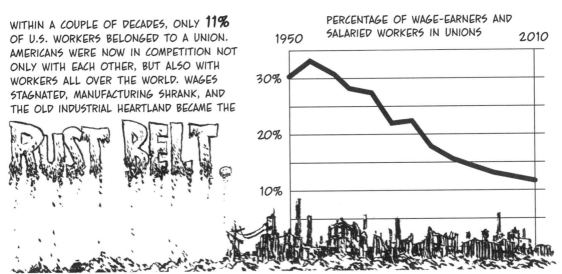

PERCENTAGE OF WAGE-EARNERS AND SALARIED WORKERS IN UNIONS

1950   2010

30%

20%

10%

WITH UNIONS WEAKENED, BUSINESS FOUND A NEW WAY TO PIT WORKERS AGAINST EACH OTHER: MAKE THEM

INDEPENDENT CONTRACTORS.

FROM NOW ON, YOU WORK AT ARM'S LENGTH!

BUT YOUR ARMS ARE SO SHORT...

AS AN EMPLOYEE, A WORKER IS ENTITLED TO HEALTH BENEFITS, EXTRA PAY FOR OVERTIME, UNEMPLOYMENT INSURANCE, ETC., AND ALL AT THE COMPANY'S EXPENSE.

WHAT EVER HAPPENED TO SELF-RELIANCE?

AS A SELF-EMPLOYED CONTRACTOR, THE WORKER ASSUMES RESPONSIBILITY FOR ALL THAT STUFF PERSONALLY.

WHY IS THERE NO LAW AGAINST PAYING YOURSELF A DOLLAR AN HOUR??!

HENCE THE "GIG ECONOMY," IN WHICH PEOPLE SCRAMBLE FOR FREELANCE JOBS. THE NUMBER OF CONTRACT AND TEMPORARY WORKERS IN THE U.S. ROSE BY **50%** BETWEEN 2009 AND 2015.

SOME OF US GET GIGS, ALGI GETS GIGGLES...

PROGRAMMERS, WRITERS, TAXI- AND TRUCK DRIVERS, NURSES, JANITORS, AND EVEN COLLEGE PROFESSORS ARE ALL IN THE SAME BOAT—AND ALL ARE IN COMPETITION WITH EACH OTHER.

AND FREE-LANCERS CAN'T FORM UNIONS—ARE YOU PAYING ATTENTION, CLASS?

AS THE FREE-LANCE TEACHER JUST SAID, INDEPENDENT CONTRAC-TORS ARE LEGALLY BARRED FROM FORMING UNIONS. THIS IS A GOVERNMENT-IMPOSED LIMIT ON WORKERS' ABILITY TO IMPROVE WAGES AND/OR WORKING CONDITIONS... AND IT ISN'T THE ONLY WAY GOVERNMENT SIDES WITH BUSINESS AGAINST WORKERS.

AN ESPECIALLY FLAGRANT BIT OF GOVERNMENT-BUSINESS COLLUSION WAS THE CASE OF THE **MARIANAS ISLANDS.**

CHINA

JAPAN

PHILIPPINES

IN THE 1990S, A GROUP OF AMERICAN RETAILERS, POLITICIANS, AND LOBBYISTS HATCHED A SCHEME TO EXPLOIT THE ISLANDS' POSITION: NEAR ASIA, U.S.-OWNED, AND LEGALLY MURKY.

EVERYONE WINS BUT THE WORKERS!

THE AMERICANS INVITED CHINESE COMPANIES TO OPEN SEWING FACTORIES IN THE MARIANAS, WHERE GARMENTS WOULD GET SPECIAL TAX TREATMENT AND CARRY "MADE IN USA" LABELS.

THE TOWERS AND MOAT ARE AN EXPECIALLY NICE TOUCH.

ASIAN WORKERS WERE SURPRISED TO FIND THEMSELVES WORKING FOR LOW WAGES IN NEAR-PRISON CONDITIONS, INSTEAD OF LIVING IN THE LAND OF THE FREE.

TO BE FAIR, WE'RE FREE TO SWIM AS FAR AS WE CAN...

COMPANIES USING THE MARIANAS INCLUDED SOME FAMILIAR BRANDS.

WHEN THE SCANDAL BROKE IN 2002, THE U.S. SENATE VOTED TO END THE SCAM, BUT THE HOUSE OF REPRESENTATIVES BALKED. SPEAKER **TOM DELAY** REFUSED TO CALL A VOTE, BECAUSE, HE SAID, THE MARIANAS WERE:

"A PERFECT PETRI DISH OF CAPITALISM... EVERYTHING THAT IS GOOD ABOUT WHAT WE ARE TRYING TO DO IN AMERICA."

SORRY, I REFUSE TO DRAW HIS FACE.

BUT—

BUT—

CLOSER TO HOME IS THE ISSUE OF THE

MINIMUM WAGE,

A GOVERNMENT-IMPOSED FLOOR UNDER THE LABOR MARKET.

WHO NEEDS A FLOOR WHEN YOU CAN LIE ON THE COLD, HARD GROUND?

THE MINIMUM WAGE, FIRST SET IN THE 1930S, ROSE STEADILY TO KEEP PACE WITH INCREASING PRICES, UNTIL ABOUT 1980.

YOU JUST CAN'T GET AWAY FROM OL' RONNIE!!

$4
$3
$2
$1

1940   1960   1980

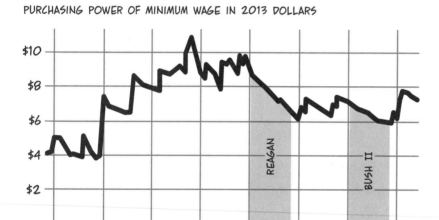

PURCHASING POWER OF MINIMUM WAGE IN 2013 DOLLARS

$10
$8
$6
$4
$2

REAGAN

BUSH II

1940   1960   1980   2000

REAGAN FROZE THE MINIMUM WAGE FOR 8 YEARS, DURING WHICH TIME INFLATION ERODED ITS VALUE BY A THIRD. BUSH II DID THE SAME. THE WAGE ROSE SLIGHTLY UNDER BOTH CLINTON AND OBAMA, BUT ITS PURCHASING POWER IS STILL LOWER THAN AT ANY TIME BETWEEN 1956 AND 1985.

MEANWHILE, EXEC-UTIVE PAY ZOOMED (SEE P. 15). FOR EXAMPLE, IN 2014 CHIPOTLE MEXICAN GRILL'S CEO **STEVE ELLS** MADE $28.9 MILLION, MORE THAN **1,500** TIMES AS MUCH AS DID HIS AVERAGE EMPLOYEE (MEDIAN PAY WAS $19,000.)

YOU GO, GUY!

IF ELLS WERE TO MAKE "ONLY" $6 MILLION AND DIVIDE THE BALANCE AMONG HIS 48,500 HOURLY WORKERS, EVERY ONE OF THEM WOULD SEE **$470** MORE PER YEAR. IN OTHER WORDS, BUSINESS CAN AFFORD TO PAY MORE.

ARITHMETIC MUSTN'T FALL INTO THE WRONG HANDS...

ANOTHER UNUSUALLY STINGY
AMERICAN LAW GOVERNS

PARENTAL LEAVE,

TIME OFF WORK FOR NEW PARENTS.

YOUR PLACE IS WHERE I SAY IT IS...

REAMS OF STUDIES SHOW THE HEALTHY EFFECTS OF TIME OFF FOR NEW PARENTS. LESS THAN THREE MONTHS' MATERNAL LEAVE PUTS NEWBORNS AT RISK, SO PARENTAL LEAVE LAWS ARE ALL BUT UNIVERSAL.

ISN'T THERE A CHEAPER WAY TO GENERATE NEW HIRES?

AND THEY SAY CORPORATIONS ARE PEOPLE...

AT THIS WRITING, ALL COUNTRIES BUT THREE REQUIRE EMPLOYERS TO GIVE NEW MOTHERS (AND SOMETIMES FATHERS) **PAID LEAVE,** USUALLY 14 WEEKS BUT OFTEN MUCH LONGER. THIS MAP SHOWS THE THREE EXCEPTIONS: THE U.S., SURINAME, AND PAPUA NEW GUINEA.

THE U.S. STANDARD IS 12 WEEKS OF **UNPAID** LEAVE.

HEY, TIME IS MONEY!

ACTUALLY, NO... **MONEY** IS MONEY...

113

BESIDES REGULATING LABOR RELATIONS IN THE PRIVATE SECTOR, GOVERNMENT ALSO DIRECTLY EMPLOYS PEOPLE, MILLIONS OF THEM. WHAT KIND OF BOSS IS THE GOVERNMENT?

IN A WORD, IT VARIES...

IN 1981, WHEN FEDERALLY-EMPLOYED AIR TRAFFIC CONTROLLERS WENT ON STRIKE, PRESIDENT REAGAN FIRED THEM ALL AND HIRED NONUNION NEWBIES TO ROUTE AIRPLANE FLIGHT PATHS.

ISN'T COMPE-TITION MUCH MORE EXCITING?

SINCE THEN, GOVERNMENT WORKERS HAVE DONE SOMEWHAT BETTER. TO ALGI'S HORROR, NEARLY HALF OF ALL UNION WORKERS IN THE U.S.— SOME 6 MILLION OF THEM—ARE NOW IN THE PUBLIC SECTOR.

JUST LOOK AT THAT BLOATED BUREAUCRACY!

THAT ONE! OVER HERE! AHEM!

U.S. Bureau of Departments

Amalgamated Gigantic, Inc. Division of Subdivisions

HYPERCAPITALISM HAS MOUNTED A TWO-PRONGED CAMPAIGN AGAINST LARGE GOVERNMENT AND ITS UNIONIZED WORKERS. FIRST, ATTACK THE UNIONS DIRECTLY...

MAKE IT STOP, PAULIE, OR WE'LL OUTSOURCE *YOU!*

AND SECOND, ATTACK THE PUBLIC SECTOR ITSELF.

WHAT COULD MAKE MORE SENSE IN AN ERA OF GIANT BUSINESSES THAN HAVING A SMALL GOVERNMENT?

WHICH BRINGS US TO...

Thou shalt PRIVATIZE.

IN OTHER WORDS, LET PRIVATE BUSINESSES
TAKE OVER GOVERNMENT FUNCTIONS.

THE TACTICS ARE CLEVER: FIRST PUSH FOR TAX CUTS, THEN STARVE GOVERNMENT AGENCIES,
THEN COMPLAIN THAT THESE UNDERSTAFFED AGENCIES ARE INCOMPETENT!

SINCE THE 1980S,
PRIVATE COMPANIES
HAVE TAKEN CHARGE
OF TOLL ROADS, PARKS,
WATER SYSTEMS, FIRE
DEPARTMENTS, AND
EVEN MILITARY AND
INTELLIGENCE DUTIES.

PRIVATIZATION CAN MAKE FUNNY THINGS HAPPEN, AS IN THE CASE OF THE

CHICAGO PARKING METERS.

FEED ME, FEED MY OWNER...

IN 2009, THE CITY OF CHICAGO LEASED ITS PARKING METERS FOR **75 YEARS** TO A COMPANY CALLED CPM, LLC. CPM GAVE CASH-STRAPPED CHICAGO A ONE-TIME PAYMENT OF $1.2 BILLION.

I'VE ALWAYS LOVED WHAT'S INSIDE PARKING METERS!

CPM QUICKLY RAISED METER RATES UP TO 400%.

PLEASE INSERT ATM CARD AND STEP AWAY FROM THE METER...

THE CITY LOST A REVENUE STREAM THAT USED TO GO TO MASS TRANSIT IMPROVEMENT, SO FORGET THAT.

%$#&%#!!

THE LEASE PROMISED CPM A TOTAL OF 36,000 METERS. REMOVING METERS (EVEN TEMPORARILY, AS FOR STREET REPAIR) OBLIGATES CHICAGO TO PAY A PENALTY.

WHANG WHANG WHANG

CPM NOW BRINGS IN ABOUT **$130 MILLION** PER YEAR, A RETURN ON INVESTMENT OF MORE THAN **10%** PER YEAR. THE CITY REALIZED IT HAD SOLD THE LEASE FOR **HALF** WHAT IT WAS WORTH...

BUT DON'T WORRY! YOU'LL HAVE 'EM BACK IN 69... 68... 67 YEARS!

DEFINITELY LESS FUNNY, BECAUSE THEY'RE NOT JUST ABOUT MONEY, ARE

PRIVATE PRISONS.

BRANDING IS ALL.

PRIVATE COMPANIES—CCA AND GEO ARE THE BIGGEST—PROMISE TO RUN PRISONS "MORE EFFICIENTLY." THEY STILL USE TAX DOLLARS, BUT THEORETICALLY SPEND LESS PER PRISONER.

UM.. YOU HAVE SALARIES... BENEFITS... BUILDING UPKEEP... FOOD... UNIFORMS... **PLUS** PROFIT. HOW CAN THAT BE **LESS?**

BECAUSE **CAPITALISM!**

EFFICIENCY LOOKS LIKE THIS: OVER THE YEARS, CCA AND GEO HAVE BEEN ACCUSED OF:

  *POOR MAINTENANCE (NOT FIXING LOCKS!)

  *FAILING TO PAY INTO EMPLOYEES' PENSION AND HEALTH ACCOUNTS

  *CUTTING STAFF BELOW SAFE LEVELS

IN SHORT, CHEATING GUARDS AND RISKING LIVES.

BUT EFFICIENTLY!

NOT TO MENTION THAT PRIVATE COMPANIES MAKE MORE MONEY BY KEEPING PRISONS FULL. AS IN CHICAGO, TAXPAYERS PAY A PENALTY FOR LOW USAGE, AND CCA, GEO, AND THEIR ILK LOBBY FOR HARSH SENTENCES, THREE-STRIKES LAWS, AND ANYTHING ELSE THAT PUTS PEOPLE AWAY.

HMM... HOW FEW PEOPLE COULD WE HAVE **OUT THERE**...

TO SUPPORT KEEPING EVERYBODY **ELSE** IN **HERE**...?

WE'RE NOT ARGUING THAT GOVERNMENT SHOULD RUN EVERYTHING—FAR FROM IT! PRIVATE ENTERPRISE DOES GREAT THINGS. REMEMBER BETTY'S BUNS? DELICIOUS!

BUT WHEN THE "PRODUCT" IS A PUBLIC SERVICE, THE PROFIT MOTIVE CAN RUN DIRECTLY AGAINST THE COMMON GOOD.

CRIMINAL-TRAINING SEMINARS WOULD GROW THE BUSINESS!!

INNOVATIVE!

DISRUPTIVE!

OUTSIDE THE BOX!

PUNICORP

ANOTHER GOOD EXAMPLE IS THE U.S. HEALTHCARE SYSTEM, IF YOU CAN CALL IT A SYSTEM. FOR DECADES, GOVERNMENTS AND CHURCHES PROVIDED MOST U.S. HOSPITAL SERVICES, BUT IN THE 1980S, FOR-PROFIT HOSPITALS ENTERED THE HEALTH CARE SCENE.

STUDIES SHOW THAT FOR-PROFIT HOSPITALS ARE MORE LIKELY TO OFFER MONEY-MAKING SERVICES LIKE OPEN-HEART SURGERY, AND LESS LIKELY TO OFFER LESS-PROFITABLE, BUT STILL NEEDED, SERVICES LIKE HOME HEALTH CARE AND EMERGENCY SERVICES.

$$ NO MERCY INCORPORATED $$

THE INCREASING DOMINANCE OF THE PROFIT MOTIVE IN HEALTH CARE ALSO INFLUENCES DOCTORS, AS THEY TEND TO OVER-PRESCRIBE DIAGNOSTIC TESTS WHEN THEY STAND TO BENEFIT FINANCIALLY.

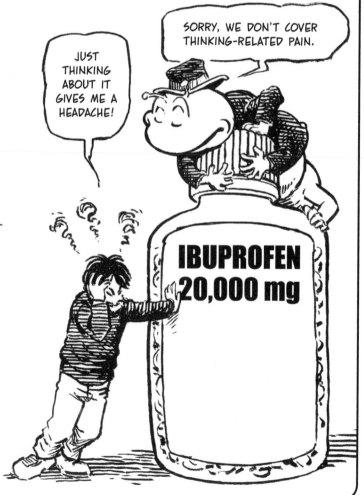

JUST THINKING ABOUT IT GIVES ME A HEADACHE!

SORRY, WE DON'T COVER THINKING-RELATED PAIN.

IBUPROFEN 20,000 mg

NOTE THAT A PRIVATE PRISON OR PARKING METER COLLECTOR IS VERY DIFFERENT FROM BETTY'S BUN SHOP. CPM, FOR INSTANCE, HAS ONLY ONE "CUSTOMER," THE CITY OF CHICAGO... AND IF CHICAGO DOESN'T LIKE CPM, THE CITY CAN HARDLY GO SHOPPING FOR A BETTER DEAL—NOT FOR SIXTY-SOME YEARS, ANYWAY.

HOW SINCERE (WE MIGHT ASK) ARE THE ARGUMENTS FOR PRIVATIZATION? DOES ALGI REALLY BELIEVE THAT "THE MARKET" WILL STREAMLINE OPERATIONS? OR ARE CORPORATE INTERESTS SIMPLY LOOKING FOR WAYS TO DIVERT TAX MONEY INTO THEIR BANK ACCOUNTS?

119

THIS CONCLUDES OUR TOUR OF
HYPERCAPITALISM'S FIVE COMMANDMENTS.

I WONDER
WHY GOD
DIDN'T
THINK OF
THESE?

CONSUME
GLOBALIZE
DEREGULATE
CUT WAGES
PRIVATIZE

WE'VE REVIEWED THEIR HISTORY AND EFFECTS: EVER-PRESENT ADS, DEBT, STAGNANT WAGES,
DISAPPEARING JOBS, MEDIA CONSOLIDATION, BANK COLLAPSES, AND THE HIDDEN COSTS OF
PRIVATIZATION, AMONG OTHERS.

TRULY, I'M NOT THE
ONLY ONE LOST IN
THE WILDERNESS!

WHERE DO THESE DEVELOPMENTS
LEAVE OUR SIX CHARACTERS?

MAY YOU EMERGE
IN LESS THAN
FORTY YEARS...

ERNIE WAGES WORKS THREE PART-TIME JOBS, PAYS HALF HIS INCOME FOR RENT, AND SUFFERS FROM SLEEP DEPRIVATION.

ZZZZZZZz

CONNIE SUMER KEEPS ALL HER EXTRA STUFF IN TWO STORAGE UNITS, WHERE SHE CAN ALSO HIDE FROM COLLECTION AGENTS.

PAUL ITTICKS DIVIDES HIS TIME BETWEEN FUNDRAISING AND MEETING WITH ALGI'S AND CAPPY'S LOBBYISTS. EVERY SO OFTEN, HE FEELS A TWINGE OF REGRET.

IS THIS REALLY ALL THERE IS?

BETTY BAKER MADE MONEY FROM HER TIME AT BETTCO, BUT SHE FEELS USELESS AND BORED. SHE HAS LITTLE INTEREST IN GOING BACK INTO BUSINESS IF IT MEANS DEALING WITH ALGI, CAPPY, AND THEIR ALLY, PAUL ITTICKS.

ALGI AND CAPPY, MEANWHILE, ARE WORKING WITH THEIR DESIGN TEAM ON A PROJECT TO REBRAND THE ENTIRE ENTERPRISE.

HOW ABOUT WE PUT ADS ON DOLLAR BILLS?

CORPORATE FLAG
DESIGN INSPIRED BY
ADBUSTERS MAGAZINE

Chapter 6

HYPERCAPITALISM, VALUES, AND WELL-BEING

WOW... THAT WAS A GRIM AND DEPRESSING CHAPTER TO WRITE... 50 PAGES OF BAD NEWS... I HOPE **READING** IT WASN'T **TOO** UPSETTING!

ANYWAY, I HOPE YOU'LL HANG IN THERE! REMEMBER, PART II OF THIS BOOK WILL BE MUCH MORE POSITIVE!

BUT FIRST WE NEED TO TALK ABOUT ONE MORE THING, WHICH TO ME, AS A PSYCHOLOGIST, IS THE CENTRAL POINT OF THE BOOK: WHAT HYPERCAPITALISM DOES TO **VALUES** AND PEOPLE'S **WELL-BEING**.

HYPERCAPITALISM, THROUGH ITS IDEOLOGY AND ITS ADVERTISING, OFFERS A **PROMISE**. IT ASSURES US THAT UNFETTERED MARKETS AND RELENTLESS BUYING WILL PROMOTE THE **PURSUIT OF HAPPINESS!**

NOW WE ASK, IS IT TRUE? DOES HYPERCAPITALISM, DESPITE ITS SHORTCOMINGS, ENHANCE WELL-BEING? OR HAS HYPERCAPITALISM'S PROMISE TURNED OUT TO BE **FALSE?**

YOU STILL HAVE SOME INK LEFT IN YOUR BOTTLE, LARRY?

SOB!

ONE WAY TO SEE HYPERCAPITALISM'S EFFECT ON VALUES IS TO RECOGNIZE THAT NOT ALL CAPITALISM IS EQUALLY HYPER. IN NORWAY, FOR EXAMPLE, **50%** OF WORKERS BELONG TO UNIONS, COMPARED WITH ONLY 11% IN THE UNITED STATES.

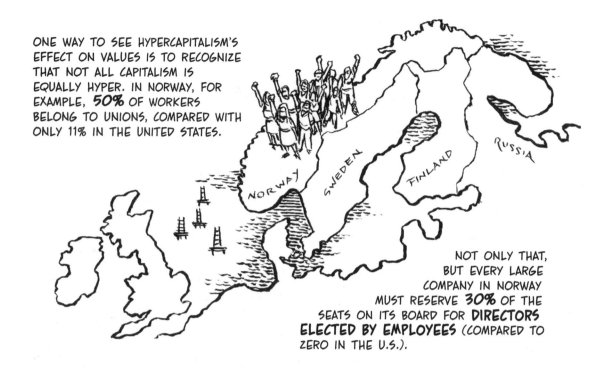

NOT ONLY THAT, BUT EVERY LARGE COMPANY IN NORWAY MUST RESERVE **30%** OF THE SEATS ON ITS BOARD FOR **DIRECTORS ELECTED BY EMPLOYEES** (COMPARED TO ZERO IN THE U.S.).

IN 2004, TWO HARVARD POLITICAL SCIENTISTS CREATED A SCORING SYSTEM THAT MEASURES A NATION'S LEVEL OF HYPERCAPITALISM. COUNTRIES WITH LOWER SCORES HAVE GREATER COMPETITION AND LITTLE LABOR INPUT OR STRATEGIC COORDINATION. HIGHER SCORES MEAN HIGHER LEVELS OF STRATEGIC PLANNING AND COORDINATION. LOWER SCORES ARE MORE HYPERCAPITALISTIC.

LET'S CALL THIS NUMBER THE S-SCORE, WITH S STANDING FOR "STRATEGIC." THE LOWER THE SCORE, THE MORE HYPER-CAPITALISTIC THE COUNTRY.

SEE? WE REALLY ARE NUMBER ONE!

S-SCORE	COUNTRY
0	U.S.A.
7	U.K.
13	CANADA
21	NEW ZEALAND
29	IRELAND
36	AUSTRALIA
51	SWITZERLAND
57	SPAIN
66	NETHERLANDS
69	FRANCE
69	SWEDEN
70	DENMARK
72	PORTUGAL
72	FINLAND
74	BELGIUM
74	JAPAN
76	NORWAY
87	ITALY
95	GERMANY
100	AUSTRIA

WE CAN USE THE S-SCORE TO EXPLORE THIS IDEA:

Differences in ECONOMIC ORGANIZATION are associated with Differences in VALUES.

IT MAKES SENSE! AFTER ALL, LAWS ARE THE RESULT OF **CHOICES.**

AYE

NO

IF A COUNTRY VALUES WORKERS OR THE ENVIRONMENT, WE EXPECT TO SEE PROTECTIVE LAWS, REGULATIONS, AND CUSTOMS IN FORCE THERE.

JA

NON

CONVERSELY, A COUNTRY'S ECONOMIC LIFE AFFECTS ITS VALUES. WE EXPECT TO SEE MORE FOCUS ON MONEY AND STATUS IN VERY COMPETITIVE SOCIETIES.

OR SO REASONED VALUE THEORIST **SHALOM SCHWARTZ,** WHEN HE BROUGHT HIS CIRCUMPLEX MODEL, HIS SURVEY RESULTS, AND HIS STATISTICAL ANALYSIS TO THE 20 S-SCORES ON THAT LIST.

SCHWARTZ'S PAST WORK HAD SHOWN THAT IT MAKES SENSE TO CONSIDER **CULTURAL** OR **NATIONAL** VALUES, AS WELL AS INDIVIDUAL VALUES. FOR EXAMPLE, WITHIN ANY COUNTRY THE INDIVIDUAL VALUES OF POWER, MONEY, AND STATUS MAY BE COMBINED INTO A SINGLE CULTURAL VALUE SCHWARTZ CALLS **HIERARCHY.**

GRAPHING COUNTRIES' HIERARCHY SCORES AGAINST THEIR S-SCORES GIVES THIS SCATTERPLOT, TO WHICH WE HAVE ADDED THE BEST-FITTING LINE TO EMPHASIZE THE TREND.

THE CORRELATION, ALTHOUGH IMPERFECT, IS CLEAR. HYPER-CAPITALIST COUNTRIES LIKE THE U.S. AND U.K. TEND TO EMPHASIZE HIERARCHY MORE THAN DO "HIGH-S" COUNTRIES LIKE GERMANY, AUSTRIA, OR NORWAY.

126

ANOTHER CULTURAL VALUE IS ONE SCHWARTZ CALLS **HARMONY.** HARMONIOUS CULTURES PURSUE GOOD RELATIONS WITH THEIR NEIGHBORS AND WITH NATURE. IN OTHER WORDS, THEY SEEK PEACE AND ENVIRONMENTAL PRESERVATION.

JOIN IN! WE NEED AN ALTO AND A FEW TENORS!

THIS GRAPH PLOTS THE 20 COUNTRIES' S-SCORES AGAINST THEIR HARMONY LEVELS. AGAIN, THE CORRELATION IS PLAIN.

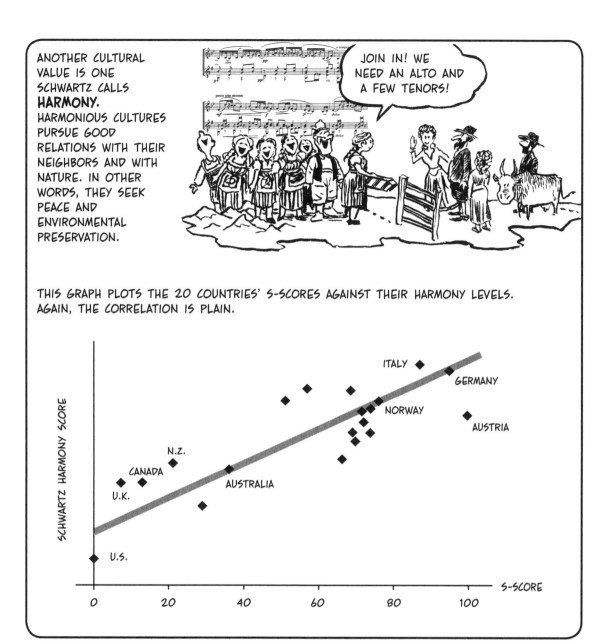

LOW S-SCORE COUNTRIES—THE MOST HYPER-CAPITALIST ONES—HAVE LOWER HARMONY VALUES. IT'S THE SEESAW EFFECT: THE PUR-SUIT OF LOOT SUPPRESSES COM-PETING VALUES.

ANYONE FEEL LIKE SINGING ALONG?

NOT ME.

NOT ME.

NO.

127

A HYPERCAPITALIST ECONOMY PUTS REAL EFFORT INTO DRUMMING MATERIALISTIC VALUES INTO ITS CITIZENS, STARTING IN CHILDHOOD. CONSUMERISM HAS TO BE TAUGHT!

IF ONLY UNBRIDLED GREED CAME NATURALLY TO EVERYONE... SNIFF...

HUSH NOW, YOU'LL STAIN YOUR TIE...

OF ALL THE VARIABLES LINKED TO NATIONAL HIERARCHY SCORES, ONE OF THE MOST HIGHLY CORRELATED IS THE AMOUNT OF TIME PER DAY SPENT BROADCASTING

TV ADS AIMED AT CHILDREN!

THE CORRELATION COEFFICIENT HERE IS A WHOPPING −0.86.

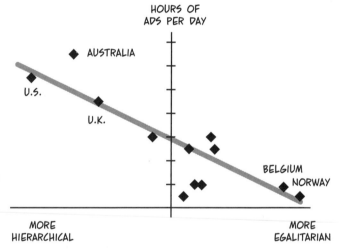

HOURS OF ADS PER DAY

AUSTRALIA

U.S.

U.K.

BELGIUM
NORWAY

MORE
HIERARCHICAL

MORE
EGALITARIAN

THAT IS, MORE-EGALITARIAN SOCIETIES BELIEVE IN SHELTERING THEIR CHILDREN FROM COMMERICAL MANIPULATION, WHICH KIDS ARE ILL-EQUIPPED TO RESIST. (SEE P. 72.)

WHAT IS WRONG WITH THOSE COUNTRIES?

HOW DO THEY PLAY WITHOUT PRODUCTS?

THE MOST HYPERCAPITALIST COUNTRIES PUT ADVERTISERS' INTERESTS FIRST.

IT'S NEVER TOO SOON TO CONSUME!

PAP

SHH!

A HOST OF RESEARCH SHOWS THAT COMMERCIAL-SOAKED CHILDREN TEND TO GROW UP INTO ADULTS WITH HIGHLY MATERIALISTIC VALUES. LET'S CALL SUCH PEOPLE "HI-MATS."

HI-MAT PARENTS ARE KNOWN TO GUIDE THEIR CHILDREN'S BEHAVIOR BY MATERIAL REWARDS MORE OFTEN THAN LOW-MAT PARENTS DO.

YOU ATE ALL YOUR KALE, KYLIE, SO YOU GET A **PONY!**

WHAT'LL YOU GIVE ME TOMORROW, **MOM?**

AND OF COURSE, ADS DON'T STOP IN CHILDHOOD. THEY CONTINUE PUMMELING US THROUGHOUT LIFE, AND POSSIBLY BEYOND, FOR ALL WE KNOW.

BUT FIRST, A WORD ABOUT **ETERNAGLOSS** WING WAX...

ALL OF WHICH RAISES A QUESTION THAT STANDS AT THE HEART OF THIS BOOK. WE'VE TALKED ABOUT VALUES; WE'VE TALKED ABOUT ECONOMICS; WE'VE TALKED ABOUT THE RELATIONSHIP BETWEEN VALUES AND ECONOMICS. BUT ONE BIG QUESTION IS STILL UNADDRESSED, AND THAT QUESTION IS...

PASTE OR LIQUID?

NO, THAT QUESTION IS—

WHAT DO THE VALUES PROMOTED BY HYPERCAPITALISM HAVE TO DO WITH **WELL-BEING?**

OH, YEAH... THAT...

WHAT DO WE MEAN BY WELL-BEING? PSYCHOLOGISTS HAVE USED THE EXPRESSION IN VARIOUS WAYS OVER THE YEARS.

*LACK OF MENTAL ILLNESS OR DISORDER

*EXPERIENCING PLEASURE

*HAVING A SENSE OF LIFE SATISFACTION

*HAVING A SENSE OF MEANING AND PURPOSE

*LIVING IN WAYS THAT DO NOT HURT ONESELF, OTHER PEOPLE, FUTURE GENERATIONS, OR THE BIOSPHERE

IT SEEMS TO ME THAT ALL OF THESE CAN GO TOGETHER! LIVING RESPONSIBLY, SUSTAINABLY, AND WITH PURPOSE IS A SOURCE OF SATISFACTION AND PLEASURE.

MEANWHILE, THE PURSUIT OF EXTRINSIC VALUES CAN LEAD TO ANXIETY AND DEPRESSION. JUST CONSIDER **CONNIE SUMER** AS SHE VISITS HER THERAPIST!

CONNIE, AS WE KNOW, IS FOCUSED ON MONEY, STATUS, IMAGE, AND POSSESSIONS...

YOU'RE **HOW** DEEP IN DEBT, CONNIE?

MANY STUDIES HAVE EXAMINED THE RELATIONSHIP BETWEEN THESE VALUES AND WELL-BEING. THE VERDICT: IT'S A NEGATIVE RELATIONSHIP.

I **AM** GOING TO GET PAID, RIGHT?

FOR EXAMPLE, RESEARCH SHOWS THAT PEOPLE WITH MATERIALISTIC VALUES TEND TO SUFFER FROM

COMPULSIVE CONSUMPTION.

THE MAIN SYMPTOM IS AN OVERWHELMING URGE TO BUY SOMETHING, ANYTHING.

THERE'S A SALE ON! I CAN SMELL IT!

TYPICALLY, A COMPULSIVE CONSUMER IS ADDRESSING NEGATIVE EMOTIONS OR FEELINGS OF EMPTINESS.

SHOPPING GIVES ME THE THRILL OF THE CHASE!

THEY DON'T CALL IT "RETAIL THERAPY" FOR NOTHING!

RUMMAGING THROUGH STUFF GIVES ME **FOCUS!**

IT OFFERS DISTRACTION, NOVELTY, AND SOMETHING LIKE PURPOSE.

CHECKING OUT GIVES ME **SATIS-FACTION!**

BUT THE NOVELTY SOON WEARS OFF.

LEAVING THE STORE GIVES ME A LET-DOWN...

A RECENT STUDY FOUND THAT PEOPLE WHO RATE MATERIALISTIC VALUES HIGHLY (HI-MATS) SPEND MORE THAN OTHERS ON NECESSITIES AND MAKE DISCRETIONARY PURCHASES MORE OFTEN.

GETTING THE BILLS GIVES ME **ACID REFLUX...**

AS A GROUP, HI-MATS ARE WORSE AT MAN-AGING MONEY AND MORE PRONE TO TAKE ON DEBT, WHICH OF COURSE FEELS BAD.

LUCKILY, **SHOPPING** WILL FIX **THAT!**

ON ANOTHER FRONT, I ANA-
LYZED SOME EXISTING DATA
TO LOOK FOR LINKS BETWEEN
A NATION'S VALUES FOR
MONEY, POWER, AND STATUS
AND THE LEVEL OF ITS

CHILDREN'S WELL-BEING.

WE **DO** ALL WANT CHILDREN'S WELL-BEING, DON'T WE?

I'M NOT SURE... IS THERE PROFIT IN IT?

RANDOM CARTOONIST JOKE →

TIM! YOU LOOK LIKE CAPTAIN HADDOCK!

AS A MEASURE OF WELL-BEING, I USED A METRIC DEVELOPED BY UNICEF, THE UNITED NATIONS CHILDREN'S EMERGENCY FUND. THIS GRAPH SHOWS THE LEVEL OF WELL-BEING OF CHILDREN IN THE 20 COUNTRIES LISTED ON P. 124, PLOTTED AGAINST HOW MUCH THOSE COUNTRIES PRIORITIZE HEIRARCHY VERSUS EGALITARIAN VALUES.

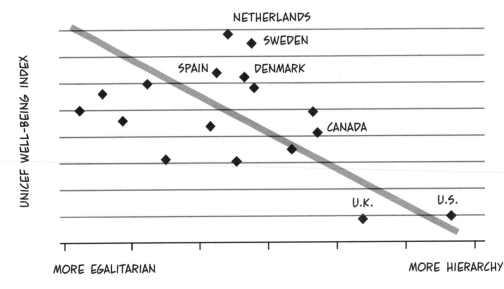

AS BEFORE, IT SHOWS A
SIGNIFICANT CORRELATION
BETWEEN HIERARCHY
VALUES (MONEY, STATUS,
POWER) AND DIMINISHED
WELL-BEING. MORE-
HIERARCHICAL COUNTRIES,
WHERE SOCIAL JUSTICE
AND EQUALITY WERE LESS
ESTEEMED, HAD LESS
HEALTHY CHILDREN ON
THE WHOLE.

VALIUM IN THE DEFENSE OF LIBERTY IS NO VICE!

THE SACRIFICE OF CHILDREN'S WELL-BEING IS AN EXAMPLE OF HOW THE PURSUIT OF MONEY, POWER, AND STATUS NOT ONLY HURTS THE PERSON PURSUING THOSE VALUES, BUT ALSO HURTS

OTHER PEOPLE

AS WELL.

RESEARCH SHOWS THAT HI-MATS ARE LIKELIER TO BELIEVE IT'S OKAY TO MANIPULATE OTHERS.

SELL YOU A BRIDGE?

BUY ME A DRESS?

HI-MATS TEND TO SHOW MORE BIAS AGAINST PEOPLE SEEN AS UNLIKE THEMSELVES.

I DISLIKE EVERYONE, SO AT LEAST I'M NOT **PREJUDICED!**

HI-MATS MORE READILY BELIEVE THAT SOME GROUPS SHOULD BE SUBORDINATED TO OTHERS.

"Y'KNOW, THE EQUALITY THING HASN'T WORKED OUT, SO MAYBE WE SHOULD FORGET IT...*

*READ ON FACEBOOK

AND IN GENERAL, THEY ARE LIKELIER TO LIE, STEAL, AND CHEAT.

I **NEVER** LIE!

WHAT I JUST SAID? THAT WAS NO LIE!

NEITHER WAS THAT!

OR THAT.

OR...

FINALLY, HI-MATS CARE LESS ABOUT **ENVIRONMENTAL SUSTAINABILITY.** HI-MATS ARE LIKELIER TO SAY THEY DON'T CARE ABOUT CLIMATE CHANGE AND THE ENVIRONMENT. THEY ARE ALSO LESS READY TO MAKE ECO-FRIENDLY LIFESTYLE CHANGES, SUCH AS RECYCLING OR USING EFFICIENT APPLIANCES OR VEHICLES.

LICENSE PLATE SEEN ON S.U.V. IN PHOENIX, ARIZONA

NOW, I MUST TELL YOU THAT ANY INDIVIDUAL STUDY HAS SOME CHANCE OF BEING **WRONG.** STATISTICAL DATA ALWAYS HAVE A DEGREE OF RANDOMNESS THAT CAN CREATE THE APPEARANCE OF AN EFFECT WHEN NONE REALLY EXISTS!

SOME COLLEAGUES AND I DECIDED TO TEST THE FINDINGS BY DOING A **META-ANALYSIS.** THIS MEANS POOLING THE RESULTS OF MANY INDIVIDUAL SURVEYS.

POOLING CREATES A VERY LARGE DATA SET, AND A LARGE DATA SET VASTLY IMPROVES OUR CONFIDENCE IN THE TRUTH OF ANY SYSTEMATIC EFFECTS THAT MAY EMERGE.

LESS p IN THE POOL!*

*RANDOM STATISTICS JOKE

RESULT: REGARDLESS OF AGE, WEALTH, OR HOMELAND, PEOPLE WHO FAVOR MATERIALISTIC, STATUS-ORIENTED VALUES, ON AVERAGE—

- feel lower life satisfaction;
- suffer more depression and anxiety;
- feel sad more often;
- experience less joy and pleasure;
- smoke and drink more;
- have lower self-esteem.

IN SUM, PEOPLE WITH MORE HUMANE, LESS-MATERIALISTIC VALUES EXPERIENCE HIGHER LEVELS OF WELL-BEING, WHILE THEIR MORE MATERIALISTIC PEERS NOT ONLY FEEL WORSE BUT ALSO ERODE THE WELL-BEING OF OTHER PEOPLE, OTHER SPECIES, AND THE VERY EARTH WE ALL SHARE.

TIME FOR A REVOLUTION OF VALUES, EH, CAPPY BOY?

UH... COUGH... LET ME CHECK WITH MY PEOPLE ABOUT THAT...

INTERLUDE

IN PART I OF THIS BOOK, WE TOLD THE STORY OF HOW CAPITALISM BEGAT HYPERCAPITALISM, THE RAPACIOUS SYSTEM THAT NOW HOLDS THE WORLD IN ITS HOT AND HEAVY EMBRACE.

BIG HUG!

WE EXPLAINED HOW THIS SYSTEM CREATES WEALTH AND POVERTY, REDUCES WORKERS TO ECONOMIC UNITS, CYNICALLY MANIPULATES CONSUMERS, AND BENDS GOVERNMENTS TO ITS WILL—WHEN IT ISN'T SIMPLY IGNORING GOVERNMENT.

JUST A LITTLE SQUEEZE!

WE ALSO DESCRIBED THE THEORY OF **VALUES,** WHICH SAYS THAT OPPOSING VALUES **COMPETE** FOR PRIORITY IN PEOPLE'S MINDS.

GOT ONE!

EXPERIMENTS, SURVEYS, AND REAL-WORLD DATA CONFIRM THE CONFLICT BETWEEN THE PURSUIT OF MATERIAL GAIN AND VALUES FOCUSED ON PEACE, EMPATHY, AND SUSTAINABILITY.

OOPS!

EXTRINSIC VALUES—FOR STATUS, IMAGE, STUFF, AND MONEY—CAN CROWD OUT **INTRINSIC** VALUES FOR PERSONAL GROWTH, LOVE, AND HELPING THE WORLD.

WE CONCLUDED THAT THE MONEY-DRIVEN, CONSUMERIST, HYPERCAPITALIST SYSTEM THREATENS OUR WELL-BEING IN MANY DIFFERENT WAYS.

THE NEXT SECTION...

IS ABOUT **CHANGE!**

IN THE FOLLOWING CHAPTERS, WE'LL INTRODUCE YOU TO PEOPLE WORKING IN MANY DIFFERENT WAYS TO CHALLENGE THE VALUES, BELIEFS, AND BEHAVIORS OF HYPERCAPITALISM.

SOME OF THESE EFFORTS CONCENTRATE ON CREATING **ALTERNATIVES:** INDIVIDUAL AND COLLECTIVE ACTIONS THAT SUPPORT INTRINSIC VALUES, WELL-BEING, SOCIAL EQUALITY, AND ECOLOGICAL SUSTAINABILITY.

OTHERS INVOLVE ACTS OF **CONFRONTATION, CHALLENGE,** AND **EXPOSURE,** WHETHER THROUGH TRADITIONAL POLITICAL MEANS OR MORE INNOVATIVE STRATEGIES.

IF PART I WAS ABOUT WHAT HYPERCAPITALISM HAS BEEN DOING TO **YOU**, THEN PART II IS ABOUT WHAT **YOU** CAN DO ABOUT **HYPERCAPITALISM!**

PART II

Chapter 7
MINDFUL BUYING
THE CONSUMPTION ASSUMPTION

AT BOTTOM, HYPERCAPITALISM DEPENDS ON CONSUMPTION. FOR THE SYSTEM TO RUN, PEOPLE ("CONSUMERS") MUST BUY AND BUY AGAIN, NOT SIMPLY SPENDING, BUT **CONSUMING,** USING THINGS UP.

OH, YEAH!

IN THE USA, ROUGHLY **70%** OF ECONOMIC OUTPUT GOES TO "CONSUMER GOODS."

IT'S HEAVEN!

THE WORDS ALONE BETRAY THE UNDERLYING VALUES. SOMETHING TO BUY IS A **GOOD,** AND BUYING EQUALS **CONSUMPTION.**

WELL, IT CONSUMES **ME!**

SO ONE WAY TO CHALLENGE THE SYSTEM IS BY **REJECTING** THE CONSUMPTION MENTALITY AND TO START **BUYING MINDFULLY!**

WHAT?

141

MEET CONNIE SUMER'S DISTANT COUSIN **CANNIE BYER.** CANNIE TAKES A DIFFERENT APPROACH TO SHOPPING. INSTEAD OF CONNIE'S DEBT-FUELED FRENZY OF IMPULSE PUR-CHASES AND RETAIL THERAPY, CANNIE STARTS BY GIVING HERSELF A **GIFT:** THE GIFT OF TIME, OF REFLECTION, OF **MINDFULNESS.**

BEFORE BUYING, CANNIE PAUSES TO CONSIDER WHETHER THE PURCHASE IS CONSISTENT WITH HER VALUES. SHE ASKS HERSELF QUESTIONS LIKE THESE:

CAN I AFFORD IT?

DO I REALLY NEED IT?

DO I REALLY NEED IT **NOW?**

IS IT DISPOSABLE, DURABLE, RECYCLEABLE?

WHAT IS IT MADE OF?

WHERE DID IT COME FROM?

WILL IT IMPROVE MY LIFE?

WILL IT IMPROVE SOMEONE ELSE'S LIFE?

WHY DO I WANT IT?

ARE THERE ANY ALTERNATIVES TO THIS PURCHASE?

WHAT COMPANY MAKES IT?

WHAT IS THE COMPANY'S RECORD ON POLITICS? LABOR? THE ENVIRONMENT?

WHERE WILL MY MONEY GO?

NO ONE IS SAYING TO STOP CONSUMING ENTIRELY. THAT WOULD BE IMPOSSIBLE—EVERYONE HAS TO CONSUME FOOD, AFTER ALL. THE IDEA HERE IS TO BE MINDFUL OF ONE'S VALUES AND ACT ACCORDINGLY WHEN BUYING THINGS.

WHO DOESN'T VALUE FOOD?

FOOD ALONE OFFERS WIDE CHOICES: VEG OR MEAT? ORGANIC OR GROWN WITH CHEMICAL FERTILIZERS AND PESTICIDES? FARMED FISH OR WILD CAUGHT? SQUISHY HAMBURGER BUNS WITH NO MORE NUTRITION THAN REFINED SUGAR? BEEF RAISED WHERE RAINFOREST ONCE GREW? COCA-COLA?

I GET IT NOW: YOU'RE ONE OF THOSE ORGANIC SPROUT-EATERS, AREN'T YOU?

UH.. IT'S POSSIBLE...

BUYING MINDFULLY INSTEAD OF COMPULSIVELY SAVES CANNIE MONEY, DECLUTTERS HER LIFE, AND ALIGNS HER BEHAVIOR WITH HER VALUES. IT MIGHT EVEN SHAKE TITANS OF INDUSTRY, IF THEY KNEW ABOUT IT.

DO YOU SENSE A DISTURBANCE IN THE FORCE, CAPPY?

STILL, ONE PERSON ALONE HAS LITTLE EFFECT, SO CANNIE SOMETIMES JOINS OTHERS IN **ORGANIZED CAMPAIGNS** OF MINDFUL BUYING.

143

THE BEST-KNOWN FORM OF ORGANIZED NON-BUYING IS THE

BOYCOTT.

BOYCOTT SUPPORTERS SHUN A PARTICULAR PRODUCT, A BUSINESS, OR EVEN A WHOLE NATION AS A WAY OF EXERTING MORAL OR ECONOMIC PRESSURE.

LARGE LOCKER

BIG SELECTION • SMALL WAGES
NO RESPONSIBILITY

A COUPLE OF BOYCOTTS FROM SEMI-RECENT HISTORY:

TABLE GRAPES

IN THE 1960S AND '70S, THE **UNITED FARM WORKERS** UNION CALLED FOR SHOPPERS TO STOP BUYING TABLE GRAPES UNTIL THE FARM OWNERS RECOGNIZED THE UNION. THIS BOYCOTT WAS ONLY PARTLY SUCCESSFUL.

PARTLY IS BETTER THAN NOTHING AT ALL!

COACHELLA VALLEY TABLE GRAPES
GROWN AND PACKED BY:
LARSON
THERMAL, CALIFORNIA 92271
UNION LABEL

SOUTH AFRICA

DURING THE APARTHEID (RACIALLY SEGREGATED) REGIME, ACTIVISTS ORGANIZED A GLOBAL BOYCOTT OF AN **ENTIRE COUNTRY,** THE UNION OF SOUTH AFRICA. THE LOSS OF TRADE, TOURISM, AND PRESTIGE HELPED TO END APARTHEID AND EXTEND EQUAL CITIZENSHIP TO ALL.

THE WHOLE WORLD HELPED!

MORE RECENTLY, IN 2008, STUDENTS CALLED FOR A BOYCOTT TO SUPPORT HONDURAN TEXTILE WORKERS WHO SEW BRANDED SPORTSWEAR FOR COLLEGES AND UNIVERSITIES.

THIS IS AN EDUCATION IN ITSELF...

WHEN THE WORKERS TRIED TO UNIONIZE, THEIR EMPLOYER, **RUSSELL ATHLETIC** (OWNED BY FRUIT OF THE LOOM, INC.), CLOSED THE FACTORY AND LOOKED FOR WORKERS ELSEWHERE.

I HEAR GUATEMALA HAS BETTER DEATH SQUADS...

ACTIVISTS CAMPAIGNED IN THE U.S., CANADA, AND AUSTRALIA. 130 UNIVERSITIES THREATENED TO CANCEL THEIR LICENSES WITH RUSSELL.

Result:

THE UNION RECOGNIZED, THE FACTORY REOPENED, A 30% RAISE, AND A LONG-TERM CONTRACT!

WE HAD TO. FRUIT OF THE LOOM COULDN'T AFFORD THE EXPOSURE.

IN THE WORDS OF AN ACTIVIST WEBSITE:

"JERZEES NUEVO DÍA [THE FACTORY] IS ONE OF THE WORLD'S ONLY GARMENT FACTORIES THAT ENJOYS STABLE ORDERS FROM A MULTINATIONAL APPAREL BRAND AND FULLY COMPLIES WITH UNIVERSITIES' LABOR CODES OF CONDUCT."

(SOURCE: WWW.USAS.ORG/2012/10/10/)

145

THE FLIP SIDE OF THE BOYCOTT IS THE **"BUYCOTT."** BESIDES WITHHOLDING MONEY FROM WRONGDOERS, CANNIE ALSO TRIES TO SUPPORT PRODUCTS THAT ARE CONSISTENT WITH HER VALUES. WHICH COMPANIES USE THE MOST SUSTAINABLE PROCESSES? WHAT SHAMPOOS ARE NOT TESTED ON ANIMALS? WHO PAYS WELL? FINDING OUT MAY NOT BE SO EASY.

SO MANY PRODUCTS, SO LITTLE INFORMATION!

THE MOST COMPREHENSIVE ONLINE SOURCE OF THIS INFORMATION, ETHICAL-CONSUMER.ORG, IS BRITISH AND OF LIMITED USE TO AMERICANS. SEVERAL MOBILE APPS ARE SUPPOSED TO RATE COMPANIES FROM A SIMPLE BARCODE SCAN, BUT NONE OF THESE WORKED WHEN WE TRIED THEM.

COME ON, APP MAKERS! HELP US OUT HERE!!

ERROR MESSAGE

ONE THING TO LOOK FOR—ON IMPORTED GOODS, ANYWAY—IS THIS LOGO, THE

FAIR TRADE

EMBLEM.

TO EARN THE FAIR TRADE LABEL, COMPANIES AND COOPERATIVES MUST PAY AT LEAST THE LOCAL MINIMUM WAGE, ACCEPT LABOR UNIONS, USE SUSTAINABLE ("GREEN") PRODUCTION METHODS, AND PROMOTE GENDER EQUITY.

THEY MUST ALSO NEVER USE FORCED LABOR OR HIRE CHILDREN.

I CAN TOTALLY SWEAR WE DON'T HAVE EVEN **ONE** CHILD EXECUTIVE!

AT THIS WRITING, AROUND 30,000 PRODUCTS CARRY THE FAIR TRADE INSIGNIA, WITH TOTAL SALES OF

$6.3 Billion.

AND NONE OF THAT MONEY COMES TO ME!!!

OF COURSE, ANYTHING FROM THE OTHER SIDE OF THE EARTH COMES AT A COST IN FUEL AND CARBON EMISSIONS. FOR ONE EXTREME EXAMPLE, REFRIGERATED PLANELOADS OF CUT FLOWERS ARRIVE DAILY ALL OVER THE UNITED STATES FROM SOUTH AMERICA.

ARE YOU INSANE?

Product of Colombia

IT IS ALMOST ALWAYS GREENER TO BUY SOMETHING THAT WAS GROWN OR MADE NEARBY.

BESIDES SAVING FUEL AND EXHAUST, BUYING LOCALLY HAS ANOTHER BENEFIT: IT KEEPS MONEY CIRCULATING IN THE NEIGHBORHOOD. LOCALLY OWNED BUSINESSES SPEND MUCH MORE OF THEIR INCOME WITHIN THE COMMUNITY THAN DO CHAIN STORES.

CONSIDER, FOR EXAMPLE, THE FINDINGS OF A STUDY DONE IN SALT LAKE CITY BY THE ORGANIZATION *CIVIC ECONOMICS*. LOCALLY OWNED BUSINESSES PUT A MUCH LARGER FRACTION OF THEIR REVENUE BACK INTO THE LOCAL ECONOMY THAN DID NATIONAL CHAINS.

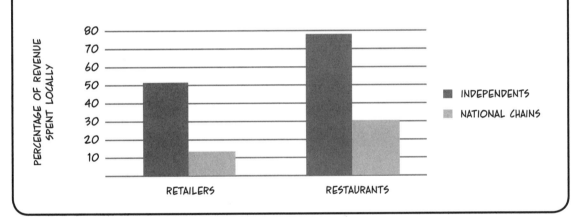

IN SHORT, BUYING LOCALLY BOOSTS THE LOCAL ECONOMY, WHILE BUYING FROM BIG CORPORATE OUTLETS TENDS TO SIPHON OFF MONEY AND SO REDUCES ITS CIRCULATION IN THE NEIGHBORHOOD.

149

A SYSTEMATIC WAY TO KEEP MONEY IN THE COMMUNITY IS BY CIRCULATING LOCAL VOUCHERS THAT ARE ACCEPTED NOWHERE ELSE. ONE FINDS THESE

COMPLE-MENTARY CURRENCIES

IN COMMUNITIES FROM MASSACHUSETTS TO KENYA.

THE DETAILS OF THEIR DESIGN, DISTRIBUTION, AND MANAGEMENT VARY, BUT THEY ALL START THE SAME WAY: ACTIVISTS OR "SOCIAL ENTREPRENEURS" PERSUADE LOCALLY OWNED BUSINESSES TO ACCEPT THE NEW PAY CHITS.

COMPLEMENTARY CURRENCIES CAN DO MORE THAN PROMOTE LOCAL BUSINESSES OVER CHAIN STORES. IN VERY POOR COMMUNITIES, LIKE KENYA'S BANGLADESH SLUM*, **BANGLA-PESA** NOTES ACTUALLY INCREASE THE TOTAL VOLUME OF TRADE, BECAUSE "OFFICIAL" MONEY IS SO SCARCE. THE NOTES HAVE ALSO HELPED PAY FOR CIVIC IMPROVEMENTS, LIKE TRASH CLEANUP.

*A SUBURB OF MOMBASA, NOT THE ASIAN COUNTRY OF THE SAME NAME

SHOPPING LOCALLY, SEEKING GREENER PRODUCTS, HONORING LABOR AND FAIR TRADE, AND OTHERWISE BUYING MINDFULLY ALL MESS UP HYPERCAPITALISM'S PLANET-DEVOURING, WORKER-PUNISHING, GLOBALIZED ENTERPRISE.

AND THEY'RE THROWING FREE-RANGE ORGANIC EGGS...

AND MORE THAN THAT: THEY MAKE PEOPLE **FEEL BETTER**.

EXCEPT THIS "PERSON!"

DATA CONFIRM THAT MINDFUL BUYING PROMOTES BUYERS' WELL-BEING. FOR EXAMPLE, A SURVEY TAKEN IN CANADA, CHINA, AND THE U.S. SHOWED THAT PEOPLE WHO SHOP AT FARMERS MARKETS AND WHO SEEK OUT ENVIRONMENTALLY FRIENDLY PRODUCTS REPORT GREATER LIFE SATISFACTION THAN PEOPLE WHO DON'T.

THIS HAPPINESS THING — IS IT STRICTLY LEGAL?

We grow what we sell!

USDA ORGANIC

IN OTHER WORDS, "PRO-SOCIAL" SPENDING—BUYING WITH THE HEALTH AND WELFARE OF OTHERS IN MIND, OR SIMPLY BUYING FOR OTHERS—PROMISES TO IMPROVE THE WELL-BEING OF THE WORLD **AND OF THE BUYER.**

KEEP THAT IN MIND!

Chapter 8
VOLUNTARY SIMPLICITY
AND THE VALUE OF TIME

FACED WITH HYPER-CAPITALISM'S RELENTLESS PRESSURE TO CONSUME, A MINDFUL BUYER RESPONDS BY EVALUATING ONE PRODUCT AT A TIME.

OTHERS GO FURTHER... THEY STRIVE TO BREAK FREE OF THE ENTIRE WORK-AND-SPEND CYCLE BY EMBRACING A MATERIALLY SIMPLER LIFE.

HISTORY OFFERS EXAMPLES OF MONKS, HERMITS, AND ASCETICS IN EVERY CULTURE. OUR DISCUSSION BEGINS WITH AN AMERICAN, THE 19TH-CENTURY WRITER, ACTIVIST, AND SOMETIME DROPOUT HENRY DAVID **THOREAU** (1818-1862).

COUGH
COUGH

IN 1845, H.D. LEFT A JOB AT HIS FATHER'S PENCIL FACTORY TO LIVE "STURDILY AND SPARTAN-LIKE" FOR TWO YEARS IN THE WOODS BY WALDEN POND IN CONCORD, MASSACHUSETTS.

PONDERING THE BREVITY OF LIFE (HE HAD TUBERCULOSIS) AND THE PORTION OF IT USUALLY SPENT EARNING MONEY, THOREAU MADE THIS STRIKING DEFINITION OF THE **COST** OF AN OBJECT.

"THE COST OF A THING IS THE **AMOUNT OF LIFE** WHICH IS TO BE EXCHANGED FOR IT."

EVERY PURCHASE, THAT IS, CARRIES A **TIME** COST: THE TIME SPENT WORKING TO EARN THE PURCHASE PRICE.

THAT'LL BE TWO AND A HALF DAYS, PLEASE.

COFF COFF

WHILE MOST OF US CAN EXPECT TO LIVE LONGER THAN THOREAU, THE FACT REMAINS THAT EVERYONE FACES A FINITE LIFESPAN, EVERY HOUR OF WHICH IS SPENT EITHER MAKING MONEY OR DOING SOMETHING ELSE.

THIS HEADSTONE COST ME SEVEN WEEKS!

Thoreau
R.I.P.
b...d...

THIS IDEA WAS FURTHER DEVELOPED BY AUTHORS **VICKI ROBIN** AND **JOE DOMINGUEZ** IN THEIR POPULAR 1992 BOOK *YOUR MONEY OR YOUR LIFE* (YMYL, FOR SHORT).

YMYL POINTS OUT THAT EVERY JOB NOT ONLY TAKES EXTRA TIME, BUT ALSO REQUIRES JOB-RELATED OUTLAYS OF CASH. OUR FRIEND **ERNIE WAGES,** STUCK IN RUSH-HOUR TRAFFIC, HAS TO AGREE!

YES, I DO...

FOR INSTANCE, BACK WHEN ERNIE WAS WORKING 40-HOUR WEEKS AT BETTCO, HE TOOK HOME $800 AFTER TAXES. NATURALLY, HE FIGURED HIS TIME WAS WORTH $20 AN HOUR.

NOT TOO BAD...

BUT IN FACT, ERNIE SPENT 40 MINUTES A DAY COMMUTING; ANOTHER 30 MINUTES PICKING UP FAST FOOD, BECAUSE HE WAS TOO FRAZZLED TO SHOP AND COOK; AND HE PARKED TWO KIDS IN DAY CARE, TOO.

WAN' ICE CREAM!

ME TOO.

I HAVE TA PEE!

ME TOO.

SO ERNIE SPENT EXTRA **TIME** AND **MONEY** JUST TO DO HIS JOB. EVERY WEEK, HIS ADDITIONAL OUTLAYS AMOUNTED TO:

	MONEY	TIME
COMMUTE	$30	3.3 HOURS
FAST FOOD	$50	2.5 HOURS
DAYCARE	$200	1.5 HOUR
TOTAL	**$280**	**7.3** HOURS

THE $280 CAME OUT OF HIS $800 PAY-CHECK, AND THE 7.3 HOURS MUST BE ADDED TO HIS 40-HOUR WORK WEEK.

THE **TRUE VALUE** OF AN HOUR OF ERNIE'S WORKTIME, THEN, WAS NOT $20, BUT AT MOST

$$\frac{800-280}{40+7.3} = \frac{520}{47.3} \approx \$11.00$$

AT LEAST IT GETS ME OUT OF THE HOUSE...

ERNIE NOW HAS TO FACE A NEW WAY TO ASSESS HIS PURCHASES: IN TERMS OF **TIME.**

FOR INSTANCE, HIS CAR PAYMENTS ARE $90 A WEEK (AVERAGE FOR THE U.S.), SO EVERY WEEK HE SPENDS

$$\frac{\$90}{\$11/hr} \approx 8 \ hours.$$

JUST LOOK WHAT I DO FOR YOU!

AN AVERAGE BEER DRINKER, ERNIE DOWNS $24 WORTH EVERY WEEK, AT A TIME COST OF

$$\frac{\$24}{\$11/hr} \approx 2 \ hours.$$

ETERNITY BEER

ERNIE STARTS DOING THE ARITHMETIC FOR ALL HIS DISCRETIONARY EXPENSES.

IT'S KIND OF FUN EXCEPT FOR THE CONTEMPLATION OF MORTALITY!

DARKVIEW

EACH NEW CALCULATION RAISES THE SAME QUESTION:

IS IT WORTH IT?

NOT EVERYONE WILL ANSWER THAT QUESTION IN THE SAME WAY ABOUT THE SAME THINGS. ERNIE MAY DECIDE THAT A CAR IS ESSENTIAL, EVEN IF IT COSTS HIM 8 HOURS A WEEK.

YEAH... MAYBE...

IS IT WORTH IT??

HIS FRIEND **THOREAU LEE SIKOVITZ,** ON THE OTHER HAND, IS READY TO **GIVE UP** THE CAR, THE BEER, AND A LOT OF OTHER THINGS.

WHO NEEDS IT? ENOUGH! I'VE HAD IT! IT'S GROSS!

HE SELLS HIS CAR AND BUYS A GOOD BICYCLE (COST: AROUND 50 HOURS TOTAL), WHICH PROVIDES ENOUGH EXERCISE THAT HE GIVES UP HIS GYM MEMBERSHIP (COST: $1\frac{1}{2}$ HOURS PER WEEK).

FOLLOWING *YMYL* GUIDELINES, T. L. PAYS OFF HIS DEBT WITH THE MONEY HE SAVES.

I FEEL SO LIGHT!

FROM THAT POINT ON, HE SAVES HIS MONEY UNTIL IT SEEMS LIKE ENOUGH.

THIS SHOULD ABOUT DO IT...

NEEDING LESS INCOME, HE CUTS BACK HIS WORK HOURS, PLANTS A VEGETABLE GARDEN, AND EVEN MAKES SOME OF HIS OWN CLOTHES. THOREAU LEE HAS BECOME A FULL-FLEDGED **VOLUNTARY SIMPLIFIER.**

THIS MAY NOT BE FOR EVERYONE...

IT HELPS TO BE THOREAU LEE SIKOVITZ...

THOREAU LEE SIKOVITZ MAY BE A CARTOON CHARACTER, BUT MILLIONS OF OTHER SIMPLIFIERS ARE 100% REAL. PROBABLY THE MOST FAMOUS AND INFLUENTIAL WERE HELEN AND SCOTT

NEARING.

THESE URBAN RADICALS, WEARY OF THE "COMPETITIVE, ACQUISITIVE, AGGRESSIVE, WAR-MAKING SOCIAL ORDER," MOVED TO A FARM IN VERMONT IN THE LATE 1930S.

TAKING ON MOST OF THE MANUAL LABOR THEMSELVES, THE NEARINGS NEEDED LITTLE MONEY; FOUR HOURS A DAY SUFFICED BOTH FOR GROWING CASH CROPS (BLUEBERRIES, MAPLE SYRUP) AND FOR ALL OTHER CHORES THAT SATISFIED THEIR MATERIAL NEEDS.

THIS DAILY SEGMENT THEY CALLED THEIR "BREAD LABOR," AND IT WASN'T ALWAYS EASY. THEY BUILT THEIR STONE HOUSE ENTIRELY BY HAND.

ANOTHER FOUR HOURS PER DAY WENT TO INTELLECTUAL AND CULTURAL PURSUITS (MAINLY WRITING), AND ANOTHER FOUR TO VOLUNTEER WORK AND COMMUNITY ACTIVITIES. IT WORKED FOR THE NEARINGS! BOTH OF THEM LIVED WELL PAST 90 YEARS OLD.

YOU DON'T HAVE TO FARM TO LIVE SIMPLY. IN 2007, "NO-IMPACT MAN"

COLIN BEAVAN

LED HIS FAMILY THROUGH A YEAR-LONG EXPERIMENT IN SIMPLE LIVING, BASED IN THEIR MANHATTAN APARTMENT.

THEY USED FOOD GROWN ONLY WITHIN A RADIUS OF 250 MILES, LITTLE PAPER, ELECTRICITY FROM A ROGUE SOLAR PANEL, NO BUSES, NO TRAINS, NO CARBON-BASED FUELS...

RESULT: THEY PAID OFF THEIR CREDIT CARDS; GOT INTO TERRIFIC SHAPE FROM ALL THE EXERCISE; ATE HEALTHIER MEALS; PLAYED CARDS AND BOARD GAMES—AND TALKED!—INSTEAD OF ZONING OUT WITH THE TUBE; AND (THEY ADMITTED), GOT VERY TIRED OF WASHING CLOTHES IN THE TUB.

IS THERE A FOOT CREAM MADE IN NEW JERSEY?

WHETHER RURAL OR URBAN, VOLUNTARY SIMPLICITY PAYS THE DIVIDEND OF **TIME.** ESCAPING THE WORK-AND-SPEND CYCLE MEANS LESS TIME DEVOTED TO SHOPPING AND WORKING FOR PAY. VOLUNTARY SIMPLIFIERS TEND TO SPEND MORE TIME AT INTRINSICALLY REWARDING ACTIVITIES, SUCH AS...

MEDITATION

SOCIALIZING WITH FRIENDS

EXERCISE

ME FOR SCHOOL BOARD

VOLUNTEERING IN THE COMMUNITY

POLITICAL ACTIVITY

PLAYING WITH THE KIDS

CREATIVE EXPRESSION

CATCHING UP ON ALL THOSE PROJECTS

IN THE PAST DECADE OR SO, PSYCHOLOGISTS HAVE STUDIED THE RELATION-SHIP BETWEEN WELL-BEING AND **"TIME AFFLUENCE."**

LET'S DO A SURVEY!

AND LET'S DO IT TOMORROW!

AND THEY HAVE FOUND:

PEOPLE WITH MORE TIME REPORT THEMSELVES AS HAVING GREATER ENGAGEMENT IN INTRINSICALLY REWARDING ACTIVITIES. THIS, IN TURN, IS ASSOCIATED WITH HIGHER LEVELS OF WELL-BEING.

THIS SURE BEATS FLIPPING BURGERS!

PEOPLE IN ECONOMICALLY DEVELOPED COUNTRIES WITH SHORTER WORK WEEKS (LIKE THESE COPENHAGEN COMMUTERS) ALSO HAVE LOWER CARBON FOOTPRINTS (AND GOOD LEG MUSCLES, TOO).

VOLUNTARY SIMPLIFIERS USE LESS ENERGY, ACT MORE ECOLOGICALLY RESPONSIBLY, SEEK ACTIVITIES THAT EMBODY MORE INTRINSIC VALUES, AND REPORT HIGHER LEVELS OF SATISFACTION THAN DO OTHER PEOPLE.

HMM... I'M NOT SICK OF IT ANYMORE... DOES THAT MEAN I SHOULD CHANGE MY NAME?

As Wayless Sikovitz and others have found, voluntary simplicity is one way to escape, at least partly, from the presence and pressures of hypercapitalism.

THOK

This route may not be for everyone, but the simplifiers do raise a question that everyone might well consider: **HOW MUCH IS ENOUGH?** HOW MUCH **STUFF** IS ENOUGH? HOW MUCH **WORK** IS ENOUGH? HOW MUCH **MONEY** IS ENOUGH?

In this chapter, we tried to provide some new ways of looking at these questions. Ultimately, we suggest, it comes down to one thing...

YOU FIGURED IT OUT, EH? **IT'S ABOUT TIME!**

UM, WELL, YES... EXACTLY!

Chapter 9
SHARING

EVEN IN THIS HYPER-CAPITALISTIC WORLD, NOT EVERYTHING IS PRIVATELY OWNED. ALL COMMUNITIES DEPEND ON THINGS HELD AND USED IN COMMON. DESPITE PRIVATIZATION'S ENCROACHMENTS, WE SHARE OUR STREETS, SIDEWALKS, AND PARKS, AS WELL AS OUR OCEANS, WATERWAYS, AND ATMOSPHERE.

THIS COLUMN OF AIR WHOLLY OWNED BY THE AMALGAMATED GIGANTIC CORPORATION. PRIVATE PROPERTY. DO NOT BREATHE.

IN THIS CHAPTER, WE DISCUSS MANY WAYS IN WHICH PEOPLE ARE SHARING WITH EACH OTHER, RATHER THAN PRIVATELY OWNING ALL THEIR POSSESSIONS. THIS APPROACH TO OWNERSHIP AIMS TO IMPROVE THE ENVIRONMENT, SAVE MONEY, AND DISCOURAGE MINDLESS CONSUMERISM.

FIRST, WE ACKNOWLEDGE THAT THE THOUGHT OF SHARING CAN MAKE PEOPLE NERVOUS. IT SOUNDS LIKE STUFF BEING TAKEN AWAY.

IN THE NAME OF THE REVOLUTION, GIVE US YOUR TOOTHBRUSH!

PURE SILK

BUT WE'RE NOT TALKING ABOUT CONFISCATION OR COERCION HERE. IN THIS CHAPTER, EVERYONE'S TOOTHBRUSH IS PRIVATE!

O.K...

WE MUST ALSO NOTE THAT, DESPITE WHAT HYPERCAPITALISM MAY SAY ABOUT SELFISH HUMAN NATURE, SHARING ACTUALLY MAKES PEOPLE FEEL GOOD. MANY EXPERIMENTS BEAR THIS OUT, LIKE THIS ONE DONE BY PSYCHOLOGIST **LARA AKNIN** AND HER COLLEAGUES AT CANADA'S SIMON FRASER UNIVERSITY.

IN THE LAB, A CHILD IS HANDED A PUPPET TO PLAY WITH AND TOLD THAT THE PUPPET "LIKES TREATS." THE CHILD THEN RECEIVES EIGHT TREATS.

AT THIS POINT, THREE THINGS HAPPEN, ONE AFTER THE OTHER. THE EXPERIMENTER PERFORMS THEM IN RANDOM ORDER, TO COUNTER ANY EFFECT THAT THE ORDER MIGHT HAVE.

1. EXPERIMENTER "FINDS" ANOTHER TREAT AND GIVES IT TO THE PUPPET.

2. EXPERIMENTER "FINDS" ANOTHER TREAT AND ASKS CHILD TO GIVE IT TO THE PUPPET.

3. EXPERIMENTER ASKS CHILD TO GIVE ONE OF HER OWN TREATS TO THE PUPPET.

THEN ASSISTANTS WATCHED VIDEOS OF THE CHILDREN AND RATED HOW HAPPY EACH CHILD APPEARED TO BE. (ASSISTANTS DID NOT KNOW WHICH TREATMENT PRECEDED EACH VIDEO CLIP.)

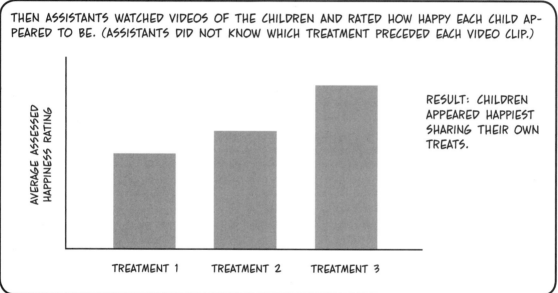

RESULT: CHILDREN APPEARED HAPPIEST SHARING THEIR OWN TREATS.

IT REALLY DOES FEEL GOOD TO SHARE! SO LET'S MOVE ON TO SEE SOME WAYS FOR PEOPLE TO DO SYSTEMATIC SHARING.

SAY, TIM... COULD I HAVE HALF YOUR SANDWICH?

BUT YOU'RE IN CALIFORNIA...

AMONG THE MOST COMMON AND
FAMILIAR FORMS OF SHARING ARE

LIBRARIES

SUPPORTED BY TAXES, THE **PUBLIC** LIBRARY OFFERS ACCESS TO THOUSANDS OF BOOKS,
MOVIES, MAGAZINES, MUSICAL ITEMS, AND REFERENCE MATERIALS, BOTH PAPER AND ONLINE.
LIBRARIES ARE ALL ABOUT SHARING: A LIBRARY BOOK MAY CIRCULATE THROUGH HUNDREDS
OF HANDS, INSTEAD OF JUST THOSE OF A PRIVATE OWNER.

USE A LIBRARY, SAVE A TREE, THEN LIE UNDER IT TO READ A BOOK! (LIBRARIES ARE
GREAT RESOURCES FOR KIDS, TOO.)

THANK YOU!

THE LENDING-LIBRARY MODEL ALSO EXTENDS BEYOND BOOKS.

TOOL LIBRARIES LEND... WELL, TOOLS. THE U.S. HAS SEVERAL DOZEN TOOL LIBRARIES, WHERE MEMBERS CAN BORROW SHOVELS, LADDERS, POWER DRILLS, AND OTHER EQUIPMENT THAT WOULD OTHERWISE MOSTLY SIT UNUSED IN SOMEONE'S GARAGE.

MOST FOLKS WON'T USE ONE OF THESE BABIES EVEN ONCE....

TOY LIBRARIES OFFER PARENTS THE LOAN OF TOYS, PUZZLES, AND GAMES. TOY LIBRARIES MAKE A LOT OF SENSE, GIVEN HOW QUICKLY KIDS CAN OUTGROW GAMES (ALTHOUGH SOMETIMES THEY DO GROW ATTACHED).

GIVE IT UP, SON! 45 YEARS OF OVERDUE FINES ARE MY LIMIT!

SEED LIBRARIES GIVE MEMBERS SEEDS FOR GARDEN OR VEGETABLE PLOTS. "BOR-ROWERS" LET SOME OF THEIR PLANTS GO TO SEED AND THEN RETURN THESE SEEDS TO THE LIBRARY. RESULT: FOOD THAT COSTS NEARLY NOTHING AND DOESN'T COME FROM A SEED-MONOPOLIZING COR-PORATION.

FOOD FROM THE EARTH: WHAT'LL THEY THINK OF NEXT?

It's also possible to share **SERVICES** as well as material goods, by means of a

TIME BANK.

A time bank consists of a group of people with a mix of skills: musicians, carpenters, accountants, cooks, yoga teachers, you name it. Each member has a "time balance" that tallies the hours the member has given and taken.

Here, for instance, **SHARON PLENTY** (at +7) has contributed seven more hours than she's taken out, while **MINNIE MINITZ** (at –4) has taken four more hours out than she has put in.

Typically, accounts are kept online. Members look at the time bank's web site to check their balances and see what services are available.

THE GROUP ALSO NEEDS PEOPLE TO MAINTAIN ITS WEB SITE!

When Minnie gives Sharon seven 1-hour mandolin lessons, Minnie's balance jumps by 7 hours, while Sharon's falls by the same amount.

$$-4+7=3 \qquad 7-7=0$$

Later, Sharon replenishes her account by helping Ernie Wages make a pie, and Minnie pays two of her hours to Wayless Sikovitz, who fixes her bicycle.

+3   –3

–2   +2

ETC.!

MODERN TIME BANKING BEGAN AROUND 1980, WHEN **EDGAR CAHN** ORGANIZED THE FIRST "SERVICE CREDIT" ORGANIZATION IN ST. LOUIS. CAHN LISTS FIVE CORE VALUES OF TIME BANKING.

1. INCLUSION: EVERYONE HAS ASSETS TO SHARE.

2. REDEFINING WORK; PEOPLE SHOULD GET CREDIT FOR SOME WORK THAT USUALLY DOESN'T PAY.

3. RECIPROCITY

4. SOCIAL NETWORKS

5. RESPECT FOR OTHERS

TIME CREDITS, LIKE THE COMPLEMENTARY CURRENCIES DISCUSSED ON P. 150, ARE AN ALTERNATIVE WAY TO EXCHANGE SERVICES. AND, LIKE KENYA'S BANGLA-PESA, TIME BANKS SEEM ESPECIALLY EFFECTIVE AT DRAWING MARGINALIZED PEOPLE INTO THE COMMUNITY.

MY SKILLS ARE WORTH MORE THAN I THOUGHT!

TIME BANKS ARE ESSENTIALLY EGALITARIAN. NO HYPERCAPITALIST 350:1 PAY RATIO HERE! AND BECAUSE OF THE 1:1 PAY RATIO, THE INTERNAL REVENUE SERVICE REGARDS TIME BANKS AS "FAVOR EXCHANGES," SO ALL SERVICES ARE RECEIVED **TAX-FREE.**

BUT PYRAMIDS ARE, UM, TRADITIONAL!

PYRAMIDS ARE **OLD!!**

THERE ARE NOW DOZENS OF ACTIVE TIME BANKS IN THE UNITED STATES. YOU'LL FIND A DIRECTORY AT HTTP://COMMUNITY.TIMEBANKS.ORG/

WHEN PEOPLE GET TOGETHER TO SHARE # HOUSING, THE RESULT IS OFTEN CALLED AN **INTENTIONAL COMMUNITY.**

CO-HOUSING IS AN INTENTIONAL COMMUNITY MODEL DEVELOPED IN SCANDINAVIA. TYPICALLY, CO-HOUSING RESIDENTS SHARE OWNERSHIP OF SOME OPEN SPACE, USUALLY WITH A GARDEN AND PLAYGROUND, AS WELL AS A COMMON BUILDING WITH A LARGE KITCHEN, LIVING ROOM, AND GUEST BEDROOMS. RESIDENTS' LIVING AREAS ARE PRIVATELY OWNED.

FOR MORE DETAILS, SEE COHOUSING.ORG.

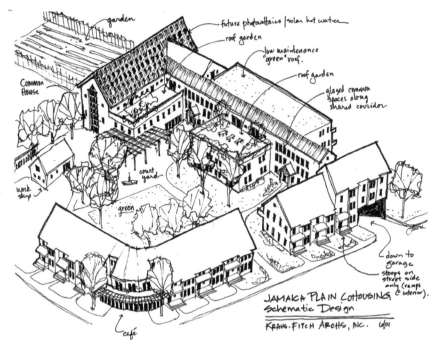

garden

future photovoltaics / solar hot water
roof garden
low maintenance "green" roof
roof garden
glazed common spaces along shared corridor

Common House

work shop

court yard

green

café

down to garage
stoops on street side only (ramps & interior)

JAMAICA PLAIN CoHousing
Schematic Design

KRAUS-FITCH ARCHS, INC.   6/01

FOR EVEN MORE SHARING, YOU CAN MOVE INTO A HOUSING CO-OP, WITH PARTIAL SHARING, OR A FULL-FLEDGED COMMUNE, WHERE NEARLY EVERYTHING IS HELD IN COMMON.

HAS ANYONE SEEN THE TOOTHBRUSH?

SHARED HOUSING TENDS TO COST LESS THAN FULLY PRIVATE LIVING, AND IT PROMOTES BETTER LAND USE AND MORE SOCIAL INTERACTION BETWEEN NEIGHBORS.

170

TRANSPORTATION

PUBLIC MASS TRANSIT IS A VERY EFFICIENT KIND OF RIDE-SHARING, BUT BUSES AND TRAINS DON'T ALWAYS GO WHERE YOU WANT. MANY CITIES NOW HAVE PROGRAMS TO SHARE BICICYLES AND CARS.

A BIKE SHARER PAYS A MONTHLY SUBSCRIPTION FEE, WHICH ALLOWS ACCESS TO BIKES AT MANY LOCATIONS AROUND TOWN. THE RIDER THEN PAYS A PER-HOUR CHARGE FOR USE OF THE RIDE. CAR SHARING WORKS THE SAME WAY.

RIDERS NEEDN'T OWN THEIR OWN RIDES; VEHICLES ARE USED MORE INTENSIVELY; AND MORE PARKING OPENS UP, TOO!

HIKING TRAILS

MANY GOVERNMENTS, INCLUDING THOSE OF CALIFORNIA, SWEDEN, AND BRITAIN, HAVE OPENED PORTIONS OF PRIVATE LAND FOR PUBLIC ACCESS. SWEDEN, FOR EXAMPLE, RECOGNIZES AN *ALLENMANSRÄTTEN* (EVERYONE'S RIGHT) TO FORAGE FOR MUSHROOMS, BERRIES, ETC., REGARDLESS OF WHO (OR WHAT) OWNS THE LAND.

YOU MAY HAVE NOTICED SOMETHING DIFFERENT ABOUT THIS CHAPTER: EVERYTHING IN IT DEPENDS ON **ORGANIZATION!**

VOLUNTARY SIMPLICITY (CHAPTER 8) IS ESSENTIALLY AN **INDIVIDUAL** DECISION. MINDFUL BUYING (CHAPTER 7) COMBINES PERSONAL CHOICES WITH SOME ORGANIZED SUPPORT, SUCH AS BOYCOTTS, FAIR TRADE NETWORKS, AND ALTERNATIVE CURRENCIES.

BY NOW IT SHOULD BE CLEAR THAT **ORGAN-IZATION** IS **ESSENTIAL.** A REVOLUTION OF VALUES WILL TAKE MORE THAN CHANGING INDIVIDUAL BELIEFS AND BEHAVIORS. SOCIAL **INSTITUTIONS** ALSO HAVE TO CHANGE.

IN THE NEXT CHAPTER, WE LOOK AT SOME THINGS THAT CAN BE DONE TO CHANGE **BUSINESS** INSTITUTIONS.

WHAT? **NO!!**

Chapter 10
BETTER BUSINESS

IT MAY SEEM THAT ENTREPRENEURS, INVESTORS, AND CORPORATIONS ARE DOOMED TO PLAY THE **VILLAIN'S** ROLE IN THE HYPERCAPITALIST DRAMA.

MAYBE **ANYONE** WHO DOES BUSINESS IS BOUND TO FALL PREY TO THE LUST FOR PROFIT...

WHEN I WAS YOUNGER, I HELD THAT OPINION, BACK THEN, I THOUGHT THERE WAS NO WAY FOR BUSINESS TO RESIST HYPERCAPITALISM. BUT NOW I REGARD THAT VIEW AS A CLOSED-MINDED **PREJUDICE.**

OVER THE YEARS, I'VE COME TO SEE THAT THE **ENTREPRENEURIAL SPIRIT** ISN'T ONLY ABOUT MAKING MONEY...

IT CAN ALSO INSPIRE PEOPLE TO FACE CHALLENGES AND RISKS IN PURSUIT OF THEIR IDEALS. MANY PEOPLE NOW GO INTO BUSINESS TO IMPROVE THE QUALITY OF HUMAN LIFE AND PLANETARY SUSTAINABILITY.

GREEN INDUSTRIAL PARK

IN THIS CHAPTER, WE SHOW HOW SOME PEOPLE ARE BRINGING **INTRINSIC VALUES** TO THE BUSINESS WORLD.

ONE WAY IS BY

CHALLENGING BUSINESS AS USUAL.

THE AMALGAMATED GIGANTIC CORPORATION DEPENDS FOR ITS SUCCESS ON FOUR BASIC PROCESSES. FIRST, ALGI BUYS RAW MATERIALS, FROM WHICH IT MAKES PLASTIC WIDGETS. RESULT: CORPORATIONS MONOPOLIZE PRODUCTION.

SECOND, THE COMPANY ADVERTISES ITS WIDGETS AND SELLS AS MANY AS POSSIBLE AT A PRICE THAT MAXIMIZES PROFIT. RESULT: MONEY FLOWS TO CORPORATIONS.

THIRD, CONSUMERS RESPOND TO ADVER-TISING BY BUYING WIDGETS, SMIDGETS, AND ALSO QUIDGETS, AND LOTS OF THEM. RESULT: OVERSPENDING AND DEBT.

FOURTH...

RESULT: POLLUTION.

THESE FOUR PROCESSES ARE BEING CHALLENGED BY NEW BUSINESSES AT THIS VERY MOMENT:

MAKERS,

AS THEIR NAME IMPLIES, ARE PEOPLE WHO MAKE THEIR OWN STUFF, AND WE'RE NOT JUST TALKING SEWING AND CANNING. NEW TECHNOLOGY GIVES INDIVIDUALS ACCESS TO AFFORDABLE, COMPUTER-CONTROLLED MANUFACTURING EQUIPMENT, LIKE MILLING MACHINES AND 3-D PRINTERS. MAKERS MAKE ROBOTS, TOO!

RESULT: INDIVIDUALS BECOME PRODUCERS.

PEER-TO-PEER SALES

THE INTERNET HAS TURNED RETAILING INTO A VIRTUAL, WORLDWIDE GARAGE SALE. ANYONE WITH INTERNET ACCESS AND SOMETHING TO SELL CAN CONNECT DIRECTLY WITH BUYERS.

NOW I CAN BUY MY VERY OWN CORPORATION-DESTROYING ROBOT ON ETSY!

RESULT: MONEY FLOWS TO INDIVIDUALS.

SHARED ACCESS

INSPIRED BY TOOL AND TOY LIBRARIES, COMPANIES LIKE **TECH SHOP** BUY DESKTOP MANUFACTURING EQUIPMENT AND PROVIDE ACCESS TO IT FOR A RENTAL FEE.

RESULT: LESS SPENDING AND CONSUMPTION.

THE CIRCULAR ECONOMY

SOME BUSINESSES RECYCLE "WASTE" PRODUCTS. **TARKETT FLOORING,** FOR EXAMPLE, WILL TAKE BACK ANY OF ITS OLD FLOORING REMOVED FROM BUILDINGS AND RECYCLE IT INTO NEW FLOORING. TARKETT HAS RESCUED 75 MILLION POUNDS OF FLOORING FROM LANDFILLS SINCE 2003.

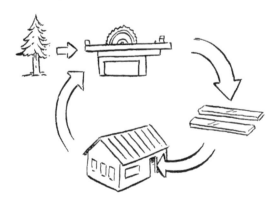

RESULT: ENVIRONMENTAL SUSTAINABILITY.

ANOTHER CHALLENGE TO HYPERCAPITALIST VALUES CAN
COME FROM INVESTORS THEMSELVES, IN THE FORM OF

RESPONSIBLE INVESTING.

REMEMBER, ANYONE WITH MONEY CAN BUY
SHARES IN A PUBLICLY TRADED COMPANY.

CAPPY FREEMARK BUYS SHARES WITH ONLY ONE THING IN MIND: GETTING THE MAXIMUM RETURN ON INVESTMENT. ONLY **MONEY** MAKES HIM SALIVATE!

IT'S LIKE PICKLED HERRING THAT WAY!

HIS BUSINESS-SCHOOL CLASS-MATE **VALERIE YU**, ON THE OTHER HAND, WANTS TO KNOW **HOW THE COMPANY BEHAVES.** INTRINSIC VALUES ARE HER THING!

I WANT TO INVEST IN A BETTER FUTURE!

VAL CAN BUY SHARES IN AN INDIVIDUAL COMPANY THAT CONFORMS TO HER VALUES, OR SHE CAN
SPREAD HER INVESTMENT AROUND VIA A **SOCIALLY RESPONSIBLE MUTUAL FUND.** A MUTUAL
FUND BUYS SHARES IN MANY COMPANIES AND SO REDUCES THE RISK ASSOCIATED WITH THE
FLUCTUATION OF A SINGLE COMPANY'S SHARE PRICE.

STRENGTH IN NUMBERS!

FOR EXAMPLE, THE **PARNASSUS ENDEAVOR FUND** AVOIDS OIL AND TOBACCO STOCKS. THE FUND INVESTS ONLY IN COMPANIES THAT MEET THE NEEDS OF EMPLOYEES WHO ARE WORKING PARENTS, PROVIDE GOOD MEDICAL INSURANCE, AND GRANT STOCK OPTIONS TO EMPLOYEES (SEE P. 179).

AND NO FISH BREATH AFTERWARD!

DISCLAIMER: COAUTHOR TIM OWNS SHARES IN THIS FUND.

SOCIALLY RESPONSIBLE INVESTING HAS A PUBLIC FACE, TOO. ONE TACTIC IS THE

DIVESTMENT CAMPAIGN.

THESE CAMPAIGNS TARGET INSTITUTIONS—UNIVERSITIES, PENSION FUNDS, FOUNDATIONS, ETC.— OWNING LARGE STOCK PORTFOLIOS. THE GOAL: TO PERSUADE THESE INVESTORS TO GET RID OF SHARES IN NOXIOUS COMPANIES. AS OF THIS WRITING, FOR INSTANCE, ABOUT 600 INSTITUTIONS HAVE SOLD OFF THEIR HOLDINGS IN **FOSSIL FUEL** COMPANIES.

DIVEST!!

DIVEST!

BUT SO MANY OF US HERE AT HARVARD HAVE A DEEP AFFINITY WITH FOSSILS...

VAL CAN ALSO INVEST STRATEGICALLY. OWNING EVEN ONE SHARE OF STOCK ALLOWS HER TO PROPOSE **SHAREHOLDER RESOLUTIONS** ABOUT CORPORATE PRACTICES. IF A RESOLUTION POLLS A THRESHOLD OF SUPPORT, IT GOES TO A VOTE OF ALL COMPANY SHAREHOLDERS. IF IT PASSES, THE COMPANY MUST CHANGE ITS POLICY.

CURSE THIS VOTING!

EVEN WITHOUT A VOTE, BAD PUBLICITY ALONE CAN EMBARRASS MANAGEMENT INTO MAKING CHANGES. FOR EXAMPLE, YUM! BRANDS (THE NAME INCLUDES THE EXCLAMATION POINT!), UNDER PRESSURE FROM SOCIALLY ACTIVE **TRILLIUM ASSET MANAGEMENT,** AGREED TO USE ONLY SUSTAINABLY RAISED PALM OIL IN YUM!'S PIZZA HUT AND TACO BELL SUBSIDIARIES.

DOING GOOD ISN'T SO BAD, IS IT?

ALTERNATIVE OWNERSHIP STRUCTURES

SO FAR IN THIS BOOK, WE'VE SEEN PRIVATE BUSINESSES, PRIVATELY HELD CORPORATIONS, AND PUBLICLY TRADED CORPORATIONS. IS THAT ALL THERE IS? OF COURSE NOT!

COOPERATIVES

CO-OPS ARE OWNED BY THE PEOPLE WHO BUY AND USE THE GOODS OR SERVICES THE BUSINESS PROVIDES. CUSTOMERS RUN THE BUSINESS INDIRECTLY, BY ELECTING MANAGEMENT. ANY CO-OP BELONGING TO THE NATIONAL CO-OP BUSINESS ASSOCIATION (NCBA) SUBSCRIBES TO THESE PRINCIPLES:

COOL!

1. VOLUNTARY AND OPEN MEMBERSHIP
2. DEMOCRATIC CONTROL
3. MEMBER PARTICIPATION
4. AUTONOMY AND INDEPENDENCE
5. EDUCATION, TRAINING, INFORMATION
6. COOPERATION AMONG CO-OPS
7. CONCERN FOR COMMUNITY

FOR MORE INFORMATION, SEE WWW.NCBA.ORG.

MEMBER-OWNED BUSINESSES INCLUDE MANY RURAL ELECTRIC COMPANIES, CREDIT UNIONS, AND FOOD CO-OPS. EXPECT GOOD SERVICE IN A CO-OP!

JUST GIVE ME A MINUTE TO GET OVER MY ECONOMIC ROLE CONFUSION...

WHAT DO YOU SAY, SUMER? YOU AND ME, WORKING TOGETHER?

EMPLOYEE-OWNED BUSINESSES

ALTHOUGH ORGANIZED DIFFERENTLY FROM MEMBER CO-OPS, WORKER-OWNED COMPANIES OFTEN SHARE CO-OPS' DEMOCRATIC PRINCIPLES, CONCERN FOR WORKERS, AND COMMUNITY ORIENTATION.

BUSINESSES CAN OFFER WORKERS A BUY-IN OPPORTUNITY THROUGH AN **EMPLOYEE STOCK OWNERSHIP PLAN (ESOP).** AN ESOP GIVES EMPLOYEES A STAKE IN THE COMPANY, AS WELL AS A MEASURE OF SECURITY IN THE FORM OF COMPANY SHARES. MORE THAN 13 MILLION AMERICANS ARE CURRENTLY ENROLLED IN AN ESOP.

WITH MORE THAN 182,000 EMPLOYEES, THE PUBLIX SUPERMARKET CHAIN IS AMERICA'S LARGEST EMPLOYEE-OWNED BUSINESS

I WANT NO PART OF THIS STUPID SCHEME!

HM... SOUNDS LIKE SOUR GRAPES...

THAT'S A DIFFERENT AESOP, BUT YES...

NOT-FOR-PROFIT BUSINESSES

YES! THEY EXIST! IN FACT, **THE NEW PRESS,** WHICH PUBLISHED THIS VERY BOOK, DEDICATES ALL PROFITS FROM SALES INTO MAKING MORE GREAT, SOCIALLY CONSCIOUS, FORWARD-LOOKING BOOKS. ANOTHER EXAMPLE IS **NEWMAN'S OWN** FOODS, WHICH SENDS ALL PROFITS DIRECTLY TO A CHARITABLE FOUNDATION.

TRY ONE OF THEIR FIG COOKIES WHILE YOU READ ON...

I HOPE YOU CAN SEE NOW WHY I THINK BUSINESS CAN HAVE A ROLE IN REVOLUTIONIZING HYPERCAPITALISM'S VALUES! YOU CAN HEAR THE RUMBLING ALREADY!

THE PROBLEM, OF COURSE, IS THAT MOST BUSINESSES STILL CARRY ON AS USUAL, OVERSELLING THEIR STUFF, PUMPING UP PROFITS, HOLDING DOWN WAGES, DODGING TAXES AND REGULATIONS...

BUT WHAT WILL HAPPEN IF THE "VALUES-DRIVEN" SECTOR **EXPANDS,** AND SOCIALLY RESPONSIBLE BUSINESSES SHOW THEMSELVES TO BE **GOOD INVESTMENTS?**

THESE COMPANIES AND ORGANIZATIONS WOULD OFFER A **MODEL** TO FUTURE INVESTORS AND ENTREPRENEURS, A NEW WAY TO CONCEIVE OF THE FUNCTIONS, RESPONSIBILITIES, AND, YES, THE **VALUES** OF BUSINESS.

AND WHO KNOWS? THANKS TO THEM, CAPITALISM'S INVISIBLE HAND MIGHT JUST PUSH ALGI ASIDE!

Chapter 11
GOVERNMENT
FOR THE PEOPLE

A FULL DISCUSSION OF GOVERNMENT AND HYPERCAPITALISM WOULD FILL A BOOK, OR TWO BOOKS, OR TEN. IT—OR THEY—WOULD HAVE TO TALK ABOUT TAXATION, LAND USE, ENERGY, TRANSPORTATION, POLLUTION, HOUSING, INTERNATIONAL TRADE, HEALTH CARE, EDUCATION, AND MILITARY AFFAIRS, AMONG OTHER THINGS.

AND WE HAVE ONLY THIS ONE MEASLY CHAPTER. IN IT, WE'LL MENTION A FEW STRATEGIES FOR RESCUING GOVERNMENT FROM CORPORATE DOMINATION; DESCRIBE SOME WAYS FOR GOVERNMENT TO BE MORE RESPONSIVE TO CITIZENS; AND LIST SOME RECENT STEPS TAKEN BY GOVERNMENTS TO ACT MORE IN LINE WITH INTRINSIC VALUES.

COME ON, WE CAN DO IT...

PUBLICLY FUNDED CAMPAIGNS

IN CASE YOU HADN'T NOTICED, AMERICAN ELECTION CAMPAIGNS ARE LONG AND SUPER-COSTLY, SO MUCH SO THAT ELECTED OFFICIALS SPEND MUCH OF THEIR TIME DIALING DONORS FOR DOLLARS (FOR THE **NEXT** CAMPAIGN!) INSTEAD OF LAW-MAKING. AND THEY'RE NOT CALLING POOR PEOPLE!

IN COUNTRIES LIKE THE U.K., WHERE GOVERNMENT BEARS THE FULL COST OF ELECTIONS, THE DEBATE SEASON LASTS WEEKS INSTEAD OF MONTHS OR YEARS, AND WAY LESS MONEY IS SPENT.

THE U.S. AND SOME STATES ALSO HAVE A SYSTEM FOR GIVING PUBLIC FUNDS TO CANDIDATES IF THEY AGREE TO LIMIT PRIVATE FUND-RAISING. THIS IS VOLUNTARY, HOWEVER. PENELOPE "PEEPS" MINTY DECIDES TO GO THIS ROUTE.

WHEN MINTY TAKES PUBLIC FUNDING, THE PUBLIC REAPS SEVERAL ADVANTAGES.

I CAN SPEND LESS TIME BEGGING FOR MONEY AND MORE TIME RESEARCHING ISSUES AND MEETING ORDINARY PEOPLE.

VOTERS ACTUALLY HAVE THE OPTION TO CHOOSE SOMEONE WHO ISN'T BOUGHT AND PAID FOR! (MY OPPONENT IS BOUGHT AND PAID FOR, BY THE WAY...)

I'M WORKING AGAINST HYPER-CAPITALISM'S FIFTH COMMANDMENT BY TAKING A PUBLIC FUNCTION OUT OF PRIVATE HANDS.

Y: A BREATH FRESH AIR

POWER TO "PEEPS!"

EVEN SO, MOST CANDIDATES STAY WITH PURELY PRIVATE MONEY. WHY?

PAUL ITTICKS EXPECTS TO WIN BY OUTSPENDING HIS OPPONENT ON POLLING, ORGANIZATION, FOCUS GROUPS, AND ESPECIALLY ADS.

THERE'S SO MUCH OF IT!!

CONCLUSION?

"PEEPS" WANTS PUBLIC FUNDING OF CAMPAIGNS TO BE **MANDATORY,** NOT OPTIONAL.

LIMITING CORPORATE RIGHTS

THE **CITIZENS UNITED** COURT CASE (SEE P. 105) REMOVED LIMITS ON CORPORATE ELECTION SPENDING. MOST AMERICANS, REGARDLESS OF POLITICAL PERSUASION, THINK THAT THIS WAS A BAD DECISION.

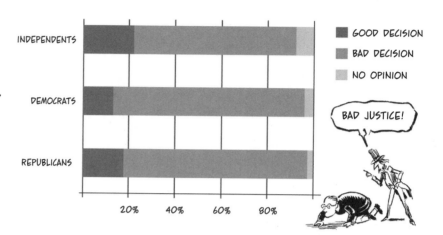

THERE IS A MOVE AFOOT TO REVERSE THE COURT'S DECISION BY **CONSTITUTIONAL AMENDMENT.** FOR A PROPOSED DRAFT OF A 28TH AMENDMENT, SEE MOVETOAMEND.ORG. THE PROPOSAL HAS TWO MAIN POINTS:

1. "THE RIGHTS PROTECTED BY THE CONSTITUTION OF THE UNITED STATES ARE THE RIGHTS OF NATURAL PERSONS ONLY" (AND NOT OF ARTIFICIAL ENTITIES).

2. "THE JUDICIARY SHALL NOT CONSTRUE THE SPENDING OF MONEY TO INFLUENCE ELECTIONS TO BE SPEECH UNDER THE FIRST AMENDMENT."

PASSING CONSTITUTIONAL AMENDMENTS IS A SLOG, BUT HUNDREDS OF ORGANIZATIONS AND CITY AND STATE GOVERNMENTS HAVE BACKED THIS ONE, AND 22 MEMBERS OF CONGRESS, SO FAR, HAVE SIGNED ON. IT'S A START!

OR, TO GO IN A DIFFERENT DIRECTION, WE COULD ASK:

WHO—or WHAT— HAS RIGHTS?

SOME PHILOSOPHERS, POLITICIANS, AND LEGAL SCHOLARS HAVE ARGUED FOR AN **EXTENSION** OF RIGHTS BEYOND INDIVIDUAL PERSONS NOW LIVING. FOR EXAMPLE, WHAT ABOUT THE RIGHTS OF **FUTURE GENERATIONS**?

WHAT ABOUT THIS IS SO HARD TO UNDERSTAND?

AND WHY NOT HERE?

THE IROQUOIS ONCE RECOGNIZED THOSE RIGHTS (SEE P. 73), AND SO DOES **GERMANY** TODAY. THE GERMAN CONSTITUTION'S ARTICLE 20a SAYS, "THE STATE... IN ITS RESPONSIBILITY FOR FUTURE GENERATIONS, PROTECTS THE NATURAL FOUNDATIONS OF LIFE..."

OTHER NATIONS AND JURISDICTIONS EXPLICITLY RECOGNIZE THE **RIGHTS OF NATURE.** ECUADOR'S CONSTITUTION DECLARES THAT NATURE HAS "THE RIGHT TO EXIST, PERSIST, MAINTAIN, AND REGENERATE ITS VITAL CYCLES." BOLIVIA HAS A SIMILAR LAW, AND NEW ZEALAND HAS GRANTED LEGAL RIGHTS TO A RIVER, THE WHANGANUI. EVEN THE CITY OF PITTSBURGH, PENNSYLVANIA, HAS AFFIRMED THE RIGHTS OF NATURE!

WHERE'S MY LAWYER?

MEASURING WHAT MATTERS

WHAT NUMBERS CAPTURE A NATION'S WELL-BEING? PRODUCTIVITY, INFLATION, INTEREST RATES, DEFICITS, OR THE DOW? OVERALL NATIONAL WEALTH IS SUPPOSED TO BE CAPTURED BY THE **GROSS DOMESTIC PRODUCT,** OR GDP, THE ECONOMY'S TOTAL OUTPUT OF GOODS AND SERVICES.

GDP IS UP... LIFE IS GOOD...

The Tao of Dow

BUT THE GDP, AND THE RELATED GNP (GROSS NATIONAL PRODUCT),* ARE STRICTLY ABOUT MONEY, AND SO, IN THE WORDS OF **ROBERT F. KENNEDY,**

"GROSS NATIONAL PRODUCT COUNTS AIR POLLUTION AND CIGARETTE ADVERTISING. IT COUNTS SPECIAL LOCKS ON OUR DOORS AND THE JAILS FOR PEOPLE WHO BREAK THEM. IT COUNTS THE DESTRUCTION OF THE REDWOOD... NUCLEAR WARHEADS AND ARMORED CARS FOR THE POLICE... THE TELEVISION PROGRAMS WHICH GLORIFY VIOLENCE IN ORDER TO SELL TOYS TO OUR CHILDREN. YET... NOT... THE HEALTH OF OUR CHILDREN, THE QUALITY OF THEIR EDUCATION... THE BEAUTY OF OUR POETRY OR THE STRENGTH OF OUR MARRIAGES, THE INTELLIGENCE OF OUR PUBLIC DEBATE OR THE INTEGRITY OF OUR PUBLIC OFFICIALS... IT MEASURES EVERYTHING, IN SHORT, EXCEPT THAT WHICH MAKES LIFE WORTHWHILE."

CONSIDER, FOR EXAMPLE, WHAT FACES ERNIE WAGES WHEN HIS MOTHER IS DYING. IF ERNIE TAKES TIME OFF WORK TO CARE FOR HER, HE DEPRESSES GDP. BUT IF HE WORKS EXTRA HOURS FOR MONEY THAT HE SPENDS ON A NURSING HOME, HE INCREASES GDP.

SUCH A GOOD BOY!

ERNIE, YOU HEARTLESS COG!

*THE GDP OF THE UNITED STATES IS THE TOTAL OUTPUT OF ALL AMERICAN COMPANIES WITHIN U.S. TERRITORY. GNP IS THE TOTAL OUTPUT OF ALL AMERICAN-OWNED COMPANIES BOTH AT HOME AND ABROAD.

IN OTHER WORDS, THE EXPRESSION OF INTRINSIC VALUES CAN HOLD DOWN GDP. INSTEAD OF GDP, THEN, WHAT WOULD BE A BETTER MEASURE OF A SOCIETY'S HEALTH? IN THE 1970S, THE HIMALAYAN NATION OF **BHUTAN** BEGAN DEVELOPING AN ALTERNATIVE MEASURE CALLED THE **GROSS NATIONAL HAPPINESS (GNH)** INDEX. GNH HAS NINE SEPARATE COMPONENTS.

THIS MODEL HAS SPARKED A WORLDWIDE DISCUSSION. SEVERAL NATIONS, INCLUDING THE U.K., FRANCE, AND THAILAND, ARE EXPLORING SIMILAR "ASSESSMENT METRICS." HERE IN THE U.S., A NUMBER OF CITIES (E.G., JACKSONVILLE, FLORIDA) NOW USE SIMILAR MULTI-FACETED INDICATORS TO INFORM POLICY CHOICES.

A BETTER DEAL FOR WORKERS

HYPERCAPITALISM HAS SLAMMED MILLIONS OF WORKERS (SEE PP. 107–114). ONE SIMPLE WAY TO LIMIT THEIR MISERY WOULD BE TO **RAISE THE MINIMUM WAGE.** THE FEDERAL GOVERNMENT SEEMS IN NO MOOD FOR AN INCREASE, BUT MANY STATES HAVE ENACTED MINIMUM WAGE LAWS BETTER THAN THE STINGY NATIONAL PROVISION, IF ONLY BY A LITTLE.

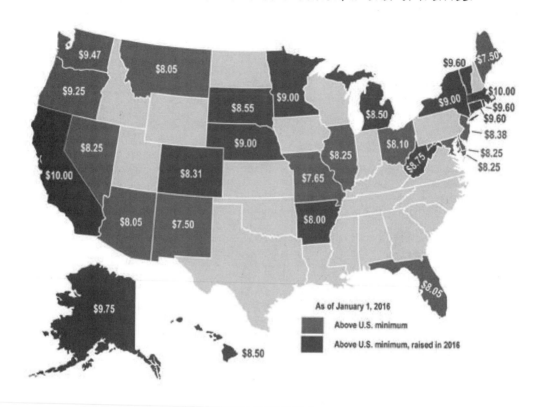

As of January 1, 2016

Above U.S. minimum

Above U.S. minimum, raised in 2016

AT THE SAME TIME, EXECUTIVE PAY HAS ZOOMED (SEE P. 15). THE FEDS HAVE NO PLANS TO RAISE TAXES ON THESE STUPENDOUS INCOMES, BUT THE CITY OF PORTLAND, OREGON, HAS AT LEAST FOUND A WAY TO RAISE AWARENESS OF THE ISSUE:

ANY COMPANY DOING BUSINESS IN PORTLAND MUST NOW PAY **EXTRA CITY TAX** IF THE COMPANY'S CEO MAKES MORE THAN **100 TIMES** THE MEDIAN PAY OF THE COMPANY'S WORKERS. THE CITY EXPECTS TO REALIZE ABOUT **$3 MILLION** A YEAR FROM THIS SURTAX, WHICH MANY COMPANIES ACCUSE OF BEING "ANTI-BUSINESS."

HISTORICALLY, WORKERS HAVE DONE BEST THROUGH **COLLECTIVE BARGAINING.** BUT HYPERCAPITALISM DEMONIZES UNIONS, AND U.S. LAW MAKES THEM HARD TO ORGANIZE.

DON'T DO ANY-THING RASH...

FIRST, LET'S HAVE A FAIR, FRANK, LONG-WINDED EXCHANGE OF VIEWS WITH MY LAWYERS.

ALGI UNFAIR!

UNION NOW!

TO ORGANIZE A WORKPLACE, EMPLOYEES ARE POLLED, FILLING OUT **AUTHORIZATION CARDS** STATING WHETHER THEY WISH TO JOIN A UNION.

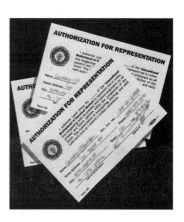

IF A MAJORITY FAVORS THE UNION, MANAGEMENT STILL HAS ENDLESS OPPORTUNITIES TO DELAY, BULLY, LITIGATE, AND WEAR PEOPLE DOWN BEFORE A **SECOND** ELECTION IS HELD. THIS SECOND VOTE OFTEN REVERSES THE OUTCOME OF THE ORIGINAL "CARD CHECK."

STRANGE, BUT NONE OF THE ORIGINAL "YES" VOTERS WORK HERE ANYMORE...

IN CANADA, BY CONTRAST, THE CARD CHECK **IS** THE ELECTION. IF THE CARDS SAY YES, THE UNION IS IN. WHY NOT HERE?

YEAH, WHY NOT?

AND SPEAKING OF NOT HERE, HOW ABOUT PAID FAMILY LEAVE FOR ALL NEW PARENTS? THAT'S WHAT THE REST OF THE WORLD ENJOYS! (SEE P. 113.)

I'D BETTER GET TO WORK ON THE REST OF THE WORLD, THEN...

CONTROLLING ADVERTISING

YOU WANT TO ADVERTISE STUFF? WELL, STUFF YOU!

HYPERCAPITALISM PUSHES ITS CONSUMERIST VISION THROUGH ADS, SO GOVERNMENT CAN PROMOTE INTRINSIC VALUES BY REINING IN ADS.

SAN FRANCISCO, FOR EXAMPLE, BARS ALL BRAND IMAGES AND LOGOS FROM ITS PUBLIC SCHOOLS. VERMONT LIMITS THE SIZE AND PLACEMENT OF OUTDOOR ADVERTISING. NO BILLBOARDS ON VERMONT HIGHWAYS!

WHAT AM I SUPPOSED TO LOOK AT?

FARTHER AFIELD, BRAZILIAN LAW BANS ADVERTISING TO CHILDREN, DESCRIBING IT AS "ABUSIVE." PEEPS MINTY (AND YOUR AUTHORS) WOULD LIKE TO SEE A TOTAL BAN ON ADS AIMED AT KIDS, WHO MIGHT THEN GROW UP BETTER ABLE TO RESIST CONSUMERISM'S CYNICAL MANIPULATION.

IF YOU CAN'T CYNICALLY MANIPULATE CHILDREN, WHOM CAN YOU CYNICALLY MANIPULATE?

GOVERNMENT COULD ALSO CHANGE ITS **TAX TREATMENT** OF ADVERTISING.

SINCE ADS COST MONEY, BUSINESSES SEE ADVERTISING AS A COST LIKE ANY OTHER. THE GOVERNMENT, AGREEING WITH THIS POINT OF VIEW, LETS BUSINESSES **DEDUCT** THE COST OF ADVERTISING WHEN CALCULATING TAXABLE INCOME.

IT'S GOOD TO SEE EYE TO EYE.

AS FAR AS I'M CONCERNED, BUYING ADS IS JUST LIKE RAISING CHILDREN, EXCEPT UNLIMITED.

IT LOOKS DIFFERENT TO THE REST OF US. ADS ARE AN INVASION OF PUBLIC SPACE, SOMETHING LIKE A **TAKING,** IN LEGAL TERMS. ADVERTISING TAKES AWAY A PRECIOUS SHARE OF PEOPLE'S TIME, ATTENTION, AND PEACE OF MIND; AND FROM THIS POINT OF VIEW, BUSINESSES **OWE** THE PUBLIC SOMETHING FOR EVERY AD THEY PRODUCE.

SO WHY NOT

TAX

ADVERTISING INSTEAD OF SUBSIDIZING IT?

BECAUSE WHO NEEDS IT?

SUCH PROTECTIVE PROPOSALS, BY THE WAY, ARE OFTEN DERIDED AS CREATING A "NANNY STATE" THAT TURNS THE PUBLIC INTO A BUNCH OF CRY-BABY CITIZENS.

DIDDA BIG, BAD ALGI-MONSTER GIVE OO A BOO-BOO?

WE PREFER TO THINK OF GOVERNMENT'S ROLE HERE AS THAT OF A TOUGH, MUSCULAR BOUNCER, TASKED WITH KEEPING BAD CORPORATE ACTORS IN LINE!

GLEEP! NANNY?

YOU GO, PEEPS!

THIS CHAPTER HAS OFFERED UP A SHORT, INCOMPLETE LIST OF IDEAS FOR GOVERNMENT ACTION AGAINST SOME OF HYPERCAPITALISM'S TROUBLESOME TRENDS...

OTHER NATIONS HAVE MADE PROGRESS IN SOME AREAS WE'VE DISCUSSED, BUT IN THE U.S., REFORMS HAVE COME MAINLY IN STATES AND LOCALITIES. STILL, I THINK THEY'RE IMPORTANT!!

Sanity Zone

FIRST, WHEN A LOCALITY SUCCESSFULLY ENACTS POLICIES THAT EXPRESS INTRINSIC VALUES, IT GIVES **VISIBLE EVIDENCE** THAT HYPERCAPITALISM CAN BE RESISTED.

SECOND, LOCAL ACTION CAN SPREAD NATIONWIDE. WOMEN COULD VOTE IN WYOMING 40 YEARS BEFORE THE 19TH AMENDMENT... AND JUST LOOK AT RECENT PROGRESS ON GAY MARRIAGE...

THIRD, IT IS USUALLY EASIER FOR PEOPLE TO MAKE CHANGES LOCALLY, ON A SCHOOL BOARD OR CITY COUNCIL, THAN AT THE NATIONAL LEVEL.

AND THAT BRINGS US TO OUR **FINAL CHAPTER**...

IT'S ABOUT **PROTEST.**

Chapter 12
PROTEST

THE LAST FIVE CHAPTERS DESCRIBED ACTS OF **ECONOMIC** RESISTANCE. BOYCOTTS PUT FINANCIAL PRESSURE ON A TARGETED COMPANY; VOLUNTARY SIMPLICITY IS ABOUT CONSUMPTION AND WORK; AND SO ON. WHEN DEPLOYING THESE STRATEGIES, OUR CARTOON FRIENDS ALL STAYED "IN CHARACTER," PLAYING ROLES DEFINED BY HYPERCAPITALIST ECONOMICS.

SEEK HIGHER PAY AND BETTER WORKING CONDITIONS

BUY MIND-FULLY

SHARE SERVICES

INVEST RESPONSIBLY

OPT OUT OF MATERIALISM, BUY LITTLE, LIVE SIMPLY

START A CO-OP

NOW THE ACTORS IN OUR HYPERCAPITALIST DRAMA ARE GOING TO STEP OUT OF THEIR ECONOMIC ROLES AND ACT AS HUMAN BEINGS WITH HEARTS, MINDS, AND VOICES. THEY'LL BE LOUD, VISIBLE, AND SOMETIMES DISRUPTIVE. THIS CHAPTER IS ABOUT THE **PUBLIC AFFIRMATION OF VALUES.**

BY THE WAY, DID YOU KNOW YOU CAN BUY BULLHORNS MADE OF RECYCLED PLASTIC?

AT ITS ROOT, THE WORD **PROTEST** MEANS TO AFFIRM PUBLICLY. IN LATIN, *PRO-* IMPLIES "FORWARD" WHILE *TESTARI* MEANS "TO ASSERT," AS IN *"TESTIFY."*

WE STRESS THIS POINT BECAUSE PEOPLE USUALLY THINK OF PROTEST AS SOMETHING PURELY IN **OPPOSITION,** BUT IN FACT, IT HAS ITS POSITIVE, AFFIRMATIVE SIDE, TOO. PROTEST TYPICALLY SPRINGS FROM DEMANDS FOR IMPROVEMENT, FOR OUTCOMES LIKE GREATER TRANSPARENCY, EQUALITY, JUSTICE, AND ENVIRONMENTAL SUSTAINABILITY. MOST PROTESTS **AGAINST** HYPERCAPITALISM ARE ALSO PROTESTS **FOR** CERTAIN INTRINSIC VALUES.

THIS IS IMPORTANT FOR TWO REASONS!

1. AS WE'VE SEEN, THE EXPRESSION OF INTRINSIC VALUES TENDS TO SUPPRESS COMPETING MATERIALISTIC VALUES (THE SEESAW EFFECT OF P. 63). THE SHEER ACT OF PROTESTING ITSELF UNDERMINES ONE OF HYPERCAPITALISM'S BASIC SUPPORTS!

EEK!

2. AFFIRMING INTRINSIC VALUES IS ALSO ASSOCIATED WITH GREATER WELL-BEING, SO IT'S NO SURPRISE THAT RESEARCH SHOWS ENHANCED WELL-BEING AMONG POLITICALLY ACTIVE PEOPLE.

Disclaimer:

JUST TO BE CLEAR, WE'RE NOT URGING YOU TO PROTEST JUST BECAUSE IT FEELS GOOD! NONETHELESS, IT IS A SIMPLE TRUTH THAT ACTING IN SUPPORT OF ONE'S POLITICAL BELIEFS IS MORE SATISFYING THAN, SAY, SHOPPING FOR SWEATERS (EVEN IF SHOPPING FITS WITH YOUR CORE BELIEFS).

SWEATERS ARE A FALSE GOD...

WHAT FOLLOWS IS A BRIEF, CHRONOLOGICAL TOUR OF SOME RECENT PROTESTS AGAINST HYPERCAPITALISM.

THEY SEEM RECENT TO ME, ANYWAY.

1996: BILLBOARD LIBERATION

THE **BILLBOARD LIBERATION FRONT,** A GROUP OF ARTISTS AND DESIGNERS, MADE THEIR MISSION THE "IMPROVEMENT" OF OUTDOOR ADVERTISING. BY NIGHT, THEY WOULD QUIETLY REPLACE BILLBOARDS' FALSE AND FATUOUS SLOGANS WITH MESSAGES SOMEWHAT CLOSER TO THE TRUTH.

THE POINT, OF COURSE, WAS TO REMIND EVERYONE THAT WE ALL SEMI-UNCONSCIOUSLY ENDURE A CACOPHONY OF ABSURD CLAIMS— AS WELL AS TO MAKE PUBLIC STATEMENTS ABOUT CONSUMERISM AND COMMERCIAL PERSUASION. SOME SAMPLES:

VANDALS! TRESSPASSERS! TORTIOUS MEDDLERS! WHY DON'T THEY BUY THEIR OWN BILLBOARDS?

196

1999: WTO MEETING, Seattle

THE **WORLD TRADE ORGANIZATION** (WTO), A PAN-GOVERNMENTAL GROUP LIKE THE IMF, FORMED IN 1995 TO REWORK TRADING ARRANGEMENTS FOR A GLOBALIZED AGE. RICH COUNTRIES WANTED THE WTO TO PROMOTE PRIVATIZATION, DEREGULATION, AND FREE TRADE, TO THE DETRIMENT OF POOR FARMING COUNTRIES AND THE ENVIRONMENT. (SEE PP. 93–95 AND 100–101).

GREAT CHAIRS AT THESE MEETINGS!

IN THE FIRST FEW WTO GET-TOGETHERS, HEATED ARGUMENTS ERUPTED BETWEEN RICH NATIONS AND POOR. BY THE 1999 MEETING, IN SEATTLE, WASHINGTON, THE RICH COUNTRIES' DEMANDS HAD SPARKED WORLDWIDE OUTRAGE.

40,000 PROTESTERS CLOGGED SEATTLE'S STREETS AND INTER-SECTIONS, SUFFERED TEAR GAS AND POLICE CHARGES, AND SUCCESSFULLY DISRUPTED THE MEETING. DIPLOMATS HAD TO GO HOME, AND SUDDENLY THE WORD "GLOBALIZATION" ENTERED THE GLOBAL VOCABULARY.

AS IF SEATTLE TRAFFIC WASN'T BAD ENOUGH...

2001: THE GOLDEN MARBLE TIM'S FIRST PROTEST

IN 1998, A MEDIA ORGANI-ZATION CALLED **KIDSCREEN** CREATED THE **GOLDEN MARBLE,** AN AWARD HONORING ADS AIMED AT CHILDREN.

IN 2001, I JOINED PSYCHOLOGIST **SUSAN LINN** AND OTHERS AT A COUNTER-CEREMONY SHE ORGANIZED IN ANOTHER ROOM OF THE SAME HOTEL THAT WAS HOSTING THE GOLDEN MARBLE FESTIVITIES.

MARKETERS! UGH!

AFTER A MORNING OF ACA-DEMIC PAPERS, WE MARCHED LOUDLY THROUGH THE HOTEL AND OUT TO THE SIDEWALK FOR OUR OWN PRIZE-GIVING.

OUR "HAVE YOU LOST YOUR MARBLES?" AWARDS WENT TO **LUCY HUGHES** FOR WRITING *THE NAG FACTOR* (SEE P. 17), AND TO THE **TELETUBBIES** TV SHOW FOR PEDDLING JUNK FOOD TO VERY SMALL KIDS.

BECAUSE, GOSH, KIDS NEED HELP DECIDING!

SINCE NONE OF THE DIS-HONOREES WERE ON HAND, THEIR AWARDS WERE ACCEPTED BY OUR FRESHLY-MINTED MAS-COT, **GOLDIE THE WEASEL.**

IT'S GOOD TO BE VALIDATED!

WE ALSO AWARDED SOME REAL HONORS. ONE WENT TO **TRISTAN KADISH,** A HIGH-SCHOOLER WHO SPOKE OUT AGAINST MCDON-ALD'S WHILE IT RE-CRUITED WORKERS ON CAMPUS. ANOTHER WENT TO THE **SWEDISH GOV-ERNMENT** FOR ITS OPPOSITION TO CHILD-ORIENTED ADS.

A REPRESENTATIVE FROM THE SWE-DISH CONSULATE CAME TO ACCEPT HIS GOVERNMENT'S AWARD.

THANK YOU FOR RECOGNIZING NON-WEASELS, TOO.

KIDSCREEN STOPPED GIVING THE GOLDEN MARBLE AWARDS IN 2003.

GOAL!

2002: WORLDCOM WHISTLED

SOMETIMES PROTEST COMES FROM INSIDE A COMPANY, WHEN A BRAVE EMPLOYEE UNCOVERS WRONGDOING AND SPEAKS OUT. ONE SUCH "WHISTLEBLOWER" WAS

CYNTHIA COOPER,

WHO WORKED AS AN AUDITOR FOR **WORLDCOM**, THEN A TELE-COMMUNICATIONS GIANT.

COOPER NOTED IRREGULARITIES IN WORLDCOM'S FINANCIAL RECORDS AND QUIETLY ASSIGNED A TEAM TO INVESTIGATE THEM. SHE AND HER TEAM FOUND THAT WORLDCOM'S PROFITS WERE LARGELY INVENTED BY FRAUDULENT BOOKKEEPING PRACTICES. SO—

CYNTHIA COOPER BLEW THE WHISTLE BY TAKING HER FINDINGS TO THE BOARD OF DIRECTORS.

DANG, CYNTH! NOT SO LOUD!

GOVERNMENT AUTHORITIES HEARD THE BLAST, FILED CHARGES, AND SENT SEVERAL WORLDCOM EXECUTIVES TO PRISON. THE COMPANY ITSELF WENT BANKRUPT AND DISAPPEARED.

WHAT WE HAVE HERE IS A FAILURE TO COMMUNICATE!

2010: GUERRILLA GARDENS

EXTREME INEQUALITY HAS RAVAGED POOR NEIGHBORHOODS IN AMERICA'S CITIES. RESIDENTS LIVE IN DECAYING BUILDINGS AMONG VACANT LOTS IN "FOOD DESERTS" WHERE THE ONLY "SUSTENANCE" COMES FROM CONVENIENCE STORES AND FAST FOOD OUTLETS.

THERE IS AN URBAN FARMING MOVEMENT THAT TRIES TO START FARMS ON VACANT LOTS, BUT IT FACES ZONING RESTRICTIONS, RELUCTANT LANDOWNERS, AND OTHER SNAGS. CAN GREEN VEGETABLES OVERCOME RED TAPE?

RON FINLEY,

OF SOUTH-CENTRAL LOS ANGELES, SIMPLY SKIPPED THE FORMALITIES AND PLANTED AN UNPERMITTED ORGANIC "GANSTA GARDEN" ON A VACANT STRIP OF CITY-OWNED LAND IN FRONT OF HIS HOUSE. OF COURSE, THE CITY AND COUNTY OF LOS ANGELES CRIED FOUL.

ER, UM, I SAY...

RENEGADE FARMER

AFTER A PETITION DRIVE AND MORE THAN A FEW MEETINGS, THE CITY RELENTED, AND NOW FINLEY WORKS TO BRING ORGANIC FARMING TO VACANT LAND ALL OVER THE VAST LOS ANGELES BASIN.

"THEY'RE USED TO PEOPLE CAVING IN, AND WE'RE NOT PLANNING ON CAVING IN!"

2011: OCCUPY MOVEMENT

AFTER THE 2008 FINANCIAL CRISIS, SOME **10 MILLION** PEOPLE LOST THEIR HOMES, AND MANY BIG BANKS BECAME INSOLVENT.

THE BUSH AND OBAMA ADMINISTRATIONS RESPONDED BY BAILING OUT THE BANKS, WHILE MOSTLY LEAVING THE DISPOSSESSED TO FEND FOR THEMSELVES. BY 2011, INEQUALITY WAS AS BAD AS EVER.

MEANWHILE, BANK EXECUTIVES WERE TREATING THEMSELVES TO HUGE BONUSES, PAID FROM FEDERAL BAIL-OUT FUNDS. THIS TRANSFER OF MONEY TO THE RICH FROM THE PUBLIC DID NOT SIT WELL WITH THE PUBLIC.

ON SEPTEMBER 17, **OCCUPY WALL STREET** SET UP CAMP IN THE NEW YORK FINANCIAL DISTRICT. THE PROTESTERS MADE NO SPECIFIC DEMANDS, BUT HAD A GREAT SLOGAN ABOUT WEALTH INEQUALITY: **"WE ARE THE 99%."**

THE MOVEMENT, WHICH SPREAD TO MANY CITIES AROUND THE WORLD, FELL APART IN THE END DUE TO LACK OF ORGANIZATION, BUT THE IDEA OF THE 99% LIVES ON.

2016: DAKOTA ACCESS PIPELINE

IN 2014, THE **DAKOTA ACCESS** PIPELINE WAS PROPOSED TO CARRY OIL FROM NORTH DAKOTA'S OIL FIELDS TO A TRANSIT HUB IN ILLINOIS.

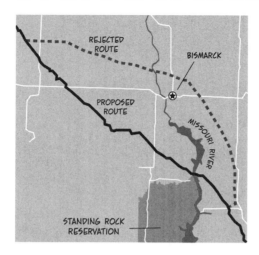

REJECTED ROUTE

BISMARCK

PROPOSED ROUTE

MISSOURI RIVER

STANDING ROCK RESERVATION

FEARING LEAKS INTO DRINKING WATER, PLANNERS ROUTED THE PIPELINE'S PATH AWAY FROM THE CITY OF BISMARCK TO A RIVER CROSSING CLOSE BY THE **STANDING ROCK** SIOUX RESERVATION.

FIRST OUR LAND, THEN OUR WATER? HELL, NO!

THE SIOUX, WHO LIKE CLEAN WATER TOO, BUILT A CAMP AT STANDING ROCK TO PROTEST AGAINST THIS ROUTE. THOUSANDS OF OTHER PEOPLE FROM ACROSS THE COUNTRY JOINED THEM; POLICE ROLLED IN; AND THE TWO SIDES FACED OFF THROUGH THE WINTER, WHILE THE WORLD WATCHED.

NO!

YES!!

IN LATE 2016, PRESIDENT OBAMA SIDED WITH THE PROTESTORS BY DENYING PERMITS TO BUILD ALONG THE DISPUTED ROUTE. BUT AFTER THE NOVEMBER ELECTION, NEW PRESIDENT DONALD TRUMP REVERSED THE DECISION.

AS OF THIS WRITING, THE CHALLENGE CONTINUES IN COURT.

THE WAY OF THE COURT IS A LONG WAY.

THIS PROTEST, LIKE SEVERAL OTHERS, MAY SEEM TO HAVE LOST. THE PIPELINE GOES FORWARD; THE WTO STILL EXISTS; AND THE 1% IS STILL FATTENING LIKE HOGS AT A TROUGH.

I SEE WHY THEY CALL BANKS "PIGGY!"

BUT THAT ISN'T THE WHOLE STORY! EVERY PROTEST HAS **INTANGIBLE** EFFECTS, TOO!

STANDING ROCK SHONE A LIGHT ON OIL COMPANIES READY TO LEAK POISON IN PURSUIT OF PROFIT.

CAN'T A CORPORATION EAT IN PEACE?

THANKS TO OCCUPY, EVERYONE IS AWARE OF THE **1%.**

AND DON'T FORGET THE 0.01%!!

URBAN FARMING STILL FACES OBSTACLES, BUT IT DOES CHALLENGE IDEAS ABOUT PROPERTY AND PROVIDE MUCH-NEEDED NUTRITION.

AS A GUERRILLA GARDENER MIGHT SAY, PROTESTING IS LIKE PLANTING A SEED.

203

IT TAKES TIME TO GERMINATE,
MATURE, AND BEAR FRUIT!

EPILOGUE

MUCH OF THE INFORMATION AND INSPIRATION FOR THIS BOOK COMES FROM *ALTERNATIVES TO CONSUMERISM*, A CLASS I TAUGHT OCCASIONALLY AT KNOX COLLEGE BETWEEN 2004 AND 2013.

THE CLASS COVERED MANY OF THE TOPICS IN PART II OF THIS BOOK: WE DISCUSSED SHARING, MINDFUL BUYING, CO-OPS, PROTEST, AND MORE.

STUDENTS CAME INTO THE CLASS, BY AND LARGE, FEELING PESSIMISTIC AND HOPELESS. AFTER THEIR PREVIOUS STUDY OF THE MODERN ECONOMY (A PRE-REQUISITE FOR MY COURSE) THEY SEEMED FAIRLY BEATEN DOWN—AT AGE 20!

BUT EVERY TIME I TAUGHT *ALTERNATIVES TO CONSUMERISM*, I NOTICED A PALPABLE SHIFT TOWARD **HOPE.** I NEVER KNEW EXACTLY WHY, BUT IT ALWAYS HAPPENED...

I CLEARLY REMEMBER THE OCCASION ONE PARTICULAR YEAR. IT WAS A FINE SPRING DAY, AND THE STUDENTS PROPOSED THAT WE HOLD OUR CLASS OUTDOORS.

WE SAT IN A CIRCLE ON THE GRASS UNDER NEWLY GREEN TREES. I CAN'T RECALL THE TOPIC UNDER DISCUSSION THAT DAY...

BUT I DO REMEMBER THAT TOWARD THE END OF CLASS, A STUDENT NAMED MARY SAID SOMETHING LIKE THIS:

I USED TO THINK THAT I HAD TO DO **EVERYTHING** TO FIGHT AGAINST THESE PROBLEMS.

BUT WHAT I'VE COME TO SEE IS THAT I DON'T HAVE TO DO EVERYTHING. I HAVE TO DO THE THINGS THAT I **CAN** DO.

THEN I HAVE TO **TRUST** THAT DAVID WILL DO WHAT HE CAN DO, AND KIMBERLY WILL DO WHAT SHE CAN DO, AND MARKUS WILL DO WHAT HE CAN DO, AND SO ON!

THAT'S WHAT'S GOING TO WORK, AND IT FEELS LIKE A GREAT RELIEF TO ME.

I THINK WHAT MARY REALIZED WAS THIS:

EVEN THOUGH MANY OF THE STRATEGIES WE'VE DESCRIBED MAY LOOK SMALL COMPARED TO THE HYPERCAPITALIST JUGGERNAUT, THAT JUGGERNAUT MAY NOT BE AS POWERFUL AS IT LOOKS.

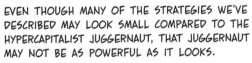

HONK
RUMBLE
SQUEAK

IN THE END, HYPERCAPITALISM IS ONLY ONE SOCIAL SYSTEM AMONG MANY, AND SOCIAL SYSTEMS CAN CHANGE IF MANY PEOPLE, INDIVIDUALLY AND COLLECTIVELY, WORK TO BRING ABOUT CHANGE WHEREVER THEY ARE AND HOWEVER THEY CAN.

REFERENCES

ALL WEBSITE REFERENCES WERE ACCURATE AND WORKING AT THE TIME WE COMPLETED THE BOOK IN THE SPRING OF 2017.

Preface

A FEW OF KASSER'S PRIMARY WRITINGS ABOUT MATERIALISM AND CAPITALISM:

T. KASSER, *THE HIGH PRICE OF MATERIALISM* (CAMBRIDGE, MA: MIT PRESS, 2002).

T. KASSER, "MATERIALISTIC VALUES AND GOALS," *ANNUAL REVIEW OF PSYCHOLOGY*, 67 (2016), 489-514.

T. KASSER, S. COHN, A. D. KANNER, & R. M. RYAN, "SOME COSTS OF AMERICAN CORPORATE CAPITALISM: A PSYCHOLOGICAL EXPLORATION OF VALUE AND GOAL CONFLICTS," *PSYCHOLOGICAL INQUIRY* 18 (2007), PP. 1-22.

T. KASSER & R. M. RYAN, "A DARK SIDE OF THE AMERICAN DREAM: CORRELATES OF FINANCIAL SUCCESS AS A CENTRAL LIFE ASPIRATION," *JOURNAL OF PERSONALITY & SOCIAL PSYCHOLOGY* 65 (1993), 410-22.

Chapter 1

JEFFERSON, PROPERTY, AND *EUDAIMONIA*:

C. HAMILTON, "THE SURPRISING ORIGINS AND MEANING OF THE 'PURSUIT OF HAPPINESS.'" AVAILABLE AT historynewsnetwork.org/article/46460.

R. M. RYAN & E. L. DECI, "ON HAPPINESS AND HUMAN POTENTIALS: RESEARCH ON HEDONIC AND EUDAIMONIC WELL-BEING," *ANNUAL REVIEW OF PSYCHOLOGY* 52 (2001), 141-166.

QUOTES:

SOCRATES: PLATO'S *APOLOGY OF SOCRATES*

ARISTOTLE: *NICHOMACHEAN ETHICS*

EPICURUS: *INTERNET ENCYCLOPEDIA OF PHILOSOPHY* AT www.iep.utm.edu/epicur/#SH5a

MLK: SPEECH GIVEN IN NEW YORK, NY, ON APRIL 4, 1967. THE ENTIRE SPEECH IS AVAILABLE AT: kingencyclopedia.stanford.edu/encyclopedia/documentsentry/doc_beyond_vietnam/; THE REACTION OF THE U.S. GOVERNMENT IS DESCRIBED AT billmoyers.com/2015/01/18/revolution-values/.

MOSES: *EXODUS* 20:17

JESUS: *MATTHEW* 6:24 & *MARK* 10:25

SEARLES: QUOTED IN B. BENNETT, "UNIFORMS AID STUDENT PERFORMANCE, ACADEMICS: NOT ONLY DO UNIFORMS ELIMINATE STATUS WARS, THEY HELP STUDENTS CONCENTRATE ON SCHOOLWORK," *LOS ANGELES TIMES*, DECEMBER 10, 1989.

HUGHES: AS APPEARING IN M. ACHBAR, J. BAKAN, & J. ABBOTT, *THE CORPORATION* (FILM), 2005.

OVERVIEWS OF THE PSYCHOLOGY OF VALUES:

G. R. MAIO, *THE PSYCHOLOGY OF HUMAN VALUES* (LONDON, UK: ROUTLEDGE, 2017).

M. ROKEACH, *THE NATURE OF HUMAN VALUES* (NEW YORK: FREE PRESS, 1973).

CHANGES IN YOUNG PEOPLE'S VALUES OVER TIME:

J. M. TWENGE, W. K., CAMPBELL, & E. C. FREEMAN, "GENERATIONAL DIFFERENCES IN YOUNG ADULTS' LIFE GOALS, CONCERN FOR OTHERS, AND CIVIC ORIENTATION, 1966–2009," *JOURNAL OF PERSONALITY AND SOCIAL PSYCHOLOGY* 102 (2012), 1045-1062; FOR MORE RECENT DATA, SEE ALSO heri.ucla.edu/pr-display. php?prQry=111.

USE OF "CONSUMER" VS. "CITIZEN":

G. SHRUBSOLE (2012). CONSUMERS OUTSTRIP CITIZENS IN BRITISH MEDIA: www.opendemocracy.net/ ourkingdom/guy-shrubsole/consumers-outsrip-citizens-in-british-media.

WEALTH INEQUALITY:

E. SAEZ & G. ZUCMAN, "WEALTH INEQUALITY IN THE UNITED STATES SINCE 1913: EVIDENCE FROM CAPITALIZED INCOME DATA," *THE QUARTERLY JOURNAL OF ECONOMICS* 131 (2016), 519-578.

PIE CHART BASED ON 2007 DATA FROM TABLE 2 IN APPENDIX B OF E. N. WOLFF, "WORKING PAPER NO. 589: RECENT TRENDS IN HOUSEHOLD WEALTH IN THE UNITED STATES: RISING DEBT AND THE MIDDLE-CLASS SQUEEZE—AN UPDATE TO 2 007," LEVY ECONOMICS INSTITUTE OF BARD COLLEGE, PP. 44, MARCH 2010.

NOTE THAT THESE NUMBERS VARY FROM YEAR TO YEAR, DEPENDING ON VARIOUS ECONOMIC FACTORS.

FOR DATA ON CEO-TO-WORKER PAY RATIOS AND DIFFERENCES IN RAISES, SEE L. MISHEL & A. DAVIS, "CEO PAY CONTINUES TO RISE AS TYPICAL WORKERS ARE PAID LESS," WASHINGTON DC: ECONOMIC POLICY INSTITUTE, JUNE 12, 2014.

AMOUNT SPENT ON ADVERTISING:

www.mediapost.com/publications/article/283458/us-ad-growth-to-hit-record-178-billion.html

Chapters 2 & 3

THERE ARE NUMEROUS SOURCES THAT ARE CLASSICS AND/OR HAVE INFORMED OUR GENERAL DISCUSSIONS OF CONSUMERISM, CAPITALISM, AND HYPERCAPITALISM. WE WILL NOT BE CITING EACH AND EVERY ONE OF THEM OVER AND OVER. BUT HERE ARE SOME OF THE MOST IMPORTANT.

M. ACHBAR, J. BAKAN, & J. ABBOTT, *THE CORPORATION* (FILM), 2005.

J. CAVANAGH & J. MANDER (EDS.), *ALTERNATIVES TO ECONOMIC GLOBALIZATION*, 2ND EDITION (SAN FRANCISCO, CA: BERRETT-KOEHLER PUBLISHERS, 2004).

J. DE GRAAF & D. K. BATKER, *WHAT'S THE ECONOMY FOR, ANYWAY? WHY IT'S TIME TO STOP CHASING GROWTH AND START PURSUING HAPPINESS* (NEW YORK: BLOOMSBURY PRESS, 2011).

J. DE GRAAF, D. WANN, & T. H. NAYLOR, *AFFLUENZA: THE ALL-CONSUMING EPIDEMIC* (SAN FRANCISCO, CA: BERRETT-KOEHLER, 2001).

M. FRIEDMAN, *CAPITALISM AND FREEDOM*, 40TH ANNIVERSARY EDITION (CHICAGO: UNIVERSITY OF CHICAGO PRESS, 1962/2002).

M. FRIEDMAN, *FREE TO CHOOSE* (FILM SERIES) (1980).

E. FROMM, *TO HAVE OR TO BE* (NEW YORK: HARPER & ROW, 1976).

C. HAMILTON, *REQUIEM FOR A SPECIES* (CROWS NEST NSW: ALLEN & UNWIN, 2010).

O. JAMES, *THE SELFISH CAPITALIST* (LONDON: VERMILLION, 2008).

T. JACKSON, *PROSPERITY WITHOUT GROWTH* (LONDON: EARTHSCAN, 2009).

A. D. KANNER & R. G. SOULE, "GLOBALIZATION, CORPORATE CULTURE, AND FREEDOM," IN T. KASSER & A. D. KANNER (EDS.), *PSYCHOLOGY AND CONSUMER CULTURE: THE STRUGGLE FOR A GOOD LIFE IN A MATERIALISTIC WORLD* (WASHINGTON DC: AMERICAN PSYCHOLOGICAL ASSOCIATION, 2004), PP. 49-67.

M. KELLY, *THE DIVINE RIGHT OF CAPITAL: DETHRONING THE CORPORATE ARISTOCRACY* (SAN FRANCISCO: BERRETT-KOEHLER, 2003).

N. KLEIN, *THE SHOCK DOCTRINE: THE RISE OF DISASTER CAPITALISM* (NEW YORK: PICADOR, 2008).

N. KLEIN, *THIS CHANGES EVERYTHING: CAPITALISM VS. THE CLIMATE* (NEW YORK: SIMON & SCHUSTER, 2014).

D. C. KORTEN, *THE POST-CORPORATE WORLD: LIFE AFTER CAPITALISM* (WEST HARTFORD, CT: KUMARIAN PRESS, 1999).

D. C. KORTEN, *WHEN CORPORATIONS RULE THE WORLD* (SAN FRANCISCO, CA: BERRETT-KOEHLER, 1996).

A. LEONARD, *THE STORY OF STUFF* (NEW YORK: FREE PRESS, 2010).

D. MILLER, "THE NORM OF SELF-INTEREST," *AMERICAN PSYCHOLOGIST* 54 (1999), 1053-1060.

T. PRINCEN, M. MANIATES, & K. CONCA (EDS.), *CONFRONTING CONSUMPTION* (CAMBRIDGE, MA: MIT PRESS, 2002).

J. B. SCHOR, *BORN TO BUY: THE COMMERCIALIZED CHILD AND THE NEW CONSUMER CULTURE* (NEW YORK: SCRIBNER, 2004).

J. B. SCHOR, *THE OVERSPENT AMERICAN: WHY WE WANT WHAT WE DON'T NEED* (NEW YORK: HARPERPERENNIAL, 1999).

J. B. SCHOR, *THE OVERWORKED AMERICAN: THE UNEXPECTED DECLINE OF LEISURE* (NEW YORK: BASIC BOOKS, 1991).

J. B. SCHOR, *TRUE WEALTH: HOW AND WHY MILLIONS OF AMERICANS ARE CREATING A TIME-RICH, ECOLOGICALLY LIGHT, SMALL-SCALE, HIGH-SATISFACTION ECONOMY* (NEW YORK: PENGUIN, 2011).

E. F. SCHUMACHER, *SMALL IS BEAUTIFUL: ECONOMICS AS IF PEOPLE MATTERED* (NEW YORK: HARPERPERENNIAL, 1973/1989).

B. SCHWARTZ, *THE COSTS OF LIVING: HOW MARKET FREEDOM ERODES THE BEST THINGS IN LIFE* (NEW YORK: NORTON, 1994).

A. SMITH, *AN INQUIRY INTO THE NATURE AND CAUSES OF THE WEALTH OF NATIONS* (NEW YORK: RANDOM HOUSE, 1776/1996).

J. G. SPETH, *THE BRIDGE AT THE EDGE OF THE WORLD: CAPITALISM, THE ENVIRONMENT, AND CROSSING FROM CRISIS TO SUSTAINABILITY* (NEW HAVEN, CT: YALE UNIVERSITY PRESS, 2008).

M. G. STEGER & R. K. ROY, *NEOLIBERALISM: A VERY SHORT INTRODUCTION* (NEW YORK: OXFORD UNIVERSITY PRESS, 2010).

G. TROY, *THE REAGAN REVOLUTION: A VERY SHORT INTRODUCTION* (NEW YORK: OXFORD UNIVERSITY PRESS, 2009).

T. VEBLEN, *THE THEORY OF THE LEISURE CLASS* (NEW YORK: PENGUIN, 1899/1979).

QUOTES THAT END CHAPTER 2:

GEORGE WASHINGTON: LETTER TO BENJAMIN HARRISON, OCTOBER 10, 1784.

MILTON FRIEDMAN: FROM *COMMANDING HEIGHTS* (PBS DOCUMENTARY), INTERVIEW CONDUCTED OCTOBER 1, 2000.

WILLIAM GRIEDER: *THE SOUL OF CAPITALISM* (NEW YORK: SIMON & SCHUSTER, 2003).

AYN RAND: A. RAND, *CAPITALISM: THE UNKNOWN IDEAL* (NEW YORK: SIGNET, 1967).

BARACK OBAMA: SPEECH GIVEN SEPTEMBER 14, 2009.

TED CRUZ: TWEET SENT MARCH 16, 2015.

CORPORATE POWER:

THE COURT CASE GIVING CORPORATIONS THE RIGHTS OF PERSONS WAS U.S. SUPREME COURT, *SANTA CLARA COUNTY V. SOUTHERN PACIFIC R. CO.*, 118 U.S. 394 (1886); MANY MORE HAVE UPHELD AND EXTENDED THIS PRIVILEGE SINCE THEN (SEE movetoamend.org/timeline).

THE CHART COMPARING THE RELATIVE WEALTH OF NATIONS AND CORPORATIONS COMES FROM blogs.worldbank.org/publicsphere/world-s-top-100-economies-31-countries-69-corporations.

Chapter 4

VALUE CIRCUMPLEX MODELS:

THE CLASSIC ARTICLE DESCRIBING THE VALUE CIRCUMPLEX IS S. H. SCHWARTZ, "UNIVERSALS IN THE CONTENT AND STRUCTURE OF VALUES: THEORY AND EMPIRICAL TESTS IN 20 COUNTRIES," *ADVANCES IN EXPERIMENTAL SOCIAL PSYCHOLOGY*, 25, ED. M ZANNA (NEW YORK: ACADEMIC, 1992), PP. 1–65.

MORE INFORMATION ABOUT THE SCHWARTZ VALUE SURVEY IS AVAILABLE IN S. H. SCHWARTZ, *DRAFT USERS MANUAL: PROPER USE OF THE SCHWARZ VALUE SURVEY, VERSION 14 JANUARY 2009,* COMPILED BY ROMIE F. LITTRELL. (AUCKLAND, NEW ZEALAND: CENTRE FOR CROSS CULTURAL COMPARISONS, 2009), AVAILABLE AT www.crossculturalcentre.homestead.com.

THE SAME CIRCUMPLEX STRUCTURE ALSO EMERGES WITH A DIFFERENT MEASURE OF VALUES, THE PORTRAIT VALUES QUESTIONNAIRE IN S. H. SCHWARTZ, G. MELECH, A. LEHMANN, S. BURGESS, M. HARRIS, & V. OWENS, "EXTENDING THE CROSS-CULTURAL VALIDITY OF THE THEORY OF BASIC HUMAN VALUES WITH A DIFFERENT METHOD OF MEASUREMENT," *JOURNAL OF CROSS-CULTURAL PSYCHOLOGY* 32 (2001), 519-542.

THE DISTINCTION BETWEEN INTRINSIC AND EXTRINSIC GOALS WAS INTRODUCED IN T. KASSER & R. M. RYAN, "FURTHER EXAMINING THE AMERICAN DREAM: DIFFERENTIAL CORRELATES OF INTRINSIC AND EXTRINSIC GOALS," *PERSONALITY & SOCIAL PSYCHOLOGY BULLETIN* 22 (1996), 280-287. THIS DISTINCTION DRAWS ON A LONG RESEARCH TRADITION ON THE DIFFERENCES BETWEEN INTRINSIC AND EXTRINSIC MOTIVATION, AS DESCRIBED IN E. L. DECI & R. M. RYAN, *INTRINSIC MOTIVATION AND SELF-DETERMINATION IN HUMAN BEHAVIOR* (NEW YORK: PLENUM, 1985). THE VALUE CIRCUMPLEX BASED ON THIS WORK WAS FIRST DESCRIBED IN F. M. E. GROUZET, T. KASSER, A. AHUVIA, J. M. FERNANDEZ-DOLS, Y. KIM Y, ET AL., "THE STRUCTURE OF GOAL CONTENTS ACROSS 15 CULTURES," *JOURNAL OF PERSONALITY & SOCIAL PSYCHOLOGY* 89 (2005), 800-816.

THE EXPERIMENTAL EVIDENCE FOR THE EFFECTS OF PRIMING CERTAIN VALUES ON THE VALUE CIRCUMPLEX THAT WAS MENTIONED IN THE CHAPTER INCLUDES:

M. BAUER, J. E. B. WILKIE, J. K. KIM, & G. V. BODENHAUSEN, "CUING CONSUMERISM: SITUATIONAL MATERIALISM UNDERMINES PERSONAL AND SOCIAL WELL-BEING," *PSYCHOLOGICAL SCIENCE* 23 (2012), 517–523.

E. M. CARUSO, K. D. VOHS, B. BAXTER, & A. WAYTZ, "MERE EXPOSURE TO MONEY INCREASES ENDORSEMENT OF FREE-MARKET SYSTEMS AND SOCIAL INEQUALITY," *JOURNAL OF EXPERIMENTAL PSYCHOLOGY: GENERAL* 142 (2013), 301–306.

K. D. VOHS, N. L. MEAD, & M. R. GOODE, "THE PSYCHOLOGICAL CONSEQUENCES OF MONEY," *SCIENCE* 31 (2006), 1154–1156.

OTHER IMPORTANT WORK ON PRIMING THAT SUPPORTS CONCLUSIONS FROM THE VALUE CIRCUMPLEX INCLUDES:

B. S. FREY & F. OBERHOLZER-GEE, "THE COST OF PRICE INCENTIVES: AN EMPIRICAL ANALYSIS OF MOTIVATION CROWDING OUT," *AMERICAN ECONOMIC REVIEW* 87 (1997), 746-755.

A. GASIOROWSKA, L. N. CHAPLIN, T. ZALESKIEWICZ, S. WYGRAB, & K. D. VOHS, "MONEY CUES INCREASE AGENCY AND DECREASE PROSOCIALITY AMONG CHILDREN: EARLY SIGNS OF MARKET-MODE BEHAVIOR," *PSYCHOLOGICAL SCIENCE* 27 (2016), 331-344.

A. GASIOROWSKA, T. ZALESKIEWICZ, & S. WYGRAB, "WOULD YOU DO SOMETHING FOR ME? THE EFFECTS OF MONEY ACTIVATION ON SOCIAL PREFERENCES AND SOCIAL BEHAVIOR IN YOUNG CHILDREN," *JOURNAL OF ECONOMIC PSYCHOLOGY* 33 (2012), 603-608.

N. LEKES, N. H. HOPE, L. GOUVEIA, R. KOESTNER, & F. L. PHILIPPE, "INFLUENCING VALUE PRIORITIES AND INCREASING WELL-BEING: THE EFFECTS OF REFLECTING ON INTRINSIC VALUES," *JOURNAL OF POSITIVE PSYCHOLOGY* 7 (2012), 249–261.

G. R. MAIO, A. PAKIZEH, W-Y. CHEUNG, & K. J. REES, "CHANGING, PRIMING, AND ACTING ON VALUES: EFFECTS VIA MOTIVATIONAL RELATIONS IN A CIRCULAR MODEL," *JOURNAL OF PERSONALITY & SOCIAL PSYCHOLOGY* 97 (2009), 699–715.

THE OIL INDUSTRY AND CLIMATE SCIENCE:

UNION OF CONCERNED SCIENTISTS, *THE CLIMATE DECEPTION DOSSIERS* (CAMBRIDGE, MA: AUTHOR, 2015). QUOTE ABOUT "VICTORY" IS FROM HERE.

UNION OF CONCERNED SCIENTISTS, *SMOKE, MIRRORS, & HOT AIR* (CAMBRIDGE, MA: AUTHOR, 2007).

THE FTC AND ADVERTISING TO KIDS:

A. BARBARO & J. EARP. *CONSUMING KIDS: THE COMMERCIALIZATION OF CHILDHOOD* (FILM). (NORTHAMPTON, MA: MEDIA EDUCATION FOUNDATION, 2008). QUOTE FROM FURTH IS FROM HERE.

T. WESTEN, "GOVERNMENT REGULATION OF FOOD MARKETING TO CHILDREN: THE FEDERAL TRADE COMMISSION AND THE KID-VID CONTROVERSY," *LOYOLA OF LOS ANGELES LAW REVIEW* 39 (2006), 78–91.

THE RELEVANT PORTION OF THE FTC IMPROVEMENTS ACT CONCERNING CHILDREN CAN BE FOUND IN SECTION 11 OF *PUBLIC LAW 96-252* – MAY 28, 1980.

QUOTE FROM THE IROQUOIS:

S. C. TUCKER (ED.), *THE ENCYCLOPEDIA OF NORTH AMERICAN INDIAN WARS, 1607-1890.* (SANTA BARBARA, CA: ABC-CLIO, 2011).

Chapter 5

COMMANDMENTS 2, 3 & 5 ARE ADAPTED FROM M. G. STEGER & R. K. ROY, *NEOLIBERALISM: A VERY SHORT INTRODUCTION* (NEW YORK: OXFORD UNIVERSITY PRESS, 2010).

COMMANDMENT 1 - THOU SHALT CONSUME:

R. SHELDON & E. ARENS, *CONSUMER ENGINEERING: A NEW TECHNIQUE FOR PROSPERITY* (NEW YORK: HARPER, 1932).

IN A FUNNY TWIST OF FATE, EARNEST ELMO CALKINS GRADUATED FROM KNOX COLLEGE, WHERE TIM KASSER HAS BEEN A PROFESSOR SINCE 1995. QUOTE FROM E. E. CALKINS, "ADVERTISING, BUILDER OF TASTE," *THE AMERICAN MAGAZINE OF ART*, SEPTEMBER 1930.

REGARDING TYPES OF **STEALTH MARKETING**, SEE R. WALKER, "THE HIDDEN (IN PLAIN SIGHT) PERSUADERS," *NEW YORK TIMES MAGAZINE*, DECEMBER 5, 2004. FOR MORE ON THE GIRLS INTELLIGENCE AGENCY, SEE J. B. SCHOR, *BORN TO BUY: THE COMMERCIALIZED CHILD AND THE NEW CONSUMER CULTURE* (NEW YORK: SCRIBNER, 2004). FUBU EXAMPLE FROM http://www.marketing-schools.org/types-of-marketing/stealth-marketing.html.

ROWE'S QUOTE ON THE **GOLDENPALACE.COM MONKEY** CAN BE FOUND AT www.send2press.com/wire/2005-040-0413-004/.

GRAPH SHOWING **HOUSEHOLD DEBT** IS FROM R. GLICK & K. J. LANSING, "CONSUMERS AND THE ECONOMY, PART I: HOUSEHOLD CREDIT AND PERSONAL SAVING," *FEDERAL RESERVE BANK OF SAN FRANCISCO ECONOMIC LETTER*,JANUARY 10, 2011. NUMBERS FOR **STUDENT AND CREDIT CARD DEBT** ARE FROM: www.newyorkfed.org/newsevents/news/research/2015/rp150217.html.

J. MITCHELL, "SCHOOL-LOAN RECKONING: 7 MILLION ARE IN DEFAULT," *THE WALL STREET JOURNAL*, AUGUST 21, 2015.

COMMANDMENT 2 - THOU SHALT OPERATE GLOBALLY:

REGARDING THE ONSET OF GLOBALIZATION, SEE C. C. MANN, *1493* (NEW YORK: ALFRED A. KNOPF, 2015).

REGARDING **COMPARATIVE ADVANTAGE,** SEE: www.investopedia.com/term/c/comparativeadvantage.asp.

FOR INFORMATION ON **BRETTON WOODS AND THE IMF,** SEE J. CAVANAGH & J. MANDER (EDS.), *ALTERNATIVES TO ECONOMIC GLOBALIZATION,* 2ND EDITION (SAN FRANCISCO, CA: BERRETT-KOEHLER PUBLISHERS, 2004).

L. CARLSEN, "UNDER NAFTA, MEXICO SUFFERED, AND THE UNITED STATES FELT ITS PAIN," *THE NEW YORK TIMES,* NOVEMBER 24, 2013.

REGARDING **HAITI,** SEE:

A. FULLER, "HAITI ON ITS OWN TERMS," *NATIONAL GEOGRAPHIC,* DECEMBER 2015.

E. PHILLIPS & D. D. WATSON, II, CASE STUDY #10-13, "MIAMI RICE IN HAITI: VIRTUE OR VICE?" IN P. PINSTRUP-ANDERSEN AND F. CHENG (EDITORS), *CASE STUDIES IN FOOD POLICY FOR DEVELOPING COUNTRIES* (2011) AT www.worldfuturefund.org/Reports/haiti/clintonhaiti.html.

REGARDING THE **SIXTH MASS EXTINCTION** CURRENTLY UNDER WAY, SEE:

G. CEBALLOS, P. R. EHRLICH, A. D. BARNOSKY, A. GARCIA, R. M. PRINGLE, & T. M. PALMER, "ACCELERATED MODERN HUMAN-INDUCED SPECIES LOSSES: ENTERING THE SIXTH MASS EXTINCTION," *SCIENCE ADVANCES* 1 (2015) E1400253.

WWF, *LIVING PLANET REPORT 2016: RISK AND RESILIENCE IN A NEW ERA* (GLAND, SWITZERLAND: WWF INTERNATIONAL, 2016).

COMMANDMENT 3 - THOU SHALT NOT REGULATE:

REAGAN QUOTE FROM HIS PRESIDENTIAL INAUGURAL ADDRESS, JANUARY 20, 1981.

SAVINGS & LOAN BAILOUT – T. CURRY & L. SHIBUT, "THE COST OF THE SAVINGS AND LOAN CRISIS: TRUTH AND CONSEQUENCES," *FDIC BANKING REVIEW* 26 (2000).

REGARDING **NAFTA,** SEE:

Q. KARPILOW, I. SOLOMON, A. VILLAMAR CALDERON, M. PEREZ-ROCHA, & S. TREW, *NAFTA: 20 YEARS OF COSTS TO COMMUNITIES AND THE ENVIRONMENT* (SIERRA CLUB, MARCH 2014).

REGARDING **MEDIA DE-REGULATION AND CONSOLIDATION,** SEE:

D. CAMPBELL, "INTERNET SPREADS WORD AS NETWORKS SHUN ADVERTS FOR BUY NOTHING DAY," *THE GUARDIAN,* NOVEMBER 24, 2000.

FREE PRESS, *MEDIA POLICY 101: WHAT YOU NEED TO KNOW TO CHANGE THE MEDIA* (FREE PRESS, 2008).

www.frugaldad.com/media-consolidation-infographic

www.museum.tv.eotv/deregulation.htm

TO WATCH ONE OF LASN'S VIDEOS THAT THE FOR-PROFIT MEDIA DIDN'T WANT TO RUN, SEE www.youtube.com/watch?v=luK0_jwyw_0&list+PLB6479E8E44048E78.

REGARDING **CAMPAIGN FINANCE,** SEE:

M. GILENS & B. I. PAGE, "TESTING THEORIES OF AMERICAN POLITICS: ELITES, INTEREST GROUPS, AND AVERAGE CITIZENS," *PERSPECTIVES ON POLITICS* 12 (2014) 564-581.

G. LEVY, "HOW CITIZENS UNITED HAS CHANGED POLITICS IN 5 YEARS," *U. S. NEWS & WORLD REPORT,* JANUARY 21, 2015.

SUPREME COURT OF THE UNITED STATES, "CITIZENS UNITED V. FEDERAL ELECTION COMMITTEE" NO. 08-205, DECIDED JANUARY 21, 2010.

J. P. STEVENS, "OPINION OF STEVENS, J., CITIZENS UNITED V. FEDERAL ELECTION COMMITTEE" JANUARY 21, 2010.

COMMANDMENT 4 – THOU SHALT SPEND LESS ON LABOR:

REGARDING **MEDIEVAL WAGES,** SEE D. ROUTT, "THE ECONOMIC IMPACT OF THE BLACK DEATH," EH.NET ENCYCLOPEDIA, EDITED BY ROBERT WHAPLES, JULY 20, 2008.

en.wikipedia.org/wiki/Labor_unions_in_the_United_States

biz30.timedoctor.com/employee-extinction-the-rise-of-contract-temp-workers-in-business/

DPE RESEARCH DEPARTMENT, *MISCLASSIFICATION OF EMPLOYEES AS INDEPENDENT CONTRACTORS: FACT SHEET 2016* (dpeaflcio.org, 2016).

FOR THE STORY OF THE **MARIANAS ISLANDS,** SEE:

S. PIZZO, "PART IV: DELAY'S UNREGULATED PACIFIC PARADISE," *ALTERNET,* MAY 14, 2002.

M. SHIELDS, "THE REAL SCANDAL OF TOM DELAY," cnn.com, MAY 9, 2005. BOTH QUOTES OF DELAY'S ARE HERE.

J. YDSTIE, "THE ABRAMOFF-DELAY-MARIANA ISLANDS CONNECTION," *NPR TRISTATESRADIO,* JUNE 17, 2006.

MINIMUM WAGE AND PURCHASING POWER:

C. K. ELWELL, "INFLATION AND THE REAL MINIMUM WAGE: A FACT SHEET," *CONGRESSIONAL RESEARCH SERVICE,* JANUARY 8, 2014.

REGARDING ELLS AND CHIPOTLE, CALCULATIONS WERE BASED ON DATA DOWNLOADED IN THE WINTER OF 2016 FROM

www.glassdoor.com/research/ceo-pay-ratio/

www.statista.com/statistics/221462/chipotle-net-income/

REGARDING **PAID LEAVE,** SEE:

worldpolicycenter.org/topics/adult-labor-and-working-conditions/policies)

L. M. BERGER, J. HILL, & J. WALDFOGEL, "MATERNITY LEAVE, EARLY MATERNAL EMPLOYMENT AND CHILD HEALTH AND DEVELOPMENT IN THE US," *THE ECONOMIC JOURNAL* 115 (2005) F29-F47.

C. J. RUHM, "PARENTAL LEAVE AND CHILD HEALTH," *JOURNAL OF HEALTH ECONOMICS* 19 (2000) 931-960.

COMMANDMENT 5 – THOU SHALT PRIVATIZE:

D. COHEN & S. FARMER, "WHY CHICAGO'S BOTCHED PARKING METER PRIVATIZATION IS ALSO BAD FOR THE ENVIRONMENT," *NEXT CITY,* JUNE 4, 2014.

PRIVATE PRISONS:

JUSTICE POLICY INSTITUTE, *GAMING THE SYSTEM: HOW THE POLITICAL STRATEGIES OF PRIVATE PRISON COMPANIES PROMOTE INEFFECTIVE INCARCERATION POLICIES* (WASHINGTON DC: AUTHOR, 2011).

B. W. LUNDAHL, C. KUNZ, C. BROWNELL, N. HARRIS, & R VAN VLEET, "PRISON PRIVATIZATION: A META-ANALYSIS OF COST AND QUALITY OF CONFINEMENT INDICATORS," *RESEARCH ON SOCIAL WORK PRACTICE* 19 (2009) 383-394.

J. W. WHITEHEAD, "JAILING AMERICANS FOR PROFIT: THE RISE OF THE PRISON INDUSTRIAL COMPLEX," *HUFFINGTON POST,* APRIL 10, 2012.

www.sourcewatch.org/index.php/Corrections_Corporation_of_America#cite_note-AZ_Star-22.

HEALTH CARE

J. CARREYROU, "SURGEONS EYED OVER DEAL WITH MEDICAL-DEVICE MAKERS," *WALL STREET JOURNAL*, JULY 25, 2013.

K. EGGLESTON, Y-C SHEN, J. LAU, C. H. SCHMID, & J. CHAN, "HOSPITAL OWNERSHIP AND QUALITY OF CARE: WHAT EXPLAINS THE DIFFERENT RESULTS IN THE LITERATURE?" *HEALTH ECONOMICS* 17 (2008) 1345-1362.

J. R. HORWITZ, "MAKING PROFITS AND PROVIDING CARE: COMPARING NONPROFIT, FOR-PROFIT, AND GOVERNMENT HOSPITALS," *HEALTH AFFAIRS* 24 (2005), 790-801.

R. Y. HSIA, A. L. KELLERMAN, & Y-C SHEN, "FACTORS ASSOCIATED WITH CLOSURES OF EMERGENCY DEPARTMENTS IN THE UNITED STATES," *JAMA* 305 (2011), 1978-1985.

M. P. LUNGREN, T. J. AMRHEIN, B. E. PAXTON, R. C. SRINIVASAN, H. R. COLLINS, J. D. EASTWOOD, & R. K. KILANI, "PHYSICIAN SELF-REFERRAL: FREQUENCY OF NEGATIVE FINDINGS AT MR IMAGING OF THE KNEE AS A MARKER OF APPROPRIATE UTILIZATION," *RADIOLOGY* 269 (2013).

R. PEAR, "DOCTORS WHO PROFIT FROM RADIATION PRESCRIBE IT MORE OFTEN, STUDY FINDS" *NEW YORK TIMES*, AUGUST 18, 2013.

Chapter 6

NORWAY'S UNIONS AND BOARD LAWS:

www.worker-participation.eu/National-Industrial-Relations/Countries/Norway/Trade-Unions

www.worker-participation.eu/National-Industrial-Relations/Countries/Norway/Board-level-Representation

CONFLICTING VALUES IN CAPITALISM:

OUR ARGUMENT FOR THE EFFECTS OF CAPITALISM ON VALUES WAS FIRST PRESENTED IN T. KASSER, S. COHN, A. D. KANNER, & R. M. RYAN, "SOME COSTS OF AMERICAN CORPORATE CAPITALISM: A PSYCHOLOGICAL EXPLORATION OF VALUE AND GOAL CONFLICTS," *PSYCHOLOGICAL INQUIRY* 18 (2007), PP. 1-22.

SCHWARTZ WROTE A COMMENTARY ON OUR PAPER IN WHICH HE CORRELATED VALUES AND THE S-SCORES: S. H. SCHWARTZ, "CULTURAL AND INDIVIDUAL VALUE CORRELATES OF CAPITALISM: A COMPARATIVE ANALYSIS," *PSYCHOLOGICAL INQUIRY* 18 (2007), 52–57.

HE TOOK THE S-SCORES FROM: P. A. HALL & D. W. GINGERICH, *VARIETIES OF CAPITALISM AND INSTITUTIONAL COMPLEMENTARITIES IN THE MACROECONOMY: AN EMPIRICAL ANALYSIS* (MPIFG DISCUSSION PAPER 04/5) (COLOGNE, GERMANY: MAX PLANCK INSTITUTE FOR THE STUDY OF SOCIETIES, 2004). SINCE THEN, SCHWARTZ'S FINDINGS HAVE BEEN REPLICATED USING A DIFFERENT MEASURE OF HYPERCAPITALISM (THE INDEX OF ECONOMIC FREEDOM); SEE TABLE 1 OF T. KASSER & S. LINN, "GROWING UP UNDER CORPORATE CAPITALISM: THE PROBLEM OF MARKETING TO CHILDREN, WITH SUGGESTIONS FOR POLICY SOLUTIONS," *SOCIAL ISSUES AND POLICY REVIEW* 10 (2016), 122-150.

RECENTLY, A PHILOSOPHER HAS MADE SIMILAR ARGUMENTS ABOUT HOW MARKETS CROWD OUT MORALS: M. SANDEL, *WHAT MONEY CAN'T BUY: THE MORAL LIMITS OF MARKETS* (NEW YORK: FARRAR, STRAUS, & GIROUX, 2013).

CORRELATIONS OF CULTURAL VALUES WITH TV ADS AND CHILDREN'S WELL-BEING:

T. KASSER, "CULTURAL VALUES AND THE WELL-BEING OF FUTURE GENERATIONS: A CROSS-NATIONAL STUDY," *JOURNAL OF CROSS-CULTURAL PSYCHOLOGY* 42 (2011), 206–215.

RESEARCH ON HOW THE DEVELOPMENT OF MATERIALISM IS RELATED TO PARENTING, TELEVISION, AND OTHER MATERIALISTIC MODELS INCLUDES:

R. BANERJEE & H. DITTMAR, "INDIVIDUAL DIFFERENCES IN CHILDREN'S MATERIALISM: THE ROLE OF PEER RELATIONS," *PERSONALITY & SOCIAL PSYCHOLOGY BULLETIN* 34 (2008), 17–31.

J. E. BRAND & B. S. GREENBERG, "COMMERCIALS IN THE CLASSROOM: THE IMPACT OF CHANNEL ONE ADVERTISING," *JOURNAL OF ADVERTISING* 34 (1994), 18–21.

M. BUIJZEN, "REDUCING CHILDREN'S SUSCEPTIBILITY TO COMMERCIALS: MECHANISMS OF FACTUAL AND EVALUATIVE ADVERTISING INTERVENTIONS," *MEDIA PSYCHOLOGY* 9 (2007), 411–30.

M. BUIJZEN & P. M. VALKENBURG, "PARENTAL MEDIATION OF UNDESIRED ADVERTISING EFFECTS," *JOURNAL OF BROADCASTING & ELECTRONIC MEDIA* 49 (2005), 153–65.

M. E. GOLDBERG & G. J. GORN, "SOME UNINTENDED CONSEQUENCES OF TV ADVERTISING TO CHILDREN," *JOURNAL OF CONSUMER RESEARCH* 5 (1978), 22–29.

J. GOOD, "SHOP 'TIL WE DROP? TELEVISION, MATERIALISM AND ATTITUDES ABOUT THE NATURAL ENVIRONMENT," *MASS COMMUNICATION & SOCIETY* 10 (2007), 365–83.

T. KASSER, R.M. RYAN, M. ZAX M, & A. J. SAMEROFF, "THE RELATIONS OF MATERNAL AND SOCIAL ENVIRONMENTS TO LATE ADOLESCENTS' MATERIALISTIC AND PROSOCIAL VALUES," *DEVELOPMENTAL PSYCHOLOGY* 31 (1995), 907–14.

A. NAIRN, J. ORMROD, & P. BOTTOMLEY, *WATCHING, WANTING AND WELLBEING: EXPLORING THE LINKS* (LONDON: NATIONAL CONSUMER COUNCIL, 2007).

H. V. NGUYEN, G. P. MOSCHIS, & R. SHANNON, "EFFECTS OF FAMILY STRUCTURE AND SOCIALIZATION ON MATERIALISM: A LIFE COURSE STUDY IN THAILAND," *INTERNATIONAL JOURNAL OF CONSUMER STUDIES* 33 (2009), 486–95.

S. J. OPREE, M. BUIJZEN, E. A. VAN REIJMERSDAL, & P. M. VALKENBURG, "CHILDREN'S ADVERTISING EXPOSURE, ADVERTISED PRODUCT DESIRE, AND MATERIALISM: A LONGITUDINAL STUDY," *COMMUNICATION RESEARCH* 41 (2014), 717–35.

M. L. RICHINS & L. N. CHAPLIN, "MATERIAL PARENTING: HOW THE USE OF GOODS IN PARENTING FOSTERS MATERIALISM IN THE NEXT GENERATION," *JOURNAL OF CONSUMER RESEARCH* 41 (2015), 1333–57.

A. RINDFLEISCH, J. E. BURROUGHS, & F. DENTON, "FAMILY STRUCTURE, MATERIALISM, AND COMPULSIVE CONSUMPTION," *JOURNAL OF CONSUMER RESEARCH* 23 (1997), 312–25.

L. J. SHRUM, J. LEE, J. E. BURROUGHS, & A. RINDFLEISCH, "AN ONLINE PROCESS MODEL OF SECOND-ORDER CULTIVATION EFFECTS: HOW TELEVISION CULTIVATES MATERIALISM AND ITS CONSEQUENCES FOR LIFE SATISFACTION," *HUMAN COMMUNICATION RESEARCH* 37 (2011), 34–57.

M. J. SIRGY, E. GUREL-ATAY, D. WEBB, M. CICIC, M. HUSIC, ET AL., "LINKING ADVERTISING, MATERIALISM, AND LIFE SATISFACTION," *SOCIAL INDICATORS RESEARCH* 107 (2012), 79–101.

J. M. TWENGE & T. KASSER, "GENERATIONAL CHANGES IN MATERIALISM AND WORK CENTRALITY, 1976–2007: ASSOCIATIONS WITH TEMPORAL CHANGES IN SOCIETAL INSECURITY AND MATERIALISTIC ROLE-MODELING," *PERSONALITY & SOCIAL PSYCHOLOGY BULLETIN* 39 (2013), 883–97.

EMPIRICAL WORK ON THE CORRELATES OF MATERIALISM:

E. BRIGGS, T. LANDRY, & C. WOOD, "BEYOND JUST BEING THERE: AN EXAMINATION OF THE IMPACT OF ATTITUDES, MATERIALISM, AND SELF-ESTEEM ON THE QUALITY OF HELPING BEHAVIOR IN YOUTH VOLUNTEERS," *JOURNAL OF NONPROFIT & PUBLIC SECTOR MARKETING* 18 (2007), 27–45.

P. COHEN & J. COHEN, *LIFE VALUES AND ADOLESCENT MENTAL HEALTH* (MAHWAH, NJ: ERLBAUM, 1996).

J. R. DECKOP, R. A. GIACALONE, & C. JURKIEWICZ, "MATERIALISM AND WORKPLACE BEHAVIORS: DOES WANTING MORE RESULT IN LESS?" *SOCIAL INDICATORS RESEARCH* 121 (2015), 787–803.

H. DITTMAR, R. BOND, M. HURST, & T. KASSER, "THE RELATIONSHIP BETWEEN MATERIALISM AND PERSONAL WELL-BEING: A META-ANALYSIS," *JOURNAL OF PERSONALITY & SOCIAL PSYCHOLOGY* 107 (2014), 879–924.

B. DURIEZ, M. VANSTEENKISTE, B. SOENENS, & H. DE WITTE, "THE SOCIAL COSTS OF EXTRINSIC RELATIVE TO INTRINSIC GOAL PURSUITS: THEIR RELATION WITH SOCIAL DOMINANCE AND RACIAL AND ETHNIC PREJUDICE," *JOURNAL OF PERSONALITY* 75 (2007), 757–82.

C. FLANAGAN, L. S. GALLAY, S. GILL, E. GALLAY, & N. NAANA, "WHAT DOES DEMOCRACY MEAN? CORRELATES OF ADOLESCENTS' VIEWS," *JOURNAL OF ADOLESCENT RESEARCH* 20 (2005), 193–218.

L. FOULKES, A. SEARA-CARDOSO, C. S. NEUMANN, J. S. C. ROGERS, & E. VIDING, "LOOKING AFTER NUMBER ONE: ASSOCIATIONS BETWEEN PSYCHOPATHIC TRAITS AND MEASURES OF SOCIAL MOTIVATION AND FUNCTIONING IN A COMMUNITY SAMPLE OF MALES," *JOURNAL OF PSYCHOPATHOLOGY & BEHAVIORAL ASSESSMENT* 36 (2014), 22–29.

M. HURST, H. DITTMAR, R. BOND, & T. KASSER, "THE RELATIONSHIP BETWEEN MATERIALISTIC VALUES AND ENVIRONMENTAL ATTITUDES AND BEHAVIORS: A META-ANALYSIS," *JOURNAL OF ENVIRONMENTAL PSYCHOLOGY* 36 (2013), 257–69.

J. W. MCHOSKEY, "MACHIAVELLIANISM, INTRINSIC VERSUS EXTRINSIC GOALS, AND SOCIAL INTEREST: A SELF-DETERMINATION THEORY ANALYSIS," *MOTIVATION & EMOTION* 23 (1999), 267–83.

K. M. SHELDON, M. S. SHELDON, & R. OSBALDISTON, "PROSOCIAL VALUES AND GROUP ASSORTATION IN AN N-PERSON PRISONER'S DILEMMA," *HUMAN NATURE* 11 (2000), 387–404.

Chapter 7

70% OF ECONOMY DUE TO CONSUMER SPENDING:

W. R. EMMONS, *DON'T EXPECT CONSUMER SPENDING TO BE THE ENGINE OF ECONOMIC GROWTH IT ONCE WAS* (ST. LOUIS: FEDERAL RESERVE BANK OF ST. LOUIS, 2012).

MINDFULNESS:

K. W. BROWN, R. M. RYAN, & J. D. CRESWELL, "MINDFULNESS: THEORETICAL FOUNDATIONS AND EVIDENCE FOR ITS SALUTARY EFFECTS," *PSYCHOLOGICAL INQUIRY* 18 (2007), 211–237.

J. KABAT-ZINN, "MINDFULNESS-BASED INTERVENTIONS IN CONTEXT: PAST, PRESENT, AND FUTURE," *CLINICAL PSYCHOLOGY: SCIENCE & PRACTICE* 10 (2003), 144–156.

E. J. LAGNER, *MINDFULNESS* (READING, MA: ADDISON WESLEY, 1989).

FAIR TRADE:

SEE www.fairtrade.net FOR PLENTY OF INFORMATION ON FAIR TRADE, CASE STUDIES, ETC.

R. SMITHERS, "GLOBAL FAIRTRADE SALES REACH £4.4BN FOLLOWING 15% GROWTH DURING 2013," *THE GUARDIAN*, SEPTEMBER 3, 2014.

QUOTE REGARDING HONDURAN WORKERS:

http://usas.org/2012/10/10/3-years-after-signing-of-historic-agreement-honduran-workers-and-fruit-of-the-loom-lead-the-way/

LOCAL SPENDING & CURRENCIES:

FOR GENERAL INFORMATION AND FOR RESEARCH ON **SALT LAKE CITY, UTAH:**

www.civiceconomics.com/indie-impact.html

http://nebula.wsimg.com/09d4a3747498c7e97b42657484cae80d?AccessKeyId=8E410A17553441C49302&disposition=0&alloworigin=1

ijccr.net IS AN ON-LINE JOURNAL ABOUT COMPLEMENTARY CURRENCIES; SPECIFIC INFORMATION ABOUT THE BANGLA-PESA CAN BE FOUND IN W. O. RUDDICK, M. A. RICHARDS, & J. BENDELL, "COMPLEMENTARY CURRENCIES FOR SUSTAINABLE DEVELOPMENT IN KENYA: THE CASE OF THE BANGLA-PESA," *INTERNATIONAL JOURNAL OF COMMUNITY CURRENCY RESEARCH* 19 (2015), 18-30.

PRO-SOCIAL SPENDING AND HAPPINESS:

L. B. AKNIN, C. P. BARRINGTON-LEIGH, E. W. DUNN, J. F. HELIWELL ET AL., "PROSOCIAL SPENDING AND WELL-BEING: CROSS-CULTURAL EVIDENCE FOR A PSYCHOLOGICAL UNIVERSAL," *JOURNAL OF PERSONALITY & SOCIAL PSYCHOLOGY* 104 (2013), 635-652.

E. W. DUNN, L. B. AKNIN, M. I. NORTON, "SPENDING MONEY ON OTHERS PROMOTES HAPPINESS," *SCIENCE* 319 (2008), 1687-1688.

M. T. SCHMITT, L. B. AKNIN, J. AXSEN, & R. L. SHWOM, *PRO-ENVIRONMENTAL BEHAVIOR AND LIFE SATISFACTION: THE ROLES OF COSTS, SOCIAL INTERACTION, AND PERCEIVED ECOLOGICAL THREAT* (UNPUBLISHED MANUSCRIPT, SIMON FRASER UNIVERSITY, 2017).

J. J. XIAO & H. LI, "SUSTAINABLE CONSUMPTION AND LIFE SATISFACTION," *SOCIAL INDICATORS RESEARCH* 104 (2011), 323-329.

A MORE GENERAL REVIEW OF PAPERS ON THE ASSOCIATION BETWEEN WELL-BEING AND ENGAGING IN PRO-ENVIRONMENTAL BEHAVIORS IS T. KASSER, "LIVING BOTH WELL AND SUSTAINABLY: A REVIEW OF THE LITERATURE, WITH SOME REFLECTIONS FOR FUTURE RESEARCH, INTERVENTIONS, AND POLICY," *PHILOSOPHICAL TRANSACTIONS OF THE ROYAL SOCIETY – A* 375 (2017).

Chapter 8

VOLUNTARY SIMPLICITY BOOKS TO WHICH WE DIRECTLY REFER:

C. BEAVAN, *NO IMPACT MAN: THE ADVENTURES OF A GUILTY LIBERAL WHO ATTEMPTS TO SAVE THE PLANET, AND THE DISCOVERIES HE MAKES ABOUT HIMSELF AND OUR WAY OF LIFE IN THE PROCESS* (NEW YORK: FARRAR, STRAUS AND GIROUX, 2009).

J. DOMINGUEZ & V. ROBIN, *YOUR MONEY OR YOUR LIFE: TRANSFORMING YOUR RELATIONSHIP WITH MONEY AND ACHIEVING FINANCIAL INDEPENDENCE* (NEW YORK: PENGUIN, 1992).

H. NEARING & S. NEARING, *LIVING THE GOOD LIFE: HOW TO LIVE SANELY AND SIMPLY IN A TROUBLED WORLD* (NEW YORK: SCHOCKEN BOOKS, 1954).

H. D. THOREAU, *WALDEN; OR, LIFE IN THE WOODS* (BOSTON: HOUGHTON MIFFLIN, 1893).

OTHER IMPORTANT VS BOOKS:

S. ALEXANDER & A. MCLEOD, *SIMPLE LIVING IN HISTORY: PIONEERS OF THE DEEP FUTURE* (MELBOURNE, AUSTRALIA: SIMPLICITY INSTITUTE, 2014).

C. ANDREWS & W. URBANSKA (EDS.), *LESS IS MORE: EMBRACING SIMPLICITY FOR A HEALTHY PLANET, A CARING ECONOMY, AND LASTING HAPPINESS* (GABRIOLA ISLAND, BC: NEW SOCIETY, 2009).

D. ELGIN, *VOLUNTARY SIMPLICITY: TOWARD A WAY OF LIFE THAT IS OUTWARDLY SIMPLE, INWARDLY RICH* (REVISED EDITION) (NEW YORK: WILLIAM MORROW, 1993).

C. HOLST (ED.), *GET SATISFIED: HOW TWENTY PEOPLE LIKE YOU FOUND THE SATISFACTION OF ENOUGH* (WESTPORT, CT: EASTON STUDIO, 2007).

L. B. PIERCE, *CHOOSING SIMPLICITY: REAL PEOPLE FINDING PEACE AND FULFILLMENT IN A COMPLEX WORLD* (CARMEL, CA: GALLAGHER PRESS, 2000).

D. SHI, *THE SIMPLE LIFE: PLAIN LIVING AND HIGH THINKING IN AMERICAN CULTURE* (NEW YORK: OXFORD UNIVERSITY PRESS, 1985).

M. SUNDEEN, *THE MAN WHO QUIT MONEY* (NEW YORK: RIVERHEAD BOOKS, 2012).

BOOKS ON TIME AFFLUENCE AND TIME POVERTY:

J. DE GRAAF, *TAKE BACK YOUR TIME: FIGHTING OVERWORK AND TIME POVERTY IN AMERICA* (SAN FRANCISCO, CA: BERRETT-KOEHLER, 2003).

J. B. SCHOR, *THE OVERWORKED AMERICAN: THE UNEXPECTED DECLINE OF LEISURE* (NEW YORK: BASIC BOOKS, 1991).

EMPIRICAL RESEARCH ON VOLUNTARY SIMPLICITY:

L. BOUJBEL & A. D'ASTOUS, "VOLUNTARY SIMPLICITY AND LIFE SATISFACTION: EXPLORING THE MEDIATING ROLE OF CONSUMPTION DESIRES," *JOURNAL OF CONSUMER BEHAVIOR* 11 (2012), 487–494.

K. W. BROWN & T. KASSER, "ARE PSYCHOLOGICAL AND ECOLOGICAL WELL-BEING COMPATIBLE? THE ROLE OF VALUES, MINDFULNESS, AND LIFESTYLE," *SOCIAL INDICATORS RESEARCH* 74 (2005), 349–368.

E. H. KENNEDY, H. KRAHN, & N. T. KROGMAN, "DOWNSHIFTING: AN EXPLORATION OF MOTIVATIONS, QUALITY OF LIFE, AND ENVIRONMENTAL PRACTICES," *SOCIOLOGICAL FORUM* 28 (2013), 764–783.

S. A. RICH, S. HANNA, & B. J. WRIGHT, "SIMPLY SATISFIED: THE ROLE OF PSYCHOLOGICAL NEED SATISFACTION IN THE LIFE SATISFACTION OF VOLUNTARY SIMPLIFIERS," *JOURNAL OF HAPPINESS STUDIES* 18 (2016), 89–105.

EMPIRICAL RESEARCH ON TIME AFFLUENCE:

R. J. BURKE, M. KOYUNCU, L. FIKSENBAUM, & H. DEMIRER, "TIME AFFLUENCE, MATERIAL AFFLUENCE AND WELL-BEING AMONG TURKISH MANAGERS," *CROSS CULTURAL MANAGEMENT* 16 (2009), 386–397.

F. GINO & C. MOGILNER, "TIME, MONEY, AND MORALITY," *PSYCHOLOGICAL SCIENCE* 25 (2014), 414-421.

A. HAYDEN & J. M. SHANDRA, "HOURS OF WORK AND THE ECOLOGICAL FOOTPRINT OF NATIONS: AN EXPLORATORY ANALYSIS," *LOCAL ENVIRONMENT* 14 (2009), 575–600.

H. E. HERSHFIELD, C. MOGILNER, & U. BARNEA, "PEOPLE WHO CHOOSE TIME OVER MONEY ARE HAPPIER," *SOCIAL PSYCHOLOGICAL AND PERSONALITY SCIENCE,* 7 (2016), 697-706.

T. KASSER & K. M. SHELDON, "TIME AFFLUENCE AS A PATH TOWARDS PERSONAL HAPPINESS AND ETHICAL BUSINESS PRACTICE: EMPIRICAL EVIDENCE FROM FOUR STUDIES," *JOURNAL OF BUSINESS ETHICS* 84 (2009), 243–255.

K. W. KNIGHT, E. A. ROSA, & J. B. SCHOR, "COULD WORKING LESS REDUCE PRESSURES ON THE ENVIRONMENT? A CROSS-NATIONAL PANEL ANALYSIS OF OECD COUNTRIES, 1970–2007," *GLOBAL ENVIRONMENTAL CHANGE* 23 (2013), 691–700.

C. MOGILNER, "THE PURSUIT OF HAPPINESS: TIME, MONEY, AND SOCIAL CONNECTION," *PSYCHOLOGICAL SCIENCE* 21 (2010), 1348-1354.

J. NASSEN & J. LARSSON, "WOULD SHORTER WORKING TIME REDUCE GREENHOUSE GAS EMISSIONS? AN ANALYSIS OF TIME USE AND CONSUMPTION IN SWEDISH HOUSEHOLDS," *ENVIRONMENT & PLANNING & GOVERNMENT & POLICY* 33 (2015), 726–745.

D. ROSNICK & M. WEISBROT, "ARE SHORTER WORK HOURS GOOD FOR THE ENVIRONMENT? A COMPARISON OF U.S. AND EUROPEAN ENERGY CONSUMPTION," *INTERNATIONAL JOURNAL OF HEALTH SERVICES* 37 (2007), 405–417.

Chapter 9

SHARING AND HAPPINESS:

L. B. AKNIN, T. BROESCH, J. K. HAMLIN, & J. W. VAN DE VONDERVOORT, "PROSOCIAL BEHAVIOR LEADS TO HAPPINESS IN A SMALL-SCALE RURAL SOCIETY," *JOURNAL OF EXPERIMENTAL PSYCHOLOGY: GENERAL* 144 (2015), 788-795.

L. B. AKNIN, J. K. HAMLIN, & E. W. DUNN, "GIVING LEADS TO HAPPINESS IN YOUNG CHILDREN," *PLOS-ONE* (2012), doi.org/10.1371/journal.pone.0039211.

A VIDEO OF CANADIAN CHILDREN IN THE STUDY CAN BE FOUND BY SCROLLING DOWN TO "SHARING STUDY" AT cic.psych.ubc.ca/Example_Stimuli.html.

OTHER DATA SHOW THAT AMERICANS WHO PARTICIPATE IN SHARING INSTITUTIONS FREQUENTLY (COMPARED TO RARELY) REPORT HIGHER LIFE SATISFACTION; SEE TABLE 2 OF T. KASSER, "LIVING BOTH WELL AND SUSTAINABLY: A REVIEW OF THE LITERATURE, WITH SOME REFLECTIONS FOR FUTURE RESEARCH, INTERVENTIONS, AND POLICY," *PHILOSOPHICAL TRANSACTIONS OF THE ROYAL SOCIETY – A* 375 (2017).

GOOD GENERAL RESOURCES ON **SHARING** ARE:

https://www.newdream.org/programs/collaborative-communities/community-action-kit/sharing

www.shareable.net/

TYPES OF LIBRARIES:

localtools.org/

www.navdanya.org/home

www.richmondgrowsseeds.org/

www.usatla.org/USA_Toy_Library_Association/
Welcome_to_the_USA_Toy_Library_Association.
html

TIME BANKS:

timebanks.org/

E. CAHN & J. ROWE, *TIME DOLLARS: THE NEW CURRENCY THAT ENABLES AMERICANS TO TURN THEIR HIDDEN RESOURCE – TIME – INTO PERSONAL SECURITY AND COMMUNITY RENEWAL* (EMMAUS, PA: RODALE PRESS, 1992).

E. COLLOM, "THE MOTIVATIONS, ENGAGEMENT, SATISFACTION, OUTCOMES, AND DEMOGRAPHICS OF TIME BANK PARTICIPANTS: SURVEY FINDINGS FROM A U.S. SYSTEM," *INTERNATIONAL JOURNAL OF COMMUNITY CURRENCY RESEARCH* 11 (2007), 36-83.

G. SEYFANG, "GROWING COHESIVE COMMUNITIES ONE FAVOUR AT A TIME: SOCIAL EXCLUSION, ACTIVE CITIZEN-SHIP AND TIME BANKS," *INTERNATIONAL JOURNAL OF URBAN AND REGIONAL RESEARCH* 27 (2003), 699-706.

G. SEYFANG, "TIME BANKS: REWARDING COMMUNITY SELF-HELP IN THE INNER CITY?" *COMMUNITY DEVELOPMENT JOURNAL* 39 (2004), 62-71.

SHARED HOUSING:

cohousing.org/

www.ic.org/

PUBLIC HIKING:

J. L. ANDERSON, "BRITAIN'S RIGHT TO ROAM: REDEFINING THE LANDOWNER'S BUNDLE OF STICKS," *GEORGETOWN INTERNATIONAL LAW REVIEW* 19 (2006-2007), 375-435.

J. L. ANDERSON, "COMPARATIVE PERSPECTIVES ON PROPERTY RIGHTS: THE RIGHT TO EXCLUDE," *JOURNAL OF LEGAL EDUCATION* 56 (2006), 539-550.

Chapter 10

DISRUPTING BUSINESS AS USUAL:

T. BAJARIN, "WHY THE MAKER MOVEMENT IS IMPORTANT TO AMERICA'S FUTURE," *TIME*, MAY 19, 2014.

A. LAROCCA, "ETSY WANTS TO CROCHET ITS CAKE, AND EAT IT TOO," *NEW YORK MAGAZINE*, APRIL 4, 2016.

K. FRENKEN, "POLITICAL ECONOMIES AND ENVIRONMENTAL FUTURES FOR THE SHARING ECONOMY," *PHILOSOPHICAL TRANSACTIONS OF THE ROYAL SOCIETY A 375 (2017).*

B. MORIN, "WHAT IS THE MAKER MOVEMENT AND WHY SHOULD YOU CARE?" *HUFFINGTON POST*, MAY 2, 2013.

J. PRABHU, "FRUGAL INNOVATION: DOING MORE WITH LESS FOR MORE," *PHILOSOPHICAL TRANSACTIONS OF THE ROYAL SOCIETY A 375 (2017).*

www.ellenmacarthurfoundation.org/circular-economy

www.newdream.org/blog/2011-10-patagonia

www.patagonia.com/worn-wear.html

http://www.tarkettna.com/sustainability/restartreclamationrecyclingprogram

http://www.tarkett.com/en/content/tarkett-rewarded-company-transition-prize-2015-circular-economy-trophy-paris-france

www.techshop.ws/

SOCIALLY RESPONSIBLE INVESTMENT AND DIVESTMENT:

www.brightscope.com/financial-planning/advice/article/5838/Socially-Responsible-Investing-An-Overview/

www.ceres.org/investor-network/resolutions/

www.gofossilfree.orgf/commitments

www.greenmoneyjournal.com/fall-2013/parnassus/

www.trilliuminvest.com/approach-to-sri/shareholder-proposals/

ALTERNATIVE BUSINESS STRUCTURES:

www.esopinfo.org/

http://www.ncba.coop/about-us/organization/7-cooperative-principles

www.nceo.org/articles/research-prevalence-effects-employee-ownership

www.nceo.org/articles/studies-employee-ownership-corporate-performance.

www.newmansown.com/charity/

www.thenewpress.com/about/about-new-press

Chapter 11

CAMPAIGN FINANCE REFORM:

FOR GENERAL INFORMATION ABOUT THE MONEY SPENT ON CAMPAIGNS, AND WHO IS "DONATING" TO WHOM, SEE www.opensecrets.org/overview/cost.php.

PREVIOUS ATTEMPTS TO REGULATE CAMPAIGN FINANCE WERE THE *FEDERAL ELECTION CAMPAIGN ACT OF 1971* (FECA, PUB. L. 92-225, 86 STAT.3) AND THE *BIPARTISAN CAMPAIGN REFORM ACT OF 2002* (BCRA, MCCAIN-FEINGOLD ACT, PUB. L. 107-155, 116 STAT.81).

www.azcleanelections.gov/about-us

www.mainecleanelections.org/mission

WHO HAS RIGHTS?:

THE POLL RESULTS REFLECT THE PERCENTAGE OF AMERICANS RESPONDING TO THE QUESTION "DO YOU THINK THE FOLLOWING SUPREME COURT RULINGS WERE GOOD DECISIONS OR SHOULD BE OVERTURNED: RULED THAT CORPORATIONS AND UNIONS MAY SPEND UNLIMITED AMOUNTS ON POLITICAL CAUSES." FINDINGS ARE IN G. STOHR, "BLOOMBERG POLL: AMERICANS WANT SUPREME COURT TO TURN OFF POLITICAL SPENDING SPIGOT," Bloomberg.com, SEPTEMBER 28, 2015.

FOR THE **PROPOSED 28TH AMENDMENT**, SEE: movetoamend.org/wethepeopleamendment; FOR CONGRESSIONAL SUPPORT, SEE: www.congress.gov/bill/114th-congress/house-joint-resolution/48/cosponsors.

FOR AN ENGLISH TRANSLATION OF THE **GERMAN CONSTITUTION**, SEE www.servat.unibe.ch/icl/gm00000_.html. ARTICLE 20A IS THE SOURCE OF THE QUOTE REGARDING THE RESPONSIBILITY FOR FUTURE GENERATIONS.

FOR MORE ON THE **RIGHTS OF NATURE**, SEE:

M. MARGIL & B. PRICE, "PITTSBURGH BANS NATURAL GAS DRILLING," *YES! MAGAZINE*, NOVEMBER 16, 2010.

www.celdf.org/rights/rights-of-nature/rights-nature-resources/

www.treehugger.com/environmental-policy/river-new-zealand-granted-legal-rights-person.html

MEASURING WHAT MATTERS:

ROBERT F. KENNEDY'S QUOTE IS FROM A SPEECH HE GAVE AT THE UNIVERSITY OF KANSAS ON MARCH 18, 1968.

INFORMATION ABOUT BHUTAN AND ITS APPROACH TO **GROSS NATIONAL HAPPINESS** CAN BE FOUND AT gnhcentrebhutan.org/. OTHER ARTICLES ARE AVAILABLE AT businessbhutan.bt/gnh-defies-wto/ AND www.economist.com/node/3445119.

T. HÁK, S. JANOU KOVÁ, S. ABDALLAH, C. SEAFORD, & S. MAHONY, *REVIEW REPORT ON BEYOND GDP INDICATORS: CATEGORISATION, INTENSIONS AND IMPACTS. FINAL VERSION OF BRAINPOOL DELIVERABLE 1.1, A COLLABORATIVE PROJECT FUNDED BY THE EUROPEAN COMMISSION UNDER THE FP7 PROGRAMME (CONTRACT NO. 283024).* (PRAGUE: CUEC, 2012)

J. WALLACE & K. SCHMUECKER, *SHIFTING THE DIAL: FROM WELLBEING MEASURES TO POLICY PRACTICE* (DUNFERMLINE, UK: CARNEGIE UK TRUST, 2012).

RAISING THE MINIMUM WAGE:

D. CARD & A. B. KREUGER, "TIME-SERIES MINIMUM-WAGE STUDIES: A META-ANALYSIS," *THE AMERICAN ECONOMIC REVIEW* 85 (1995), 238-243.

CONGRESSIONAL BUDGET OFFICE, *REPORT ON THE EFFECTS OF A MINIMUM-WAGE INCREASE ON EMPLOYMENT AND FAMILY INCOME* (WASHINGTON DC: AUTHOR, 2014).

P. COY, "SEVEN NOBEL ECONOMISTS ENDORSE A $10.10 MINIMUM WAGE," *BLOOMBERGBUSINESSWEEK*, JANUARY 14, 2014.

H. DOUCOULIAGOS & T. D. STANLEY, "PUBLICATION BIAS IN MINIMUM-WAGE RESEARCH? A META-REGRESSION ANALYSIS," *BRITISH JOURNAL OF INDUSTRIAL RELATIONS* 47 (2009), 406-428.

P. MOORE, "POLL RESULTS: MINIMUM WAGE," *HUFFINGTON POST*, APRIL 13, 2016.

INFORMATION FOR THE MINIMUM WAGE MAP IS FROM time.com/4274938/minimum-wage-state-map/.

FORMING A UNION IN CANADA:

www.usw.ca/join/how

www.yorku.ca/ddoorey/hrm3422/blog/wp-content/files/Certification-Process-Chart.doc

INCREASING TIME AFFLUENCE:

M. A. MANDELMAN & A. B. MESSIGIAN, "NUMBER OF PAID SICK LEAVE LAWS EXPANDS RAPIDLY IN 2016," *THE NATIONAL LAW REVIEW*, DECEMBER 22, 2016.

NATIONAL PARTNERSHIP FOR WOMEN AND FAMILIES, *CHILDREN BENEFIT WHEN PARENTS HAVE ACCESS TO PAID LEAVE: FACT SHEET* (WASHINGTON DC: AUTHOR, 2015).

NATIONAL PARTNERSHIP FOR WOMEN AND FAMILIES, *PAID LEAVE WORKS IN CALIFORNIA, NEW JERSEY, AND RHODE ISLAND: FACT SHEET* (WASHINGTON DC: AUTHOR, 2016).

www.dol.gov/general/topic/workhours/sickleave

CONTROLLING ADVERTISING:

TABLE 2 OF T. KASSER & S. LINN, "GROWING UP UNDER CORPORATE CAPITALISM: THE PROBLEM OF MARKETING TO CHILDREN, WITH SUGGESTIONS FOR POLICY SOLUTIONS," *SOCIAL ISSUES AND POLICY REVIEW* 10 (2016), PP. 122-150 PRESENTS DATA SHOWING THAT THERE IS SUBSTANTIAL BIPARTISAN SUPPORT FOR THESE SORTS OF LAWS. FOR EXAMPLE, 54% OF REPUBLICANS, 68% OF INDEPENDENTS, AND 78% OF DEMOCRATS SUPPORT A 1% TAX ON ALL BROADCAST ADVERTISING, WITH REVENUE DEDICATED TO K-12 EDUCATION, AND 61% OF REPUBLICANS, 65% OF INDEPENDENTS, AND 70% OF DEMOCRATS SUPPORT PROHIBITING ADVERTISING IN SCHOOLS, TEXTBOOKS, AND SCHOOL BUSES.

LIBRARY OF CONGRESS, "BRAZIL: NEW RESOLUTION BANS ADVERTISING TO CHILDREN UNDER AGE 12," APRIL 22, 2014.

T. NUDD, "VERMONT CELEBRATES 40 BILL-BOARD-FREE YEARS," *ADWEEK*, JANUARY 16, 2008.

SAN FRANCISCO'S LAW IS THE *"COMMERCIAL-FREE SCHOOLS ACT,"* AMENDMENT TO RESOLUTION NO. 95-25A6 (VERSION NO. 3), PASSED IN JUNE 1999.

J. J. THORNDIKE, "SHOULD WE TAX ADVERTISING?" *TAX HISTORY PROJECT*, AUGUST 8, 2013.

UNITED NATIONS, *REPORT OF THE SPECIAL RAPPORTEUR IN THE FIELD OF CULTURAL RIGHTS* (2014, DOWNLOADED NOVEMBER 20, 2015 FROM http://www.un.org/en/ga/search/view_doc.asp?symbol=A/69/286).

Chapter 12

UNDERMINING MATERIALISTIC VALUES BY ACTIVATING INTRINSIC VALUES:

P. CHILTON, T. CROMPTON, T. KASSER, & A. NOLAN, *COMMUNICATING BIGGER-THAN-SELF PROBLEMS TO EXTRINSICALLY-ORIENTED AUDIENCES* (COMMON CAUSE REPORT, VALUESANDFRAMES.ORG, JANUARY 2012).

N. LEKES, N. H. HOPE, L. GOUVEIA, R. KOESTNER, & F. L. PHILIPPE, "INFLUENCING VALUE PRIORITIES AND INCREASING WELL-BEING: THE EFFECTS OF REFLECTING ON INTRINSIC VALUES," *JOURNAL OF POSITIVE PSYCHOLOGY* 7 (2012), PP. 249-261 ON, SOME OTHER STUDIES INCLUDE:

G. R. MAIO, A. PAKIZEH, W-Y. CHEUNG, & K. J. REES, "CHANGING, PRIMING, AND ACTING ON VALUES: EFFECTS VIA MOTIVATIONAL RELATIONS IN A CIRCULAR MODEL," *JOURNAL OF PERSONALITY & SOCIAL PSYCHOLOGY* 97 (2009), PP. 699-715.

K. M. SHELDON, C. P. NICHOLS, & T. KASSER, "AMERICANS RECOMMEND SMALLER ECOLOGICAL FOOTPRINTS WHEN REMINDED OF INTRINSIC AMERICAN VALUES OF SELF-EXPRESSION, FAMILY, AND GENEROSITY," *ECOPSYCHOLOGY* 3 (2011), 97-104.

N. WEINSTEIN, A. K. PRZYBYLSKI, & R. M. RYAN, "CAN NATURE MAKE US MORE CARING? EFFECTS OF IMMERSION IN NATURE ON INTRINSIC ASPIRATIONS AND GENEROSITY," *PERSONALITY AND SOCIAL PSYCHOLOGY BULLETIN* 35 (2009), 1315-1329.

WELL-BEING'S RELATIONSHIP WITH POLITICAL ACTIVISM AND VOLUNTEERING:

M. KLAR & T. KASSER, "SOME BENEFITS OF BEING AN ACTIVIST: MEASURING ACTIVISM AND ITS ROLE IN PSYCHOLOGICAL WELL-BEING," *POLITICAL PSYCHOLOGY* 30 (2009), 755-777.

S. MEIER & A. STUTZER, "IS VOLUNTEERING REWARDING IN ITSELF?" *ECONOMICA* 75 (2008), 39-59.

J. WILSON, "VOLUNTEERING," *ANNUAL REVIEW OF SOCIOLOGY* 26 (2000), 215-240.

PROTESTS AGAINST HYPERCAPITALISM:

www.billboardliberation.com/mission.html

www.britannica.com/event/Seattle-WTO-protests-of-1999

susanohanian.org/show_commentaries.php?id=604

D. CRARY, "COMMERCIALS AIMED AT KIDS DENOUNCED," *HONOLULU ADVERTISER*, SEPTEMBER 11, 2001.

A. RIPLEY, "CYNTHIA COOPER: THE NIGHT DETECTIVE," *TIME*, DECEMBER 20, 2002.

D. HOCHMAN, "URBAN GARDENING: AN APPLESEED WITH ATTITUDE," *NEW YORK TIMES*, MAY 3, 2013.

S. LOPEZ, "IN THE WEEDS OF BUREAUCRATIC INSANITY THERE SPROUTS A SMALL REPRIEVE," *L. A. TIMES*, AUGUST 20, 2011.

S. LOPEZ, "L. A. STILL SAYING PARKWAY VEGETABLE GARDENS MUST GO," *L. A. TIMES*, JULY 31, 2013.

en.wikipedia.org/wiki/Occupy_movement

S. MUFSON & J. EILPERIN, "TRUMP SEEKS TO REVIVE DAKOTA ACCESS, KEYSTONE XL OIL PIPELINES," *WASHINGTON POST*, JANUARY 24, 2017.

INTANGIBLE EFFECTS OF PROTESTING:

D. S. MEYER, "HOW SOCIAL MOVEMENTS MATTER," IN J. GODWIN & J. JASPERS (EDS.), *THE SOCIAL MOVEMENTS READER*, 2ND ED., (MALDEN, MA: WILEY-BLACKWELL, 2009) PP. 417-422.

INDEX

About the Authors

TIM KASSER, PH.D., IS A PROFESSOR OF PSYCHOLOGY AT KNOX COLLEGE IN GALESBURG, ILLINOIS. HE HAS WRITTEN FOUR BOOKS AND OVER ONE HUNDRED SCIENTIFIC ARTICLES, BOOK CHAPTERS, AND REPORTS ON MATERIALISM, VALUES, ECOLOGICAL SUSTAINABILITY, AND QUALITY OF LIFE, AMONG OTHER TOPICS. IN ADDITION TO TEACHING CLASSES ON PERSONALITY, CLINICAL PSYCHOLOGY, AND RESEARCH METHODS, TIM CONSULTS WITH A VARIETY OF ACTIVIST AND CIVIL SOCIETY ORGANIZATIONS. HE LIVES IN THE ILLINOIS COUNTRYSIDE WITH HIS WIFE, TWO SONS, AND ASSORTED ANIMALS.

LARRY GONICK IS THE AUTHOR/CARTOONIST BEHIND THE AWARD-WINNING *CARTOON HISTORY OF THE UNIVERSE,* AS WELL AS *THE CARTOON HISTORY OF THE UNITED STATES* AND A STACK OF *CARTOON GUIDES* TO SCIENCE AND MATH. HE HAS TRAVELED THE WORLD IN SEARCH OF MATERIAL, AND, HAVING FOUND SOME, NOW MOSTLY STAYS HOME AND DRAWS. BEFORE TAKING UP PEN, BRUSH, AND INKPOT, HE USED TO TEACH CALCULUS AT HARVARD. HE'S MARRIED WITH GROWN CHILDREN.

Publishing in the Public Interest

THANK YOU FOR READING THIS BOOK PUBLISHED BY THE NEW PRESS. THE NEW PRESS IS A **NONPROFIT, PUBLIC-INTEREST PUBLISHER.** NEW PRESS BOOKS AND AUTHORS PLAY A CRUCIAL ROLE IN SPARKING CONVERSATIONS ABOUT THE KEY POLITICAL AND SOCIAL ISSUES OF OUR DAY.

WE HOPE YOU ENJOYED THIS BOOK AND THAT YOU WILL STAY IN TOUCH WITH THE NEW PRESS. HERE ARE A FEW WAYS TO STAY UP TO DATE WITH OUR BOOKS, EVENTS, AND THE ISSUES WE COVER:

SIGN UP AT www.thenewpress.com/subscribe TO RECEIVE UPDATES ON NEW PRESS AUTHORS AND ISSUES AND TO BE NOTIFIED ABOUT LOCAL EVENTS.

LIKE US ON FACEBOOK: www.facebook.com/newpressbooks.

FOLLOW US ON TWITTER: www.twitter.com/thenewpress.

PLEASE CONSIDER BUYING NEW PRESS BOOKS FOR YOURSELF; FOR FRIENDS AND FAMILY; AND TO DONATE TO SCHOOLS, LIBRARIES, COMMUNITY CENTERS, PRISON LIBRARIES, AND OTHER ORGANIZATIONS INVOLVED WITH THE ISSUES OUR AUTHORS WRITE ABOUT.

THE NEW PRESS IS A 501(C)(3) NONPROFIT ORGANIZATION. YOU CAN ALSO SUPPORT OUR WORK WITH A TAX-DEDUCTIBLE GIFT BY VISITING www.thenewpress.com/donate.

94